The Anglophone Cameroon Predicament

Mufor Atanga

Langaa Research & Publishing CIG
Mankon, Bamenda

Publisher:
Langaa RPCIG
Langaa Research & Publishing Common Initiative Group
P.O. Box 902 Mankon
Bamenda
North West Region
Cameroon
Langaagrp@gmail.com
www.langaa-rpcig.net

Distributed in and outside N. America by African Books Collective
orders@africanbookscollective.com
www.africanbookcollective.com

ISBN: 9956-717-11-8

© Mufor Atanga 2011

DISCLAIMER
All views expressed in this publication are those of the author and do not necessarily reflect the views of Langaa RPCIG.

Dedication

Time past and future
Are in Time present
Censure not
The progenitors of
Our ignominious past.

To my daughters
Lum Anwi and Sifru
And all the inheritors of our time present.

About This Book

This study explores the fate of the former West Cameroon from 1961 until 1993 and its people in the Cameroon Republic. As a linguo-cultural minority, after reunification in the early 1960s, the Anglophones soon realised that the Francophone-led regime was not prepared to develop a federal and bilingual nation as had been agreed at reunification, but aimed at assimilating them. However, little was done by them to resist this. The calls for national integration and actions undertaken to realize it, as such, became simply a subterfuge for assimilation.

Measures undertaken to exploit the region's economy and marginalize its people took several forms. Principally the economic structures that were meant to facilitate auto-centred development were undermined and destroyed. Whilst the perception of institutionalised discrimination did not only manifest itself in the exclusion of Anglophones from positions of real authority, but also meant that the region was deprived of any meaningful development.

Part of the problem stems from the instrumentalisation of the different languages, traditions and values legated to Cameroon by the former colonial powers, Britain and France, for political objectives. The two regions had agreed to form a single country on the basis of a federation. The abolition of the federation came to be part of the strategy for assimilation.

With the advent of multi-party politics, most Anglophone Cameroonians increasingly have made vocal demands for a return to a federation, as they believe it is the only system that can adequately guarantee them their rights and equal opportunities. However, on the advice of France, the Francophone-led regime in Cameroon has refused to yield to such demands. As long as the demands of the Anglophones are not met, there is the grave danger of a violent conflict which might eventually lead to the break-up of the country.

Table of Content

List of tables...	v
List of Figures..	vi
Selected Abbreviations..	vii
Acknowledgements...	ix
Foreword..	xi
Preface...	xvii

Chapter One: General Introduction...1

The Problématique...	4
Significance of the Study...	6
Scope...	6
Literature Review...	7
Theoretical Framework...	11
Cultural Pluralism and Nation-Building......................................	11
The Federal System...	16
Political Pluralism, Integration and the Federal System............	18
Federalism and Nation-Building...	20
Basic Propositions...	22
Methodology...	23
Organisation of the Work...	23
Notes and References...	24

Chapter Two: Colonialism and the Development of Modern Political Institutions in the Cameroons.. 27

Introduction...	27
Historical Setting: The Colonization of the Cameroons............	27
The Consequences of the First World War to the Colonial Development of The Cameroons..	29
The Nature of British Colonialism and Its Influence in the Cameroons Development of Political and Administrative Institutions in the Cameroons...	30
The Nature 0f French Colonialism, and the Development of French Political and Administrative Institutions in the Cameroons....................	35
Differences Between the French and British Approach to Colonialsim and Its Implications for Political Developments in the Cameroons...............	39
Constitutional Developments in the	

Southern Cameroons Before 1960.. 42
The Politics of Reunification.. 43
The Ibo Factor in Pre-Unification Southern Cameroons Politics............. 43
Party Politics and The Reunification Issue in the Southern Cameroons, 1957-196.. 44
The Foumban Conference and Its Implications for the Constituional Developmetn of the Southern Cameroons... 48

Notes And References.. 50

Chapter Three: The Impact of Reunification
on West Cameroon.. 53

The French Connection: Cameroon, the Neo-Colonial State Par Excellence the Constitutional Implications of the Foumban Conference for the State of West Cameroon.. 53
The Erosion of Anglophone Autonomy: Party Politics and the Consolidation of Federal Authority in West Cameroon,
1961-1970... 63
The Formation of a Single National Party and the Demise of the State of West Cameroon.. 73
The Abolitionn of the Federation, 1972.. 75
The Socio-Cultural Impact of Reunification on the State of West Cameroon.. 80
The Economic Impact of Reunification on the State of
West Cameroon.. 89
Communications and Road Infrastructural Development and the Decline of the West Cameroon Economy.. 95

Notes And Refernces.. 100

Chapter Four: The Failure of National Integration: An analysis of the Biya Regime, 1982-93.. 109

The Nature of the State in Cameroon under Biya..................................... 109
President Biya and the Intensification of the Alienation of the Anglophones.. 111
The Biya Regime: Raised Hopes and Broken Promises............................ 114
Ethnicity and Regionalism in the Politics of the Biya Regime................. 120
The Ministry of Defence... 124
Presidency of The Republic... 129

The Mass-Media And Bi-Culturalism in Cameroon.................................... 129
The Development of Television in Cameroon... 130
Is The Television Audience Embarrased by the English Language?.......... 132
Television Programmes in the English Language....................................... 133
Distribution of Trasmission Time between French and English Language Programmes on Television... 134
English Language Programmes on the Radio... 137
Multipartism, the Emergence of West Cameroon "Liberation" Movements, and the Implications of the October 11, 1992 Presidential Elections for the Stability of the State... 139

Notes and References... 145

Chapter Five: Summary and Conclusion.. 147

Summary... 147
Findings.. 150
Recommendation.. 155
Conclusion.. 155

Appendices...159

Appendix I
Constitutional Position of the Southern Cameroons in the Event of It Electing to Become Part of the Republic of Cameroon............................ 159

Appendix II
Open Letter to All English-Speaking Parents of Cameroon from the English-Speaking Students of the North-West and
South-West Provinces... 163

Appendix III: The Buea Declaration of the All
Anglophone Conference... 173

Bibliography..185

List of Tables

Table 2.1a: Sources Of Revenue For The Southern Cameroons: 1954-1958(£000).. 33

Table 2.1b: Capital Programmes Of Governments, 1955-56 To 1961-62 (£ 000)... 33

Table 3.1: Distribution Of Ministers And Vice Ministers By Region In The 1972 Cabinet.. 79

Table 3.2: East And West Cameroon Primary School Enrollment 1958-1961.. 83

Table 3.3: The Development Of Primary Education In Cameroon. 1960 – 1977.. 84

Table 3.4: Staff Distribution At Yaoundé University: 1977/1978 (Anglophone/Francophone Compared)...................................... 87

Table 3.5a: Cdc Production Statistics: 1959-1964 (In Metric Tons)............ 91

Table 3.5b: Comparative Table Of The Principal Produce Exported From West Cameroon For The Years 1965 And 1966... 93

Table 3.6: Population Of The Principal Towns Of The United Republic Of Cameroon As At 1976... 97

Table 3.7: General Summary Of Tarred Road Network In Cameroon (In Km) As At 1991.. 99

Table 4.1a: Population Of The Various Provinces (Regions) In Cameroon Based On The 1987 CensusError! Bookmark not defined............... 121

Table 4.1b: Population Figures Of The 1976 Census In Cameroon.......... 122

Table 4.2a: Distribution Of Senior Personnel At The Ministry Of Defence And At The Secretariat Of State For Defence (1990 – 1991)..................... 125

Table 4.2b: Distribution Of The Officer Corps In The Armed Forces: Francophones And Anglophones Compared (March 1992)........... 126

Table 4.3: Distribution Of Posts Of Responsibility In The Republic Of Cameroon: Francophone/Anglophone Compared (March 1992).. 127

Table 4.4:English Language Programmes That Have Disappeared Without Replacement... 130

Table 4.5:The Distribution Of Posts In The Cameroon Radio And Television Corporation (1989-1990)... 131

Table 4.6a: The Distribution Of Transmission Time OnTelevision Between French And English Language Programmes For The Month Of October, 1989.. 135

Table 4.6b:Distribution Of Time Between English And French Language Including CfI Programmes... 137

Table 4.7:Distribution Of Air-Time Betweem French And English Language Programmes On The National Radio And Televsion............................... 138

List of Figures

Figure 5.1a: Diagram of Qualitative Integration... 152

Figure 5.1b: Diagram of Mal-Integration... 154

Selected Abbreviations

APA	Anglophone Patriotic Alliance
CAM	Cameroon Anglophone Movement
CCE	Caisse Centrale de la Coopération Économique
CCP	Cameroon Commoners Party
CDC	Cameroon Development Corporation
CDC	Commonwealth Development Corporation
CNU	Cameroon National Union
CPDM	Cameroon Peoples Democratic Movement
CPNC	Cameroon Peoples National Congress
CRTV	Cameroon Radio and Television Corporation
CUC	Cameroon United Congress
CFI	Canal France International.
EEC	European Economic Community
FAC	Fond d'aide et de coopération
FIDES	Fonds d'Investissements pour le Développement Economique et Social
FONADER	Fonds National de Développement Rural des Crédits pour les Petits Cultivateurs
KNC	Kamerun National Congress
KNDP	Kamerun National Democratic Party
KPP	Kamerun Peoples Party
KUNC	Kamerun United National Congress
KUP	Kamerun United Party.
LDP	Liberal Democratic Party.
MDR	Mouvement pour la Défense de la République
OCAM	Organization of Afro-Malagasy Countries
PFA	The Patriotic Front Alliance
SDF	The Social Democratic Front
SONARA	The National Refining Company Limited
SWELA	South West Elites Association
UC	Union Camerounaise
UDEAC	L'Union douanière et économique d'Afrique central
UNDP	National Union for Democracy and Progress
UPC	Union des Populations du Cameroun
UTC	United Africa Company
WCDA	West Cameroon Development Agency

Acknowledgements

During the course of the research on which this book is based I became indebted to so many people that I could not possibly mention all of them here. However, I do remain eternally grateful for their assistance and support.

During my fieldwork in Cameroon, I received invaluable assistance from Messrs Francis Wache, Tande Dibussi and Prince Henry Mbain. Messrs Nfor Nfor, Ntemfac Ofege, and Akonji Atekwana made available to me very useful material based on their own research. The late Hon. S.T. Muna also granted me access to very useful material from his personal library.

I gained invaluable insights through exchanges with colleagues amongst whom are Nantang Jua, Piet Konings and Francis Nyamnjoh – without the constant insistence of Francis this book might never have been published. Exchanges with my students at the University of Buea also helped me to hone some of the arguments advanced in this study.

Finally, I wish to thank the small circle of activists around Buea, Victoria and Douala who were instrumental in organising what became known as the *All Anglophone Conference I,* and all the people who granted me interviews.

Mufor Atanga
August 2011

Foreword

Regime members and organic scholars tended to be quite optimistic about the integration of the Anglophone minority into the Francophone-dominated post-colonial state in Cameroon. For instance, in his book *The One and Indivisible Cameroon* published in 1981, an Anglophone scholar, John W. Forje, insisted that Anglophones and Francophones belonged together for historical reasons and had come to form an inseparable whole in the aftermath of reunification in 1961. There is also no doubt that the relative absence of any open resistance in Anglophone Cameroon to the Francophone-dominated state's integration efforts from the achievement of reunification to the political liberalisation process in the early 1990s gave the false impression of the success of the integration process in the country. Cameroon actually used to be praised as Africa's sterling example of nation-building from two colonial blocs of Anglo-Saxon and Gallic origin.

In this book, the Anglophone Cameroonian political scientist, Mufor Atanga, challenges such claims of a successful Cameroonian integration process. He instead claims that what has come to be called the 'Anglophone problem' constitutes one of the severest threats to the post-colonial nation-state project in Cameroon. His study focuses on the people's perceptions and actions in the Anglophone region, which was christened West Cameroon after reunification, and it largely covers the period 1961, the start of a unique experiment in federation, to the first years of political liberalisation in the 1990s.

One of the principal merits of this book is its attempt to expose certain myths on colonialism, reunification and federalism propagated by regime members and organic scholars.

The first myth is that Cameroon has always been one. It stresses that Cameroon was already in existence before colonial time when all people in Cameroon lived together amicably and peacefully. Colonialism, it is said, fostered a rupture in pre-colonial conviviality and cordiality traditions. Atanga's book, however, convincingly shows that the colonial state was far more important than the (largely mythical) pre-colonial state in mapping out the historical trajectory of the post-colonial state. In fact, the colonial state was instrumental in 'inventing' Cameroon itself and creating two distinct communities on Cameroonian territory. The discrete British and French colonial legacies since World War I have left a wide gap between the peoples on either side of the linguistic and administrative divide. While the completely different colonial legacies were already likely to hamper the post-colonial state's integration efforts, another potential obstacle was the superior bargaining strength of the Francophone majority vis-à-vis the Anglophone minority.

The second myth is that reunification signified a long-awaited reunion of people separated for many years by arbitrarily imposed colonial borders and thus was warm-heartedly and freely embraced by both parties. Atanga's book provides ample evidence that for Anglophones reunification was more like a loveless United Nations-arranged marriage between two people who hardly knew each other. Deprived of their preferred option, an independent state, Anglophone Cameroonians were given only two options in the 11 February 1961 UN-organised plebiscite: achievement of independence either by joining Nigeria – the British mandate and trust territory had been administered as an integral part of Nigeria – or reunification with Francophone Cameroon, which had already become independent in 1960 under the new name of Republic of Cameroon. In the end, the majority of the Anglophone population voted for what they considered the lesser of two evils. Their vote in favour of reunification appeared to be more a rejection of continuous ties with Nigeria, which had proved detrimental to Anglophone Cameroon's development than a vote for union with Francophone Cameroon, a territory with a different cultural heritage and one that was then involved in a violent civil war.

A third myth is that the constitutional negotiations in Foumban in June 1961 were a historic event when estranged brothers mutually agreed upon a federal constitution for a reunified Cameroon. In this book, however, Atanga argues that for Anglophones the conference was an occasion where the Francophone majority used its superior bargaining power to control negotiations and enforce a form of federation far below Anglophone expectations. By reuniting with the former French Cameroon, the Anglophone elite had hoped to enter a loose federal union as a way of protecting their country's minority status and cultural heritage. During the constitutional talks, the Francophone elite were only prepared to accept a highly centralised federation, which was regarded merely as a transitory phase towards the formation of a unitary state. Such a federation demanded relatively few amendments to the 1960 Constitution of the Republic of Cameroon. Interestingly, Pierre Messmer, one of the last French high commissioners in Cameroon and a close advisor to President Ahidjo wrote in 1998 that he and others knew at the time that the so-called federal constitution provided merely a 'sham federation', which was 'safe for appearances, an annexation of West Cameroon'. The final version of the constitution was only approved by the Parliament of the Republic of Cameroon on 1 September 1961, just one month prior to reunification. For this reason, the All Anglophone Conference declared in 1993 that 'the union between Southern Cameroons, the former British trust territory, and the Republic of Cameroon had proceeded without any constitutional basis'.

Atanga provides substantial evidence that West Cameroon lost most of the limited autonomy it had enjoyed as part of the Nigerian federation. Even worse, a few months after reunification, President Ahidjo created a system of regional administration in which West Cameroon was designated as one of the six regions, basically ignoring the country's federal system. The regions were headed by powerful inspectors who, in the case of West Cameroon, in effect overshadowed the prime minister with whom they were in frequent conflict concerning jurisdiction. In addition, the West Cameroon government could barely function since it had to depend entirely on subventions from the federal government that controlled its major sources of revenue. When, in 1972, Ahidjo created a unitary state in blatant disregard of constitutional provisions, there was in reality little left of the federation, except perhaps in name. What was regarded as one of the last visible symbols of the 1961 union was removed in 1984 when Ahidjo's successor, Paul Biya, abolished the appellation 'United Republic of Cameroon' and replaced it with 'Republic of Cameroon', which significantly was the name of the Francophone part of the country which became independent in 1960.

Ahidjo's justification for the 1972 'glorious revolution' was that federalism fostered regionalism and impeded economic development. According to Atanga, a growing number of Anglophones were inclined to attribute the abolition of the federal state not to any shortcomings of federalism *per se* but to the hegemonic tendencies of the Francophone-dominated state. For them, the nation-state project after reunification was driven by the firm determination of the Francophone political elite to dominate the Anglophone minority and erase the cultural and institutional foundations of Anglophone identity. Atanga provides us with numerous examples of Anglophone grievances which were mainly of a political, economic and cultural nature. Essentially, Anglophones complain of a growing marginalisation in all spheres of public life and thus of being second-class citizens in their own country.

Significantly, Atanga does not go to the extent of blaming only the Francophone elite and the French colonial power for the entire Anglophone problem, as is often the case in the most radical Anglophone circles. He emphasises instead that the Anglophone political leaders bear an important share of the responsibility for the Anglophone predicament. Apparently, when they realised that their influence within the federated state of West Cameroon was beginning to whittle down, the federal arrangements no longer suited their designs, they started competing for Ahidjo's favours and aspiring for positions of power within the single party and the federal government and eventually within the unitary state, thus blatantly neglecting the defence of West Cameroon's autonomy and interests.

The co-optation of the Anglophone elite into the 'hegemonic alliance' and the autocratic nature of the post-colonial regimes prevented Anglophones from openly organising in defence of their interests until the political liberalisation process in the early 1990s. According to Atanga, Anglophones have not only played a leading role in accomplishing political liberalisation in Cameroon but also used the liberalisation of political space to create and reactivate various organisations to represent their interests. Most of these organisations initially championed a return to the federal state, but the persistent refusal of the Biya government to discuss any related constitutional reforms forced them to adopt a secessionist stand. These organisations, however, face many internal and external problems to realise their goals. One of the major problems is the internal divisions among the leadership of the various Anglophone movements and the Anglophone elite as a whole about the policies and strategies for redressing the Anglophone problem.

This is a well-researched and well-argued book. It teaches us many lessons about the post-colonial nation-state projects and federal experiments in Africa. The unitary approach to the nation-state project was the predominant choice of African leaders in the decades following independence. Usually, this amounted to a continuation of the colonial state's nation-building programme, the primary concern of which had been to integrate the diverse ethno-regional groups into the state and place them under one centralised authority. Today it is generally agreed that this approach fostered political monolithism and authoritarianism at the expense of constitutionalism. Alternative constitutional arrangements, notably federalism which basically emanates from the desire of people to form a union without necessarily losing their various identities, were either ignored or consciously violated by African leaders or, as in Nigeria, they experienced an increasing concentration of power in the federal centre. Atanga's book is a detailed narrative of the Anglophone Cameroonian minority's growing protest against their subordinate position in the Francophone-dominated unitary state and their vanguard role in demands for a rearrangement of state power.

Piet Konings,
African Studies Centre
Leiden (The Netherlands)

Chapter One

General Introduction

"We do not wish to bring the weight of our population to bear on our British brothers. We are not annexationists…"[1]

Ahmadu Ahidjo, 1959

It is very difficult to comprehend events in contemporary Africa without going back to her colonial experience. This applies as well to Cameroon's triple colonial experience[2] that has come to have a great bearing and influence in shaping events at the advent of independence and thereafter.

Cameroon, with its more than 150 distinct peoples (Johnson 1970a: vii), is one of the most pluralistic of African states.[3] In most African societies, European influences have affected the traditional cultures in one way or the other, and in most cases, turned out to be the most dominant factor in the so-called 'modernisation drive.' Cameroon has been in the mainstream of these currents in Africa. Here, however, the problem of 'cultural super-imposition' has been compounded by the fact that she had colonial powers of different distinct and opposing cultures; Germany, from 1884 until her defeat during the First World War, then Britain and France.

Cameroon has, in fact, been subjected to several external influences. Portuguese, Spanish, and Dutch trading companies operated important trading stations and missionaries set up permanent posts by 1864. Political and economic domination by Germany from 1884 ended in 1916 when France and Britain forced the Germans out (Johnson 1970a: viii).

Cameroon became a Class 'B' mandate of the League of Nations with the recognition of French and British brigandage by the 1919 Treaty of Versailles (Nfor 1984[4]: 9; Johnson 1970a: ix). Her Class 'B' status meant that the mandate received supervision from the League, and as such, Britain and France dealt with the territory as they so desired.

After the Second World War, and with the birth of the United Nations Organisation (UNO) in 1945, the territories became Trust Territories (Johnson 1970a: viii). Article 76b of the UN Charter, which promised "Self-government or independence … (according to) the freely expressed wishes of the people concerned" (Johnson 1970a: viii) provided the basis for the struggle for independence in the Cameroons. The strategy for obtaining this goal on both sides of the colonial divide, found expression partly, in the quest for re-unification (Johnson 1970a: viii).

In the British Cameroons, both Britain and Nigeria were objects of the nationalist struggle, as "…the strong emotions that drove the English-speaking Cameroonian nationalists resulted from a sense of affront and discrimination about the retardation of the Territory compared to other areas of Nigeria" (Johnson 1970a: 141). As such, home rule meant freeing the territory from the contiguous Eastern Regional Institutions, and demanding greater responsibility over local affairs.

It is worth noting that the brief period of German rule did not produce a 'Kamerun Nation," as it did not precipitate cultural and practical affinities, and did not introduce substantial economic interchange (Johnson 1970a: 143). As such, calls for reunification were mainly an expression of nationalism, or as Prof. Anomah Ngu puts it "this was based on sentiment."[5]

In the Southern Cameroons, the political parties were unable to reach agreement on the reunification issue, as the three parties, the Kamerun National Democratic Party (KNDP), the Cameroons People's National Convention (CPNC), and the One Kamerun Party (OK) were divided on the issue. The KNDP wanted independence for the Southern Cameroons before unification with the Republic of Cameroon, the CPNC stood for independence as one of the Regions in the Federation of Nigeria, while the OK party wanted immediate reunification. At a conference summoned by the British government in Mamfe in August 1959, all the parties maintained their positions (Mukong[6] 1993). The Kamerun United Party (KUP) of P.M. Kale stood for the independence of the territory as a separate political entity (Ngoh[7] 1990: 7; Mukong 1993). At the UN, a last minute consensus by the parties for independence was not followed up because the Afro-Asian Block intimated that it will block such a request (Johnson 1970a: 146).[8]

The 'Two Alternatives' of either achieving independence as one of the regions within the Federation of Nigeria, or reuniting with their 'brothers' of the Republic of Cameroon on the basis of equality, was foisted on the Southern Cameroons. The 'Third Alternative' of independence as a sovereign entity, as well as the position of the Prime Minister, Dr. John Ngu Foncha who represented the will of the majority of the people and the party in government, was not taken into consideration. The KNDP therefore had to come to terms with far less than it had desired, and settled for reunification.

The pro-reunificationists emerged victorious at the plebiscite held on February 11, 1961.[9]

The Federal Republic of Cameroon with its two superimposed foreign cultures came into being on 01 October 1961 after the Foumban Constitutional Conference. This ended 45 years of division and separate development under different colonial powers having different forms of political administration, legal and educational systems (Nfor 1984: 1). It is also important to note that the preceding 32 years of German colonial exploitation was shorter than the subsequent 45 years of French and British exploitation of the territories.

At the time of reunification, the two states differed greatly in population and landmass. East Cameroon had a landmass of 432,000 km^2 and a population of 3,200,000 people, constituting about 78%, while West Cameroon had a population of 800,000, and a land surface of area of 43,500 km^2 making up the remaining 22% (Johnson 1970a: ix; Nfor 1984: 2).

There was equally a great disparity in the level of socio- economic development. There was a degree of economic development in East Cameroon with some petty industries, a comparatively better network of roads, a few kilometres of railway and more educational facilities compared to backward West Cameroon (Nfor 1984: 2).

Herein is the genesis of what has come to be known in Cameroon as the 'Anglophone problem'[10] as adequate safeguards were not enshrined in the constitution to guarantee the rights of the people of West Cameroon as a 'distinct minority' within the Federation. The few provisions meant to provide such guarantees were subsequently undermined and discarded, with little or no challenge from the 'Anglophone community.' An analysis of the reasons for undermining the guarantees and the inadequate challenge forms an important thrust of this work.

Whilst the former British West Cameroon faced her new destiny in the Federal Republic of Cameroon, France did not relax her grip on East Cameroon. The Francophone-led regime set about annexing West Cameroon in every way but name and this contributed to intensifying the neo-colonial relationship with France. To attain this objective, France found in Ahidjo a willing tool who will implement her policies. In order to understand this, the fact that Ahidjo was never a central participant in the turbulent political conflicts of the mid-1950s is important. The French never wanted to create a precedent in Africa by negotiating with the Union des Populations du

Cameroun (UPC) who were then waging a war of liberation (Bayart[11] 1978: 46). After the removal of Andre Marie Mbida as the Prime Minister by France, she brought in Ahidjo. At the independence of the Republic of Cameroon, Ahidjo could thus pay tribute: "… to our guardian power, France, for helping us to build our nation without force and hatred" (Nfor 1984: 2). This, in spite of the fact that France was then massacring Cameroonians in *Bassaland* and the *Bamileke* region, and the UPC was waging a war of liberation against France.

This work is primarily concerned with the socio-economic and political evolution of West Cameroon and Cameroonians of English expression as a distinct minority within the Republic of Cameroon. However, an analysis of the central role that policies and developments emanating from the centre, Yaoundé, have played in shaping and influencing socio-economic and political developments in West Cameroon will be made.

The Problématique

In 1961 following the Foumban Conference[12], Cameroonians on both sides of the linguo-cultural divide formed a political union. Since the early 1990s there have been increasing demands from important and vocal constituencies within the minority Anglophone community demanding a reconfiguration of the union, including from important components, a 'reassertion of the independence' of the region. The basis for these centrifugal currents is the allegations of lack of good faith and institutionalised discrimination against the Anglophone community and the region by the Francophone-led regime. In the process, substantial evidence in support of this claim has been produced, and as one of the principal architects of reunification, John Foncha[13] puts it:

> …For 31 years, the Anglophones have been marginalised, suppressed, oppressed, cheated, brutalised and treated like underdogs, like plantation workers; all this in a bid to woo them into integrating their minds, souls and also to obliterate all the English in which we grew up[14] (Foncha 1992: 17).

Another observer, John Nchami[15] (1992) has pointed out that the English-speaking Cameroonian feels very much like an outsider in his own country, as he is fit only for the assistant or secondary roles even to the worst of mediocres. What is responsible for this deep-rooted and pervasive feeling of alienation among the population of West Cameroon? What has been the reaction of the people of West Cameroon to the perceived alienation over the years?

What has come to be known as the 'Anglophone problem' manifests through frequent complaints by Anglophones about the lack of equal opportunity in political appointments, non-participation of Anglophones in any position of real power and influence in the country's affairs, the over-centralisation of powers in Yaoundé, where English-speaking Cameroonians who do not understand French are not attended to by Francophone bureaucrats. It equally relates to the meagre share of development resources from a budget that is to a large extent funded by oil revenues that are generated in the English-speaking part of the country; the commonly held view that the Anglophones are less patriotic from whence the derogatory term of 'Biafrans.'

There is the temptation to perceive the 'anglophone problem' as one of deliberate and systematic elimination and alienation from the political process. The problem, too, is also and equally one of unbalanced regional development policies that have been pursued over the years by the Ahidjo - Biya regimes.[16]

An examination is made of how the issues of ethnic conflict and rivalry, regionalism, religious differences, status and class conflict, are subsumed by the issues of a 'linguo-cultural minority' and, by extension, the penetration of (alien) foreign cultures that seem to have become the major variable in socio-economic and political allocation of resources, and/or major determinant of socio-economic (under) development within the context of neo-colonialism.

Cameroon, as a "bilingual', albeit pluralistic society under the firm grip of authoritarianism, resisted the forces of disintegration, while with apparent opening up, seems to be yielding to centrifugal forces. Herein lies the main thrust, interest and significance of this study.

Given the foregoing, there is need to attempt a response to a number of questions:

a) Is the Anglophone/Francophone conflict simply the institutionalised use of state machinery to pursue the interests of a fraction of the ruling class against the countervailing interests of another fraction of the ruling class using the language (cultural) divide?

b) Are the instruments of state power being used to subvert the legitimate aspirations of a distinct minority, and to appropriate resources for the benefit of the ruling class (elites) irrespective of the linguo-cultural divide?

c) Did West Cameroon fare better during the era of federalism, or is it performing better within the centralised system?

d) How has Cameroon's relationship with France affected the development of the territory of West Cameroon?

e) Has language been instrumentalised for the economic exploitation of a distinct minority?

The analysis attempts at understanding these questions and in shedding a little light on them. Furthermore, an attempt is made at appreciating the factors responsible for incessant socio-political upheaval in West Cameroon and make recommendations based on the findings.

Significance of the Study

Until the 1990s, there was a general paucity of scholarly works relating to the political economy of West Cameroon. Most of the studies prior on West Cameroon approached it from the perspective of institutional and constitutional dimensions of political integration in a pluralistic state. With the wave of democratic 'reawakening' in Africa as from the early 1990s, and given the attendant challenges associated with the pluralistic nature of African states, coupled with the potential of disintegration, grievances related to significant minorities within states need to be re-examined with a view to checking latent dissent and providing political solutions to potential spots of political instability. West Cameroon provides a very good example of such a minority situation in Africa. This study thus hopes to contribute to the understanding of minority issues in Africa in general and that of West Cameroon in particular.

Scope

This study covers essentially the geographical entity which at independence became known as West Cameroon, consisting of two English-speaking regions of the North-West and the South West of present day

Republic of Cameroon. However, it makes an analysis of policies and decisions emanating from the centre, Yaoundé, as they have come to be of fundamental importance in shaping socio-political and economic developments in the region, and by extension, the influence and relation of the rest of the country to West Cameroon. In the process, the role played by the two superimposed and distinct cultures (Anglo-Saxon and French) in the political evolution of West Cameroon and in national politics is highlighted.

Literature Review

Prior to the 1990s, a number of studies had been carried out on the socio- political and economic history of Cameroon since independence. However, very few writers had undertaken an analysis of the political economy of West Cameroon.

Most of these works are of the 'Modernization school' that approached the issues against the backdrop of the different colonial experience regions of Cameroon underwent. The result has been an attempt at resolving the Francophone -Anglophone contradiction through what has come to be known as national integration. Such works include Le Vine (1964), Johnson (1970a), Jacques Benjamin (1972) and Richard Joseph (1978).

Willard Johnson (1970a) deals with the challenges of political integration in what he calls a fragmentary society, and looks at the cultural, economic and political aspects of the process. He shows how the British and French Cameroons went about the process of political reunification in 1961, which led to the formation of a federation.

Johnson examines the theory of integration of political systems and how such unions are maintained and uses this to analyse the Cameroon experience. He looks at the impact of disparate colonial legacies on the traditional cultural patterns in Cameroon, and explains the rise of the movement for political union. He then moves on to look at the character of the Cameroon union, its leaders and their differing conception of federalism, and that of other countries, such as the USA.

He concludes:
Clearly, the political structures of the two states that formed the Federation were quite different. The political cultures animating them were also different ... Prime Minister Foncha seems to have sought a

confederation of almost autonomous states. Ahidjo, on the other hand apparently wanted a non-federation, one so strong at the centre as to approximate a unitary structure (Johnson 1970a: 370).

It is this factor that has led to the predicament of West Cameroon, since the vision of the Francophone-led regime eventually prevailed.

Le Vine (1964)[17] tackles the independence of the Republic of (East) Cameroon and the birth of the Federal Republic of Cameroon, of the Union of Cameroon Republic and the former under British trusteeship. He traces the political evolution of Cameroon from its German days to when it was divided between Britain and France after the First World War. Le Vine focuses on the forces and processes that went into defining the political community of the Cameroon Republic. The work sees factors like ethnic particularism, Western influence and nationalism as being influenced by socio-political factors.

Le Vine (1970)[18] provides background information on reunification, and what it meant for the two sides involved. He asserts that before reunification West Cameroon and East Cameroon had little in common, except a brief period as a German protectorate, a minor ethnic community and the feeling that they ought to be reunited after forty years of separate administration and development under the French and British, and as such, had developed modern political systems that were mutually exclusive.

He then delves into the constitutional arrangements that envisaged a transitional period during which each unit had considerable political autonomy and could prevent federal passage of bills it opposed. However, this did not last long, as by 1962, there were already signs of dissatisfaction with the central authority by prominent actors within the state of West Cameroon.

These processes are discussed within the context of political parties in the two regions before reunification. He examines inter-party competition and their programmes, supporters and leadership before independence and reunification. The positions of various parties on reunification are elaborated, and he explains why the pro-reunificationists, especially in West Cameroon, emerged victorious eventually. He thus provides us with some good background information as to how the 'anglophone problem' emerged in Cameroon.

Bayart's (1978) article[19] deals basically with the marginalisation of Anglophone Cameroon from the political process by 1972. Ahidjo was able to capitalise on the apparent political naivety of the Anglophone leadership, coupled with the personal ambitions of some members of the leadership to bring about the rapid loss of West Cameroon power and influence in the Federation, such that by the time of the 1972 referendum, the Federation existed only on paper.

Bayart provides an anatomy of how Ahidjo gradually transferred state powers to the Federal Government, and thereby leaving the two state governments with little or no power. By 1966, Ahidjo had succeeded in merging the parties and forming one single party, the Cameroon National Union (CNU). Ahidjo equally manipulated the constitution which then empowered him to appoint state Prime ministers instead of the state legislative assemblies. The unitary constitution of 1972, as Bayart asserts was the culmination of the twin process of harmonising the administration of the federal states and the maximisation of presidential power.

Bayart concludes that West Cameroon autonomy, by the time of the referendum, was a dead letter, and the powers of the Head of State extended to every corner of the country. He states:

Although the Anglophone political class has since assured continued representation at all levels of the political system, this participation no longer involves the prerogative to act on behalf of a distinct regional and linguistic collectivity (Joseph 1978: 89-90).

Jacques Benjamin's (1972)[20] work is an analysis of how political union could be achieved between two communities through the use of the federal system. He starts off with a theoretical discussion of federalism, and how it ought to operate in a bicultural community, then moves on to the specific experience of Cameroon. There is a synopsis of the diverse use of federalism, especially in newly emerging states.

He moves on to the consequences of colonial intervention and the setting up of federal states to maintain colonial boundaries which have, at times, been dissolved immediately after independence, while at times it has led to bloodshed. He attributes this to the attempt at transferring the power of the former colonial powers to a new dominant element in a new state, and as a result of this, external colonialism is replaced by internal colonialism.

Benjamin sees reunification in the case of the Cameroons as trying to solve the problems created by imperialist expediency. He expressed his fears which have turned out to be true, that reunification might be at the expense of the minority Anglophone community, in the sense that it would likely be absorbed by the majority Francophone community. He states that this is not the goal of the Anglophone community. He asserts that the problem can only be minimised by the emergence of a new national culture.

The writer asserts that the creation of the Cameroon federation was marked with ambiguity, as only the minority Anglophones affirmed and wanted to maintain the existence of two states. From his analysis, he demonstrates the overwhelming role of the Cameroon federal institutions, vis-à-vis state institutions and consequently the lack of adequate protection for minority rights. The Federated states only enjoyed very limited autonomy. Benjamin thus, rather than seeing it as a federation, prefers to see the Cameroon Federation as a unitary state with a degree of decentralisation.

Analysing from the viewpoint that 'Federalism' is a concept in constant evolution, he objectively comes up with two models: either the Cameroon State evolves to a perfectly decentralised and bilingual state, or a unitary state in which English or the Anglo-Saxon cultural heritage plays but a subordinate role. One can state that his analysis has turned out, to a large extent, to be very precise, as Cameroon has eventually ended up as a unitary state with English playing a very subordinate role.

With a lot of empirical evidence, he demonstrates how the economic and cultural presence of France was a very strong and centralising factor, while, on the other hand in West Cameroon, British policy was a total 'hands off'. Benjamin then delves into the role of imperialism as a factor in the analysis of centripetal and centrifugal forces at work in Cameroon, and asserts that it is still the struggle for the division of the world amongst imperialist powers.

He then turns to the theoretical and empirical analysis of culture as a factor in the creation of federations and the safe-guards that protect the minorities and make the federations' workable or unworkable, taking into consideration external factors such as support of powerful states for one side or the other of the cultural minority or majority. He observes that more often than not a cultural minority is exploited economically, and cites examples such as that of the Black Americans in the USA and Irish Catholics in Britain. This aspect of the economic exploitation of a minority constitutes an essential part of this study.

Ombe Ndzana (1987)[21] focuses his study on the Cameroon Development Corporation (CDC), which is a state-owned agro-industrial enterprise and the National Refining Company Limited in the Southwest Province. While Ombe Ndzana makes an in-depth analysis of how the National Refining

Company operates and of the workers and their working conditions, he tries to situate the refinery within the context of the political economy of the region. He points out that in spite of the presence of the refinery in the province; people have benefitted little in terms of development and social benefits. He points out that it is only the multinational corporations and the state that benefit in diverse ways from the operations of the refinery.

In his analysis of the CDC, he traces the history of the Corporation to when the first German owned private plantations were established on the slopes of the Mt. Fako in 1892 and the creation of the CDC by the British in 1947. In his analysis, he dwells on the proletarinisation of the peasantry in this region and their subsequent exploitation, by the Corporation and the state, as it is only the state that benefits from the activities of the Corporation.

Ombe Ndzana argues that the perception by the people of the region that they benefit little from the presence of the two parastatals have led to a situation of disaffection amongst the population in this area. He examines the consequences of the increasing dependence of the state on oil revenues, and given the fact that the oil reserves are dwindling and the adverse consequences this could have on the state revenue.

The limiting factor in respect of Ombe Ndzana's study is that it limits itself to the analysis of the Refinery and the CDC and as such to the Southwest Province only, at the expense of other aspects of the political economy of the region.

Theoretical Framework

Cultural Pluralism and Nation-Building

For a proper understanding of the concept of culture, we need to go back to its Latin roots in which it is associated with cultivation (Fonlon[22] 1965: 5). Culture as such, implies the use of man's "knowledge, energy and skill" to influence the growth of things. Today, however, the word culture is used to refer exclusively to "the cultivation of man" (Fonlon 1965: 8).

Cultural action promotes growth for the individual and the society; since each generation is supposed to use the cultural legacy it has inherited from the past, enrich it with discoveries in science and philosophy, as well as the arts. It is important to note here that the idea of culture is to produce the perfect man. However, culture does not only mean human refinement, but equally the rich and varied content of civilisation expressed in the arts and the sciences of ethics and mores, of social institutions..." (Fonlon 1965: 9).

Schneider[23] concurs, as he states:

> Culture...is that complex whole which includes knowledge, belief, art, morals, law, custom, and any other capabilities and habits acquired by man as a member of society (Schneider 1973: 118).

Man creates culture in the process of meeting his needs, and since these needs are ever present he needs a way of satisfying them permanently. This brings us to the importance of language.

In the process of creating things, man has to think and express himself, and as such, he needs language. Here, it is appropriate to reiterate Fonlon's pertinent postulation that:

language is the first cultural necessity, the first cultural invention of man. There can be no culture without language, no language without culture. Culture and language or expression are one (Fonlon 1965: 12).

Crawford Young[24] argues that language has long been recognized as a central aspect of identity, and notes that what has been less well appreciated is the importance of bilingualism (Young 1976: 19). He points out that for most of the

> ...developing world identity patterns derived from shared language, culture. . . which are not coterminous with the territorial unit of sovereignty have been important, often crucial determinants of political alignments (Young 1976: 5).

Culture, as such, is the driving force behind human activity. Human problems are generally the same all over, and as such, there is something common to all cultures, at all places and at all times. As such, no culture is completely foreign. But cultures do differ considerably from place to place, primarily because of the prevailing nature of things under which people live or operate in different places.

In a situation of diversity in cultures in a given political union, there is need to allow each culture to live its own life and pursue an autonomous destiny. However, this is likely to happen only where the cultures are of equal strength, and where each cultural community is bent on defending its own way of life, regardless of its intrinsic worth. Switzerland, Belgium, India and Canada are notable examples.

Another situation may arise where the weight of one of the cultures is so heavy that it overshadows the others. An example of this is the hegemony of Anglo--Saxonism in the United States where immigrant communities try to become as American as they can within the shortest possible time (Fonlon 1964: 13). Fonlon[25] concludes his argument by urging that the best possible course is in recognising the intrinsic worth of each of the cultures and picking out the positive elements in each of them in order to build up a new, rich, harmonised and dynamic system (Fonlon 1964: 13).

Political events, as Crawford Young argues, are an important independent variable in determining the saliency of cultural conflict at any moment in time (Young 1976: 5) The situation becomes more complicated when 'external cultures' intrude into the national scene and become crucial determinants of political activity and political configurations. As Young rightly points out, at one moment, ethnic conflict may appear to eclipse all other factors in the political equation; a few years later, the same cleavage may appear entirely muted and quite irrelevant to the explication of the political process (Young 1976: 8). Writing on America, Robert Dahl noted that "... in spite of growing assimilation, ethnic factors continued to make themselves felt with astonishing tenacity" (quoted in Young 1976: 8).

In spite of all that has been done to contain cultural diversity in Canada, Quebecois nationalism is still very strong.[26] The growing French-Canadian nationalism was temporarily placated by trying "... to remove francophonic grievance by extensive measures to symbolize the equality of English and French in the Canadian confederation..." (Young 1976: 8). The Canadian federal government argued that French Canadians must be made to feel at home everywhere in Canada, and therefore government services should be provided in both languages. Therefore, a bilingual public service would have to be created with French Canadians occupying the same proportion of posts at all levels as they constitute part of the nation as a whole (Thorborn 1980: 157).

Perhaps there is need to pose the question: what really is pluralism? For Von Beyme[27] (1980: 80), pluralism has come to be seen as 'interest group liberalism' which posits that a system built largely upon group bargaining must be perfectly self-corrective. This relies on the balancing impacts of 'overlapping memberships' and countervailing powers.

Ehrlich[28] (1980: 35) sees pluralism, among other things, as the federalisation of states based upon the right of various social, ethnic, and cultural groups to organise themselves. He argues that pluralism is every trend of socio-political thought and each movement organised not only to oppose totalitarian regimes and authoritarian rule but also bureaucratic centralism. As such, every current which opposes uniformisation of public life is pluralist. Ehrlich adds that pluralism is not a characteristic peculiar to some concrete socio-political system or some form of state (Ehrlich 1980: 43). Smith argues that the plural society is one:

> ... composed of socially or culturally defined collectivities demarcated by wholly separate and autonomous institutional structures. The collectivities... are bound within a state framework through the domination of one group, for whom the state becomes the agency of subjugation. Thus, pluralism has as its natural corollary inequality and stratification (quoted by Young, 1976, p 17).

What all of these seem to imply is that various interest groups bound together by common background which may either be language, ethnic affiliation, religion, etc do try to capture state power and use it for their own ends, which may be at variance or even inimical to the national groups which may have similar aims as that of the ruling group or class.

Dahl[29] (1980: 20) postulates that struggles for autonomy arise out of conflicts and cleavages which in turn manifest pluralist tendencies. He argues rightly that hegemonic regimes which suppress autonomy and prevent the manifestation of conflicts make the development of a pluralistic social and political order difficult, and whenever these societal 'gags' are removed, that is political liberalisation, the tendency towards autonomy and pluralism becomes manifest in political and social life.

Young (1976: 12) gives three main components of pluralism:
- The State within which groups define themselves and interact.

- Two or more socially and politically significant aggregates whose competition, interaction and conflict constitute one important element in the overall pattern of political transactions in the polity.

- The basis for these solidarity groupings being affinities of ethnicity, language and/or territory.

In this instance, the main variable is the language/territory dichotomy, while other variables play a secondary, but equally fundamental role.

While maintaining the above divisions, we will adopt Young's propositions that:-

- The set of groupings which constitute permanent plurality are not necessarily frozen collectivities, but are in a state of flux.

- The individual actor is not necessarily assigned by birth to a single cultural aggregate; the possibility exists of two or more simultaneous cultural affiliations.
- Each cultural grouping may vary widely in the degree to which its identity pattern is given ideological formulation.[30] (Young 1976: 12-13).

Dahl qualifies pluralism as 'conflictive'. This, one may interpret as the tendency in any pluralistic society, is towards conflict resulting from the competition for the same resources or "spoils of office" by various socio-political cleavages. Dahl (1980: 22) perceives conflictive pluralism as a question of the nature of class and ideological conflicts and the variations within various cleavages determined by factors like religion, region, ethnic group and language. He argues that the strength of these subcultures has historically been underestimated. He notes that the incidence of conflictual pluralism is very high in almost all the countries of the world today. This is not to say that the amount of conflictive pluralism is the same, even in countries with the same regime types (Dahl 1980: 23).

The question of class, from Dahl's major argument, seems to be only an element in a fragmented pattern of cleavages and conflicts that is persistently pluralistic. We will try to demonstrate how each of these manifests itself in this particular study.

For Dahl, the way forward will be for particularities to give way to the general good. He, however, notes that all assertions to the nature of the general, collective, public or national interests are unless they are merely empty themselves likely to become matters of public controversy (Dahl 1980: 30). In this case, he argues that members of an advantaged majority might not necessarily agree with the point that their best interest lies in making sacrifices in favour of a relatively disadvantaged minority (Dahl 1980: 30).

Thorburn[31] (1980: 153) argues that for 'pluralism' to be successful, it requires that the nation be firmly bound together by a common culture, ideology, language and other such characteristics so that the shock of conflict and competition between groups does not tear the country apart. This, in a way, limits pluralism to a kind of 'conversion box' of various countervailing interests and 'democratic practice.' Dahl (1980: 31) proposes that the solution might lie in either centralisation or decentralisation accompanied with greater hierarchic controls or greater democratisation of subsystems depending on the nature of structures in question.

This brings us to the question of the best way in which to organise pluralistic societies so as to enhance harmony and coexistence between the various socio-political cleavages. This invariably leads to the concept of federalism.

The Federal System

It is very important to point out here that there is no perfect or an ideal federal system. Rather, there are as many federal systems as there are federal states[32] (Akinyemi et al 1979: ix). However, it is equally important to note that there are certain fundamental traits, tenets or principles that qualify a system as 'federal'.

It is not our objective here to trace the origin of federalism. We will however try to give an understanding of the concept. Writers like Jean Bodin, Otto Cosmanus, Hugo Grotius and Pufendorf viewed federalism as a voluntary form of political union, either temporary or permanent, of independent authorities for special common purposes such as defence against foreign powers, for the interest of trade and communications, or for other reasons (Dare[33] 1979: 26). It was however, only in 1787 that a new concept of federalism was introduced into the American constitution (Dare, 1979: 26).

Adele Jinadu[34] (1970: 15), understands federalism to be "...a form of government and institutional structure, deliberately designed to cope with the twin but difficult tasks of maintaining unity while also preserving diversity." The problem however, as pointed out earlier, is that there are several varieties of political arrangements to which the term has properly been applied. The classical formulation is the one in which Wheare[35] (1963: 10) states:

> ...by the federal principle, I mean the method of dividing powers so that the general and regional governments are each, within a sphere, coordinate and independent.

As Wheare points out, the ultimate test of federalism is in its practice. Friedrich's definition is, however, more encompassing. He argues that federalism "...is a general principle of social organisation...the degree of federalism is a political and not legal criteria" (Jinadu 1979: 17). This less restrictive reformulation of federalism can be found in several forms of political systems, ranging from centralized to decentralized and also to a loose structure of supranational cooperation (Jinadu 1979: 17).

What Livingston contributes to the 'federal debate' and which is worthy of note is his idea of "...the spectrum of federalism" (Jinadu 1979: 17). In it, Livingston notes that:

> ...federalism is not an absolute but a relative term; there is no specific point at which a society ceases to be unified and becomes diversified. The differences are of degree rather than of kind. All countries fall somewhere in a spectrum which runs from... a theoretically integrated society at one extreme to a theoretically wholly diversified at the other (quoted by Jinadu 1979: 19).

This tackles the problem of an ideal type of federalism. Etzioni's main contribution to the 'federal debate' is in his perception of the concept as a means of uniting diverse peoples while retaining local autonomy and peculiarities such as language, nationality (ethnicity) religion, etc (Jinadu 1979: 20).

Wheare's framework provided the basis for subsequent formulations of the federal concept. It is important to note here that no single federal framework adequately provides us with a workable prescription of what is federal. All of them, however, severally and individually contribute to the 'federal idea'.

For Livingston, a federal society is one with cleavages patterned along geographical lines. It is one with a plurality of ethnic groups with different historical, cultural and linguistic backgrounds, but in which each ethnic group occupies a marked and distinct geographical location from the others. Federalism, as such, becomes a device for reconciling unity and diversity (Dare 1979: 29).

From the foregoing, one can discern two broad definitional categories of federalism:

- the legalistic, institutional approach which stresses a formal division of powers between levels of government, and
- the process view, which sees it as a phenomenon of inter-governmental cooperation, which cuts across any formal constitutional division of powers (Akinyemi et al 1979:1)

In spite of the divergent approaches to the concept, no fundamental disagreements exist as each approach emphasizes a narrow perspective of a broad theme, of which none by itself explains the totality of the federal concept and its dynamics.

Political Pluralism, Integration and the Federal System

It is generally agreed that federalism, as has been practised over the years, is shaped and influenced by local exigencies. What has come to be known as classical federalism, however, is as practised in countries like the United States, Canada, Australia, etc. A point to note here is that these three countries have dissimilar constitutions. However, the constitutions of these countries arose, as Shridath Ramphal[36] points out, because these

> ...Communities are prepared to cooperate with each other through national regulation of a limited number of matters and for these matters only but are determined at the same time, to retain their separate identities and to remain the competent authority in their own territories for the regulation of other matters. Only federalism satisfies this desire for a national identity coincident with the retention of separate local identities and for a concomitant distribution of governmental power nationally and locally... Only

federalism fulfils the desire for unity where it co-exists with a determination not to smoother local identity and local power (Ramphal 1979: xiv).

It is within this context that we would want to examine the Cameroon Federation especially as it relates to West Cameroon before its demise in 1972, when a unitary state was proclaimed. It is on the basis of the foregoing that one will be able to propose an alternative system of government that will satisfy the particular and the general.

A discussion of federalism inevitably cannot avoid some measure of comparison. Federalism seeks to resolve the conflict between centrifugal and centripetal forces by finding a kind of middle ground.

Shridath Ramphal (1979: xv) argues that the federal option can be seen as a pragmatic method of organising government so that sovereignty and political power are combined within a single nation of several territorial units but are so distributed between national and unit governments that each within its own sphere is substantially independent of the others.

If we were to accept as starting point the principle of 'classical federalism' we will want to see its relevance to Cameroon by laying emphasis on:

> the need for a supreme written constitution, for a pre-determined distribution of authority between Federal and State Governments, for an amending process which allows revision of the federal compact but by neither the Federal Government or State Governments acting alone; for a Supreme Court exercising powers of judicial review; and for some measure of financial self-sufficiency (Ramphal 1979: xvii).

It is within these parameters that one may wish to assess the "degree of federalism" that obtained in the Cameroon Federation, and also look into the possibility of its returning to a federal state.

Tom French argues that federations do fail in spite of their initial success, because the leaders and their followers may not be able, where necessary, of over-riding most other considerations of group interest (Ramphal 1979: xix). For federations to succeed, as such, there is the need to recognise the intrinsic worth of federalism as a system of government before embarking on it.

One cardinal rule of federalism is the need for national consensus. As

Shridath Ramphal (1979: xxii) points out, federalism embodies the spirit of self-determination, and for this to be sustainable, federalism should be of such a nature that a region or minority group benefit from being in the federation, rather than seeing itself as standing to gain more from being out of the federation. He argues that as such, the national image should not be seen to be reflecting only one part of the nation.

As Pierre Trudeau[37] points out, the values to be protected must "... include the language or cultural heritage of some very large and tightly knit minority"(quoted by Ramphal 1979:xxii). It is only by tackling such real issues with decisions designed to sustain the national consensus that federalism and unity can be preserved.

Another argument in favour of federalism is that while it allows for decentralisation and devolution of power to the local authorities, it equally creates new centres of economic growth encouraged by local initiatives, which would have been submerged by central administration (or bureaucracy). Decentralisation as such leads to some sort of development, where there was none or little before, and at the same time encourages balance development (Akinyemi et al 1979: 8).

Federalism is incompatible with autocracy or totalitarian rule.[38] In essence, Wheare argues that:

Dictatorship, with its one party government and its denial of free election, is incompatible with the working of the federal principle. Federalism demands forms of government which have the characteristics usually associated with democracy or free government. There is a wide variety in the forms which such government may take. (Wheare 1963: 47).

The association of democracy and federalism has, however, been a contentious issue over the years. Some writers have argued that this amounts to an attempt at transferring Anglo-Saxon ideas to other situations and cultures, which have in most cases failed. Be that as it may, what experience has proven, however, is that it is very difficult, if not impossible, to talk of federalism within the framework of dictatorship.

Federalism and Nation-Building

From the perspective of political integration and nation-building, Wheare[39] (1962: 29-30) argues that federalism:

> ...is an appropriate form of government to offer communities or states of distinct or differing nationality who wish to remain independent and in particular to retain their own nationality in all other respects... would not this be an appropriate device for bringing nations together, for preserving them, and at the same time developing over and above their feelings of distinct nationality?

In this process of nation-building, the role of dynamic and purposeful leadership has been seen as very crucial in bringing about successful federations, and where this has been lacking, the tendency has been for the attempt to fail. Ronald Watts[40] (1966: 138) argues that federations do not just occur because there are desires for unity. These desires must be motivated and backed by dynamic leadership at the right time and where such leadership has been lacking, the process of constitution making has been protracted and controversial.

Political leadership can, however, be assessed only in relation to the centripetal and centrifugal forces within the federation. As such, its role can only be seen in relation to other factors, and not necessarily independently. Given the underlying forces to which the leadership is reacting, one can only see it as a variable. The important point to raise is on the nature of the socio-economic and cultural environment within which the political leadership is operating and the pay-offs for the various leaders (Jinadu 1979: 25).

For Max Frankel[41] (1979: 265), the federal bargain for new nations is a very risky one in that they are faced with the problem of adequately safeguarding minority rights and just representation of territorial interests, and on the other hand, very strong possibilities of secession. Frankel proposes two alternatives for new nations: to either construct a federation based on some ' classical' model and run the more than serious risk of secession and other modes of failure, or try to counteract centrifugal tendencies with strongly centripetal institutions, thus creating a system that is only federal superficially (Frankel 1979: 265).

Wheare (1962: 32) points out that there is always the underlying assumption of territorial segregation when discussing integration of differing nationalities in a single nation. In practice, however, this may not be the case, as you may have minorities within the various territories. What is essential, however, is that there should be areas in which each of the minorities is at least in a majority so that there can be a state or states in the federation to which each nationality can look to as a motherland or national homeland (Wheare 1962: 32). For Livingstone:[42]

Every society, every nation…is more or less closely integrated in accordance with its own peculiar historical, cultural, economic, political and other determinants. Each is composed of elements that feel themselves to be different from the other elements in varying degrees and that demand in varying degrees a means of self-expression. These diversities may…produce in a certain group within the population a demand for self-expression (quoted by Davis 1979: 168-169).

Davis (169) adds that for a society to be truly federal, the diversities should be 'territorialised', rather than being scattered throughout the territory. As Adele Jinadu (1979: 16) has, however, pointed out the major weakness of Wheare's presentation of federalism, as well as that of others would seem to be the emphasis on formal institutional requirements: that is, the whole retinue of checks and balances and electoral machinery at all levels of governance.

The major problem would seem to be the failure of distinguishing between an idea and its institutional manifestations. If one were to look at the federal objective as one of union and also the system of government, one is bound to see federalism as both an end and a means.

In conclusion, it is very pertinent to point out here that this has not been an argument to establish a case for federalism as an intrinsically superior form of government but rather, as a better option in a pluralistic state, if such a state wants to maintain its unity, given the centrifugal forces at play.

Basic Propositions

This study is based on the following propositions:

1. The perception of discrimination and alienation from the political process by the Anglophone community is as a result of the lack of constitutional safeguards to protect its rights as a distinct minority within the Cameroon polity.
2. The perceived assumption that Anglophone (Anglo-Saxon) culture is inferior to the Francophone (French) culture in Cameroon is a product of French assimilationist policies in Africa during the colonial era.

3. The exploitation and domination of Cameroonians of English expression by their French speaking compatriots can be attributed to the disunity within the Anglophone community and the lack of a visionary and purposeful leadership amongst them.

Methodology

The approach to the study is historical/descriptive, as well as analytical. Economic relations in a political system cannot be divorced from the political ideology, and this is reflected in this work.

Materials used are those relevant to the problematic of the study, and can be classified into two:

i) Primary sources

Fieldwork contributes significantly to the study, and these were mainly interviews with past and present politicians of West Cameroon origin, businessmen, and past and present top managerial cadres of parastatals in West Cameroon, bankers, journalists, university lecturers, trade union officials, and other persons who could provide information relating to the study. Such interviews will be recorded on tape and/or notebook.

The information obtained is of primary importance, since it came from those who were and/or remain actively involved and concerned with the issues under consideration.

ii) Secondary sources

The secondary sources are mainly documents: these include press releases, 'tracts,' memoranda on the "anglophone problem".

Also information was sourced from government archives in Cameroon as well as official publications of parastatals. Use has been made of books, theses, journals, newspapers and magazines.

Organisation of the Work

The work is organized in five chapters. Chapter One is essentially introductory and includes the theoretical framework.

Chapter Two briefly covers the colonial period, with emphasis on the role of mainly France and Britain in the development of 'modern' political institutions in the Cameroons, and the consequences that such a legacy came to play in the politics of the Cameroons leading up to independence and immediately thereafter.

Chapter Three, made up of two major parts, deals with the socio-economic and political evolution of West Cameroon from 1961-1972. The second part covers the period from 1972-1982, with its main high points being the abolition of the Federation, complete neutralization of all West Cameroon opposition to assimilation, as well as the blockage of auto-centred economic development.

Chapter Four Covers the period 1982-1993 coinciding with Biya's first decade as president of the Republic of Cameroon. It marks the intensification of the policy of Anglophone assimilation. It deals with the development of resistance to these policies and reactions to the perception of assimilation, oppression and alienation.

Chapter Five, being the concluding chapter, deals essentially with the summary, findings, and recommendations.

Notes and References

1   Ahmadu Ahidjo, then Prime Minister of the Republic of Cameroon, addressed the 13th Session of the General Assembly of the United Nations Organisation, Special 4th Committee on the Reunification of Southern Cameroons and the Republic of Cameroon in 1959.
2   Cameroon is a former colony of the German empire that was disproportionately carved up between France and Britain after the defeat of Germany in the First World War as a mandated territory of the League of Nations.
3   Johnson, Willard R. (1970), The Cameroon Federation: Political Integration in a Fragmentary society, Princeton University Press, New Jersey
4   Nfor, N. Nfor (1984), "A Federation Without Federalism: The Cameroon Experience in Nation-building, 1961-1972," unpublished Seminar Paper, Department of Political Science, Ahmadu Bello University (ABU), Zaria, July 10.
5   Interview with Professor Victor Anomah Ngu, Yaoundé, March 31, 1993.
6   Mukong, Albert 1993, "Where Things Went Wrong," unpublished paper presented at the "All Anglophone Conference," Buea, April 1993.
7   Ngoh, V. Julius (199), "A Walk Down Memory Lane: Cameroon's Reunification. A Who's Who," *Camlife*, Vol.1, No.3.

8   The Afro-Asian Bloc wanted to discourage the proliferation of 'small and economically unviable' states on the continent.
9   Gorgi-Dinka, Fongum (1990), "Seating Ambazonia at the United Nations," being a memorandum submitted to the President of the General Assembly of the United Nations.
10   This phrase is used to describe broadly the economic exploitation, the political oppression and the alienation of Cameroonians of West Cameroon origin.
11   Bayart, Jean Francois (1978) "The Birth of the Ahidjo Regime" in *Gaullist Africa: Cameroon under Ahidjo*
12   This was a constitutional conference held at the Sultan of Foumban's Palace between the then Government of the Republic of Cameroon led by Ahmadu Ahidjo and the Government of West Cameroon led by Dr. John Ngu Foncha and opposition parties. It is generally known as the Foumban Conference and modalities for reunification were agreed on pending ratification by the House of Assemblies of the Federating States. The West Cameroon House of Assembly never ratified the agreement.
13   John Foncha was the leader of the KNDP and Prime Minister of West Cameroon at the time of reunification in 1961. He became the Vice President of the Federal Republic of Cameroon at reunification.
14   Foncha, J.N. (1992), "A Memorandum on the Return to Federalism in Cameroon Part II," Bamenda, February.
15   Nchami, John (1992) "Of Constitutional Reforms and Federalism: The Anglophone Problem" in *Times and Life Magazine*, January.
16   Ahmadu Ahidjo and Paul Biya are, respectively, the first two presidents of Cameroon.
17   Le Vine, Victor (1964), *The Cameroons from mandate to independence*, Greenwood Press Publishers, Westport, Connecticut, USA.
18   Le Vine, Victor (1979)"Cameroon" in *Political Parties and National Integration in Tropical Africa* by J.S. Coleman and C.G. Roseberg, University of California Press, Berkeley.
19   Bayart, J.F. (1978), "The Neutralisation of Anglophone Cameroon" in *Gaullist Africa Cameroon under Ahmadou Ahidjo* by Richard Joseph (ed), Fourth Dimension Publishers, Enugu, Nigeria.
20   Benjamin, Jacques (1972), *Les Camerounais Occidentaux: La Minorité dans un état bicommunautaire*. Les Presses de L'Université de Montréal, Montréal.
Ndzana, V. Ombe (1987) *Agriculture, Pétrole et Politique Au Cameroun: Sortir de la Crise?* L'Harmattan, Paris.
22   Fonlon, Bernard (1965), "The Idea of Culture," pp 5-29 in ABBIA, No.11, November, Yaoundé
23   Schneider, L. and Bonjean C. (eds) The Idea of Culture in the Social Sciences. Cambridge University Press, London.
24   Young, Crawford (1976), *The Politics of Cultural Pluralism*. The University of Wisconsin Press, Wisconsin.
25   Fonlon, Bernard (1964), "Will We Make or Mar?" pp 9-33 in ABBIA, No.5,

March, Yaoundé.

26 There was a referendum in Canada in late 1992 to grant more concessions to the French Canadians and aborigines, but most Canadians voted against it. French Canadians because they felt the reforms were not far reaching enough, while other Canadians felt it gave too much to the French Canadians.

27 Von Beym, Klaus (1980), "The Politics of Limited Pluralism: The Case of West Germany," pp 80-102 in *Three Faces Pluralism: Political Ethnic and Religious* by Stanislaw, Ehrlich and Graham Wootton (eds) Gower Publishing Company Limited, England.

28 Ehrlich, Stanislaw (1980), "Pluralism and Marxism," pp 34-35 in Ehrlich and Wootton.

29 Dahl, Robert (1980), "Pluralism Revisited" pp 20-33 in Ehrlich and Wootton.

30 Crawford Young adopts this from *Crises and Sequences of Political Development* by Leonard Binder et al (Princeton: Princeton University Press, 1971).

31 Thorburn, Huge G. (1980)"Ethnic Pluralism in Canada" in Ehrlich and Wootton.

32 Akinyemi, et al (1979) in preface to *Readings on Federalism*, NIIA, Lagos, Nigeria.

33 Dare, L.O. (1979). "Perspectives on Federalism," pp 26-33 in Akinyemi et al, *Readings on Federalism*, NIIA, Lagos.

34 Jinadu, Adele (1979), "A Note on the Theory of Federalism," pp 13-25, in Akinyemi et al,

35 Wheare, Kenneth C. (1963), *Federal Government*, Fourth Edition, Oxford University Press, London.

36 Shridath Ramphal, as Secretary General of the Commonwealth, delivered a keynote address at a Conference organised by the NIIA on federalism. This address is to be found in Akinyemi et al.

37 Pierre Trudeau was the Prime Minister of Canada from 1968 to 1979 and again from 1980 to 1984.

38 This can be seen clearly in Ahidjo's dislike of the federal system since federalism is inherently about power sharing within a democratic system.

39 Wheare, K.C. (1962), "Federalism and the Making of Nations," pp 28-57, in *Federalism: Mature and Emergent* by A.W. Macmahon, Russell and Russell, Inc., New York.

40 Watts, Ronald (1966), *New Federations: Experiments in the Commonwealth*, OUP, London.

41 Frankel, Max (1979), "The Viability of the Federal Formula for New Nations" in Akinyemi et al.

42 Quoted in Rufus Davis (1978), *The Federal Principle: A Journey Through Time in Quest of Meaning*. University of California Press, Los Angeles, California.

Chapter Two

Colonialism and the Development of Modern Political Institutions in the Cameroons

... If you vote for Cameroun Republic, you will invite a new system under which everyone lives in fear of the Police and the Army. You will not be free to move about; you cannot lecture freely or discuss your political views in public; you must carry tax receipt round your neck like a dog; and you can be arrested and flogged by the police and even imprisoned without a fair trial!

Dr. E.M.L. Endeley, February 1961.

Introduction

The key to the understanding of contemporary politics in the Cameroons lies in the proper grasp of its colonial history and its extra-ordinarily rich cultural, ethnic, economic and political diversity. The Federal Republic of Cameroon came into being in 1961 as the first "bilingual" federation in Africa, bringing together peoples whose separate colonial experiences provided stark contrasts not only in language, law, administration, and education, but equally in such matters as political style and expectations. How did this come about? What were the underlying reasons for such a union? What were the forces and pressures that motivated the main actors in this enterprise?

An analysis of the various phases of colonialism in the Cameroons and the different attitudes, values and traditions that emerged thereafter will assist in providing answers.

Historical Setting: The Colonisation of the Cameroons[1]

In Africa, many factors motivated the establishment of colonies. Primary among these were: the lucrative slave trade to North America; the need for raw materials for the industrial revolution in Europe. All of these and more contributed in the struggle for, and the establishment of the Cameroons as a German colony in 1884.

Cameroon's geographical position made it of strategic importance for the slave trade to the Americas. By the end of the 17th and early 18th centuries, the Dutch, Portuguese, French, English, Swedish and Danish were active in the Cameroons coast as slave traders. By the beginning of the 19th century, Calabar, Bimbia and Douala on the Rio dos Cameroes and Rio del Rey were famous slave shipping ports on the Bight of Biafra (Eyongetah and Brain[2] 1974: 55; Le Vine 1964: 17; Johnson 1970a: 69).

With the abolition of the slave trade by the British, she opened a garrison at Fernando Po (Equatorial Guinea) so as to check slave shipments from the Bights of Benin and Biafra in 1827. She soon became the dominant power along the Nigeria and Cameroons coast (Le Vine 1964: 18). She used this advantage to encourage British trading firms to set up trading posts in the Cameroons coast. It was during this period that the use of Pidgin English began to spread (Eyongetah and Brain 1974: 56).

Another dimension to the scramble for the Cameroons was added when freed slaves began missionary activities on the Island of Fernando Po in 1827. By late 1844, they had purchased and established a church on a piece of land at Bimbia. In 1858, Alfred Saker, after purchasing a piece of land from the King of Bimbia, established the Victoria settlement (Le Vine 1964: 18). This is when the scramble for the Cameroons proper could be said to have begun.

In this struggle for the Cameroons, the British saw in the French their principal rivals. The Germans were never seen as posing any threat in this struggle for supremacy in the Cameroons. By the 1870s, the French had established trading posts at Malimba, Grand Batanga and Campo (Eyongetah and Brain 1974: 60; Le Vine 1964: 20).

Between 1877 and 1884, the local chiefs showed their marked preference for the British by directing their requests for protection and annexation to the British government, either to London or to Consul Hewett in the Gulf of Guinea (Eyongetah and Brain 1974: 59). The British seemed not to be in a hurry. It was only in 1882 that Edward Hewett was instructed to prepare a report on the Cameroons after thorough investigation. He recommended that treaties be made with the coastal chiefs, given the heavy French presence in the coastal areas. This was approved only in 1883, and Hewett was dispatched in 1884. In July 1884, he was signing treaties at Bonny.

On 20 June, 1884, the German agents of the Woermann's firm in Hamburg had received instructions to tell the local chiefs that Germany wanted to annex their territory (Eyongetah and Brain 1974: 60). By July 14, 1884, Dr. Nachtigal had arrived Douala and made treaties with the chiefs. Hewett arrived Douala on July 19, 1884, only to learn that the Germans had signed treaties of annexation with kings Bell and Akwa on July 14 (Le Vine 1964: 21).

On July 19, 1884, Dr. Buchner was installed as imperial representative and when Hewett arrived the same day, he was there to greet him. In 1887, the last obstacle to German control of the Cameroons was eliminated when the British Missionary Colony in Victoria, the Baptist Missionary Society, sold its holdings to the Basler Mission after two years of negotiation (Le Vine 1964: 24)

With the arrival of Julius Von Soden as Cameroon's first German governor on July 3 (1885 - 1891), Cameroon effectively became a German colony. Cameroon was to remain a German colony from 1884-1916, a period of 32 years (Eyongetah and Brain 1974: 95; Le Vine 1964: 25). The first German plantations on the slopes of Mt. Cameroon were established by the firms of Woerman as well as Jantzen and Thormählem, and by 1913, the plantations had closed to 40,470 acres under cultivation in the Victoria area, of which one-third was under cultivation in 1885 (Le Vine 1964: 25).

The Consequences of the First World War to the Colonial Development of the Cameroons

At the outbreak of World War I in 1914, allied forces attacked German-Cameroon from the French Congo, Chad and Nigeria. A seaborne attack was launched on Douala, using Nigerian, British and French troops. By September 26, 1914, Douala was captured. A condominium was established to administer the territory until the enemy had been completely defeated.

On March 4, 1916, Britain and France agreed to divide the Cameroons, and this allowed the respective countries to administer their respective territories as they so desired. This brought to an end the condominium. They agreed that:

1) Territories ceded to Germany in 1911 would be returned at once to the administrative aegis of French Equatorial Africa, and would initially be

treated as occupied territory.

2) The British and French zones were defined so that the French obtained four-fifths of the total remaining area and the British obtained two disconnected pieces bordering Nigeria (Le Vine 1964: 32).

By the time of World War I, Cameroon had assumed a very important strategic, economic, military and political position for the Germans. After the conquest of the Germans in 1918 it was effectively seized. On May 7, 1919, the Supreme Allied Council shared out the various German colonies in Africa to those who had conquered them. The council left the status of Togo and the Cameroons to be settled through negotiations with Britain and France (Le Vine 1964: 34).

The French were not prepared to see Togoland and the Cameroons become League of Nations mandates. France argued that it will administer the territory "without a mandate but in the spirit of a mandate" (Le Vine 1964: 35); a euphemism for colonisation. However, during protracted negotiations with the British Foreign Office, the French government eventually agreed that both Togo and the Cameroons should become League Mandates, and this was confirmed by the Council on July 20, 1922 (Le Vine 1964: 35).

The arbitrary division of Cameroon into three parts: the French Cameroons; the British Northern Cameroons and the British Southern Cameroons, meant that the territory lost whatever semblance of unity it had achieved during the German protectorate. The two Cameroons under separate administrations moved off in different directions. The division of the Cameroons led to the development of two distinctly different Cameroons with different social, economic, administrative and political traditions (Le Vine 1964: 36) as well as cultural values. This is very essential to understanding Cameroon's contemporary political vicissitudes.

The Nature of British Colonialism and Its Influence in the Development of Political and Administrative Institutions in the Cameroons

In order to understand British colonial policy, one must first of all understand the underlying motives that went into the formulation of such a policy. British exploration of other lands was initially motivated by the quest for spices, then bullion, and later raw materials after the Industrial Revolution. As such, the predilection of Britain to acquire colonies was guided by her economic interests. In this, trade was paramount. Very secondary motives related to the necessity to expand the power and prestige of Britain in relation to other European powers. There was also the need to provide security for worldwide trade (Johnson 1970a: 75).

The major objective of Britain in her colonies, especially in Africa, was not, as she would want us to believe, to bring British civilisation to the primitive peoples. Rather, the primary objective of British colonial policy at this time was to maintain a long period of external control over its possessions, and at minimal cost to the Crown (Markovitz[3] 1977: 59). As such, her emphasis on the self-sufficiency of her colonies reflected her limited moral commitment to the transformation of her colonies (Johnson 1970a: 75).

Britain justified this policy in two ways: it alleged that the ultimate goal of British colonialism was self-government for the colonised territories, in spite of the remoteness of this possibility in the minds of the British government. This self-government was to be instituted through a very gradual process of increasing the degree of participation by the indigenes in the political decision-making process set up by the colonial regimes (Markovitz 1977: 60). Of course, the real reason, however, as was pointed out earlier on, was to minimise the cost, both human and material, of administering extensive colonial possessions whilst maximising the exploitation of these territories and their peoples.

What were the instruments for carrying out this policy? The British found in Africa traditional institutions that suited their purposes: that is, the traditional rulers of various African societies. Where such institutions did not exist, they always tried to create them. Hence, their predilection of 'discovering' chiefs in acephalous societies such as in *Iboland* in Eastern Nigeria, and amongst the *Bakweris* in the Southern Cameroons. The creation of warrant chiefs and legislative councils all stemmed from this now famous concept of indirect rule. This was in pursuit of the British notion of recognising and supporting the customary authorities in African societies, the chiefs and elders (Markovitz 1977: 61).

The theory of indirect rule placed a lot of emphasis on the gradual evolution of the political institutions: the ideal African rural life was to be disturbed as little as possible and at the same time, Africans were encouraged to disrupt the traditional pattern of the economy by encouraging them to grow cash crops, such as cocoa, coffee and cotton (Markovitz 1977: 61). Disruption of the traditional economies, as well as the new opportunities this offered created powerful alliances between the European and African dominant groups (Markovitz 1977: 78).

British colonial policy was not different in Cameroon from that of her other colonies, in spite of the trusteeship status of the territory. If there was any difference, it was in the degree of social and economic neglect of the British Cameroons, in respect to other British colonies. This was compounded by the fact that Britain fused the British Cameroon to her colony, Nigeria. As an appendage of Nigeria, British Cameroons did not receive the direct attention of the administering authority. Since colonialism was essentially about economic exploitation, this meant that the territory was doubly exploited (Nfor[4] 1980: 8; Eyongetah and Brain 1974: 101). Since British Cameroon was administered as part of Nigeria, and more particularly, part of the Eastern Region, after 1952, this came to affect the nature of nationalism that developed in the territory.

During this period, the economy remained centred on the plantations which the Germans had developed. There was little government expenditure, either on social services or on public works. The territory ran on a deficit throughout the mandate and trusteeship periods and got subsidies from the Nigerian budget. In spite of its being administered as an integral part of Nigeria, contacts with Nigeria were sparse, as over land communication was very poor, since the few roads that existed were barely motorable, and only during a few months of the year. Given the overwhelming presence of the *Ibos* and their involvement in the administrative, economic, commercial and social life of the territory, Nigeria became synonymous with the *Ibos*. Cameroonian nationalism and calls for separation from Nigeria became a means of expressing anti-Ibo feelings (Nfor 1980: 8-9; Eyongetah and Brain 1974: 101; Le Vine 1964: 195).

Table 2.1A: Sources of Revenue for The Southern Cameroons: 1954-1958 (£ 000)

Period	Constitutional Grant	CDC Profits	Fed. Advances
Oct 1, 1954 - March 31, 1955	569,000	60,300	—
1955-1956	430,500	19,200	Nil
1956-1957	217,000	Nil	363,000
1957-1958	224,000	15,100	340,000

SOURCE: Colonial Office, Nigeria: Report of the Fiscal Commission presented to Parliament by the Secretary of State for the Colonies by Command of Her Majesty, 1948, p 52.

Table 2.1B: Capital Programmes of Governments, 1955-56 To 1961-62 (£ 000)

	1955-56	1956-57	1957-58 Revised Estimates	1958-59 Estimates	1959-60	1960-1961 Forecasts[a]	1961-1962
Federal	6,360	12,744	21,575	36,840	...	54,459[b]	...
North	3,476	5,724	7,000	7,240	7,186	(c)	(c)
West	5,291	4,347	7,849	10,088	8,126	(c)	(c)
East	1,017	1,551	2,303	2,933	4,835	2,984	2,992
Southern Cameroons	80	365	313	635(d)	1,189	900	827

(a) Forecasts given are dependent on availability of resources
(b) Over the three years
(c) Not available
(d) Draft estimates

SOURCE: Colonial Office, Nigeria: Report of the Fiscal Commission presented to Parliament by the Secretary of State for the Colonies by Command of Her Majesty, July 1958, p 69.

Administratively, the Southern Cameroons was under the authority of the Lieutenant-Governor of the southern provinces of Nigeria, with a Senior Resident of Cameroon Province based in Buea. In 1948, Bamenda Division was made a Province, while Kumba, Mamfe, and Victoria formed a smaller Cameroon Province. All of the territory was put under a Commissioner for the first time, responsible to the Chief Commissioner of the Eastern Provinces (Eyongetah and Brain 1974: 109; Le Vine 1964: 210).

As funds and personnel were not available to apply direct rule, a number of different Native Authorities were created based either on traditional chiefs or on councils composed of village headmen or elders. These local authorities were responsible for various aspects of local government under the supervision of district officers. They were in charge of native authority police, courts, collected taxes, and dealt with such matters as health and sanitation, and roads (Eyongetah and Brain 1974: 109; Le Vine 196: 198).

The judicial system involved two sets of courts: the supreme and magistrate courts, which administered European type justice, and the native authority courts, which were in four grades. Grade 'A' courts had full powers in civil cases, while 'B' , 'C' and 'D' grade courts dealt with civil cases with the claim not exceeding £100, £50 and £25 respectively (Eyongetah and Brain 1974: 111).

Financial arrangements depended on the central treasury of Nigeria. The rationalisation of the integration of the Southern Cameroons into Nigeria, justified both by the British and Nigerian governments, was the alleged economic unviability of the territory (Nfor 1980: 13; Eyongetah and Brain 1974: 111).

By the 1950s, the Southern Cameroons was administered by a Commissioner and two residents for the two provinces. The post of

Commissioner had been created in 1948. Until 1954, he was responsible to the Lieutenant-Governor of the Eastern Region and not to the Governor-General of Nigeria. When the Southern Cameroons attained regional status, he became head of the territory, responsible directly to the Governor-General in Lagos (Eyongetah and Brain 1974: iii).

The Nature of French Colonialism, and the Development of French Political and Administrative Institutions in the Cameroons

Aimé Césaire[5] (1966: 13), in an emotional outburst against colonialism, rightly pointed out that colonialism was not, as we have been made to believe by Western propaganda, an evangelistic nor philanthropic enterprise, nor, a determination to push back the frontiers of ignorance, sickness, or tyranny, nor was it the enlargement of God, nor the extension of law.

This encapsulates the French attitude towards colonialism: one of hypocrisy. French policy in her colonies, typified by the Cameroonian experience, in spite of its 'mandated' and later "trusteeship" status, was one of cultural assimilation. This was informed by the French purported commitment to the revolutionary slogans of "Liberty, Freedom and Equality". However, the French attachment to these values abroad did not go deep enough to sustain its promises to the subjugated peoples. The revolution while freeing the slaves, only turned to restore their chains. French colonialism was, thus, aimed at creating new societies

> "… morally and politically similar to our own as much as possible, ultimately united with it by very close friendship, which should be for our fatherland an augmentation of economic power, and in the long run, an integral part of it" (Eyongetah and Brain 1974: 113; Le Vine 1964: 89; Johnson 1970a: 74).

French colonialism, while adopting a moral flavour at the same time was unable to hide its main purpose: economic exploitation. This concept of assimilation was even reflected in the French constitution (Article 109) of 1948, which stated that "…the colonies are French territory in the same way as the metropole and enjoy the same position in private and public law" (Le Vine 1964: 89).

This policy supposedly meant that Africans were to be developed into

Black Frenchmen. As such, as far back as 1848, the inhabitants of Senegalese coastal towns were granted French citizenship and franchise. Assimilation meant a commitment to bringing the subjugated people into the dignity and freedom of man through the acquisition of federal equality (Le vine 1964: 89; Johnson 1970a: 74).

Assimilation required at least knowledge of French and acceptance of French law, which included a rejection of practices such as polygamy, and a willingness to serve in the French army, and the practice of some 'civilized' profession. As such, the African the French did succeed in turning into French men became more loyal to France than were their British educated counterparts to Britain (Le Vine 1964: 99; Eyongetah and Brain 1974: 113).

However, difficulties in implementing the policy of assimilation led to the development of the policy of 'association'. Association, unlike assimilation, sought to create a small African elite with French values. This meant the application of different policies and standards to the inhabitants of the colonies depending on the extent to which they had moved toward the French social ideal (Crowder[6] 1970: 26; Le Vine 1964: 20).

Throughout French Africa, separate legal systems came to exist, to distinguish between those Africans assimilated into French law, 'Citizens,' from those subject to native customs, 'subjects'. Citizens possessed the civil and political rights of persons of French origin, while the subjects could become citizens by showing evidence of having become europeanised through education or employment of a 'European character'. Africans strove to attain the status of citizens so as to enjoy the accompanying rights and privileges (Le Vine 1964: 90).

It is, however, in the system of summary punishment, 'indigénat,' which was highly resented by Africans, that the distinction between the two types of status became apparent. Explaining the system of indigénat while not explaining the psychology of the francophone African, partly explains his motivation for striving to become a black Frenchman. The decree establishing the indigénat in Cameroon in 1924 exempted citizens from its application. It equally exempted natives who had rendered some distinguished services to France from its application. However, this did not put those so exempted on the same status as the citizens (Le Vine 1964: 100).

The indigénat penalties of fifteen days imprisonment or fines of up to a 100 francs were not in themselves excessive but the range of violations to which they applied were more interesting: acts of disorder; organizing a game of chance; circulating rumours of a nature to disturb public peace; giving aid to malefactors, agitators, vagabonds, natives who have fled their villages and to all persons wanted by the administration; hindering traffic on public highways; vagabondage; practices of sorcery when consequences do not lead to a court appearance; reluctance in paying taxes; attempts to simulate or aggravate natural ills or wounds in order to be dismissed from a public works project; allowing dangerous animals or animal nuisances to stray onto another's property (Le Vine 1964: 100).

The administration of the indigénat was the responsibility of district officers and sub-district officers. One could make appeals even up to the Commissioner. The indigénat was used in the French Cameroons to punish natives who failed to cultivate their gardens or work on the railway, who failed to pay their taxes within three months of its levy, who failed to take off their caps in the presence of the local administrator, who spat on the floor of a government office, who had not kept an appointment with the local sub-district officer, who had come late to work on a public works project, etc. The indigénat was widely resented in Cameroon and with a lot of bitterness (Le Vine 1964: 100).

Of course, this meant that the system of dual legal status also found expression in the courts and the legal system: Before the Brazzaville Conference (1948) eliminated the indigénat and clarified the legal status of the various peoples under French control, the 'citizen' and 'subjects' were subjected to two entirely different legal systems. For 'citizens,' the full set of codes for metropolitan France was applicable (Le Vine 1964: 101). A system of justice indigene decreed in Cameroon on April 23, 1921 was administered by a tribunal de races, one or more of which was usually found in each of the administrative districts presided over by the French administrator. These tribunals followed procedure prescribed by local custom and "applied customary laws so long as they do not conflict with the principle of French civilization" (Le Vine 1964: 102).

Administratively,[7] the overall administrative officer in the colony was the Commissioner representing the Minister of the Colonies. He possessed the administrative and military powers of a colonial governor. He was in charge of appointing regional administrators, district officers, as well as an advisory body, the conseil d'administration. In effect, what all these implied was that France's hierarchical and centralised bureaucratic traditions were transplanted to Africa. The local areas were administered directly through their own administrative native staff (Le Vine 1964: 91; Johnson 1970a: 75).

The conseil d'administration was made up of important administrative personnel and European notables whom the Commissioner consulted when taking very important decisions. He was not obliged to take their advice. It was only in 1927 that two Africans became members. By 1945, only four Cameroonians were members. There were also commissions for Agriculture, Hygiene, etc (Le Vine 1964: 92).

There was also what was known as a Conseil de Notables, instituted initially, in 1925, composed of indigenes. It was normally appointed by the district officer. The councils were completely powerless, having no greater function than criticising, given that their advice was more often than not completely ignored by the administrator. The introduction of the Conseil de Notables went hand in hand with the reduction of the authority and power of the traditional rulers. While the revision of the chieftaincy system was gradual, it was complete (Le Vine 1964: 94). This was achieved through suppressing their judicial powers, then grouping them under regional councils whose head, a chef de region, was not necessarily a chief. His only qualification being his unalloyed support to the French authority. Chiefs were usually paid a percentage of taxes they collected in their localities (Le Vine 1964: 97). By 1947, local administration had evolved into a quasi-direct system of institutions and practices at the top of which you had the High Commissioner of the Cameroon, responsible to the Minister of Colonies in France.

After the Second World War, France abolished the system of forced labour in all her colonies, and extended citizenship to large 'categories' of Africans, but this did not mean universal suffrage. The constitution of the Fourth Republic gave the colonies, the right to seat representatives in metropolitan institutions, including the French National Assembly, the Council of the Republic, the Assembly of the French Union. Between 1946 and 1952, the numbers of eligible voters under one common electoral roll increased by 500 per cent. Local assemblies gained additional powers and soon acquired the status of territorial legislatures. This was legitimated by the 1956 Loi Cadre[8] (Markovitz: 69).

This was a radical shift in French colonial policy as the Loi Cadre stated that French colonial policy was geared towards autonomy for the colonies rather than independence. In a referendum, only Guinea voted against continued association. However, between 1960 and 1961, most of the French colonies were granted pseudo-independence.

Differences between the French and British Approach to Colonialism and Its Implications for Political Developments in the Cameroons

An understanding of the differences between French and British attitudes towards the administration of the mandate and trust territories is very important because reunification brought into serious conflict the results of two very different colonial policies. It would also further an understanding of why it has been rather difficult for Francophone African countries to successfully cooperate with former British colonies in Africa.[9] No where do these differences in views and attitudes clash more than in Cameroon where the two systems came and met.

One fundamental difference between the French colonial policy and that of the British is that French colonial policy was built on the colonies being permanently associated with France as remains the experience. This philosophy that emanated from the era of 'Enlightenment' in France held that Africans were to be completely assimilated and made equal citizens of France. In practice, however, only a very tiny minority did achieve French citizenship (Markovitz 1977: 63).

The French assumed that the African elites that will emerge from such a development will share the same values with them in 'a common disdain for the untutored African.' What all this amounted to is that France evolved a highly centralized, hierarchical and uniform system of government in her colonies, with little consideration for local differences. This went hand In hand with a complete juridical and administrative integration of the colonies into metropolitan institutions (Markovitz 1977: 63).

The British on the other hand, wanted traditional societies to 'maintain their uniqueness.' This was guided by their cardinal objective for colonialism; trade and commerce, while subjecting the colonies to British law. As such, the British were bent on seeing the colonies pay their way. There was thus the need to reduce overhead costs by making the indigenes administer themselves. This led to the development of the system of indirect rule (Johnson 1070a: 75; Crowder 1970: 33).

The French, like the British, did use traditional authorities to administer the territories. It is however, the nature and power of the chiefs in the two systems that made them completely different. The British claimed it was their task to preserve what they considered to be good in the indigenous institutions and assist them to develop along their own lines. As such, the relationship between the British political officer, and the chief was generally that of an adviser who interfered only in extreme circumstances with the chief and native authority (Crowder 1970: 27).

In the French system, the chief was placed in an entirely subordinate role to the district officer. He was merely an agent of the central colonial government with clearly defined duties and powers. His area of administration did not necessarily correspond to a pre-colonial political unit (Crowder 1970: 29). Chiefs did not necessarily remain chiefs of the old political units but of new administrative cantons which most often deliberately transcended the old political units. The British were scrupulous in their respect for traditional methods of selecting chiefs, but since the French were more concerned with efficiency, as they perceived the chiefs as administrative agents, more often than not, they were selected on the basis of their loyalty to the French (Markovitz 1970: 29). The Chiefs in the French system retained no traditional judicial counterparts. They were rather perceived as agents of the law and as such, were involved in the implementation of the most resented indigénat (Markovitz 1970: 29).

Since the French believed one of their objectives was to carry out a 'civilizing mission' French administrators tended to measure their success by the degree of acculturation their subjects acquired. In the process, the acquisition of French culture was made an object of worship or an end in itself. The British measured theirs by the stimulus colonialism gave to their commerce (Johnson 1970a: 78).

This French approach in contrast to that of the British, could be seen in the nature and role of education and language in their colonies. The French considered their language as la porte ouverte vers la culture, vers l'avenir, vers le progrès; that is, 'the gateway to culture, the future and progress.' In Cameroon, as such, there was a definite policy against the vernaculars, but they found it imperative to impose French not only as a language in the schools but made it mandatory to teach other subjects in French from the first day. A number of government and missionary secondary schools were opened especially immediately after World War II and during the last decade of French occupation, a sizeable number of Cameroonians were sent to France on scholarship, in mark contrast to the British attitude toward education in the Southern Cameroons (Johnson 1970a: 78; Fonlon 1976:

195).

In the British Cameroons, as Vernon Jackson (1967) points out:

> ... the school systems virtually collapsed, and no language policy was emphasized apart from the use of English by government officials arriving from Nigeria. This was followed between the wars by a resurrected, inadequately financed, slowly developing spread of primary education, mainly through missionary organizations... the government encouraged the use of vernaculars in schools... higher education for Cameroonians was available in English-speaking Nigerian institutions and was restricted numerically: study in Britain was possible only for a handful of scholarship holders (Vernon Jackson, cited by Fonlon 1976: 196).

This was in marked contrast to France's emphasis on the French language and the development of education from the onset of her colonial enterprise.[10]

France's impact on the cultural values of Cameroonians was far greater than in other African countries she colonised, given the comparatively more extensive spread of formal education in Cameroon as of the time of independence. Cameroonians were among the most numerous African student groups in French universities by 1962 and the attachment to and competence in French language and culture is greatest among this group[11] (Johnson 1970a: 82).

While the French did cultivate a native elite which was absorbed into the territorial and federal administrative services, the British, on the other hand, discouraged the formation of a class of *Europeanized Africans*, particularly at the level of central colonial administration (Crowder 1970: 34).

The most important disparity in the political super-culture which colonialism engendered concerned the attitude of Cameroonians towards language. This difference symbolizes a number of other ones of greater subtlety. An understanding and appreciation of the differences between the two official languages in Cameroon and the behaviours of the various peoples is essential to understanding their attitudes towards politics, administration, law, education, culture, etc.

Constitutional Developments in the Southern Cameroons Before 1960

Britain had received a mandate from the League of Nations to administer her occupied area of the Cameroons in 1922. Between 1922 and 1945, the Southern Cameroons was administered as part of the southern provinces of Nigeria. Then from 1946 to 1954, as an integral part of the Eastern Region of Nigeria.

During this period, the Southern Cameroons was able to achieve constitutional advancement as a province of Nigeria at various constitutional conferences (Eyongetah and Brain 1974: 119). The Clifford Constitution of 1922 set up a legislative council but with no representation from the Cameroons.

It was only with the Richards Constitution of 1946 that two Native Authority representatives, Chief Manga Williams of Victoria and Fon Galega of Bali represented the Cameroons in the Eastern House of Assembly (Le Vine 1964: 210). In 1948, the Southern Cameroons was divided into two provinces: Bamenda Province and the Cameroon Province. A commissioner answerable to the Chief Commissioner of the Eastern Provinces of Nigeria was appointed. Although with the 1946 and 1948 constitutional developments, the British Cameroons qualified for representation in the Central Legislative Council in Lagos, she was only represented in the Eastern House of Assembly (Le Vine 1964: 202).

With the increased political agitation in the Southern Cameroons, especially after 1948, for regional status, the 1952 Macpherson Constitution provided for thirteen members from the Southern Cameroons to be seated in the Eastern House of Assembly. The House of Representatives had two members from the Cameroons while of the four ministers from the Eastern Region in the Council of Ministers; one was to come from the Southern Cameroons (Eyongetah and Brain 1974: 130; Le Vine 1964: 204).

After the collapse of the Macpherson Constitution as a result of the crisis in the Eastern Regional House of Assembly there was increased agitation for a regional status for the Southern Cameroons. With the Lyttleton Constitution of 1954, this objective was attained. On October 26, 1954, the Southern Cameroons House of Assembly held its first meeting in Buea (Eyongetah and Brain 1974: 136).

The first Executive Council had Dr. E.M.L. Endeley as the Leader of Government Business. In May and June 1957, political leaders in the

Southern Cameroons attended the Nigerian Constitutional Conference in London. The London conference had agreed that the legislative assembly in the Southern Cameroons be increased from 21 to 26 members. In May 1958, with the introduction of the ministerial government, Dr. Endeley became the first Premier of the Southern Cameroons. As a result of his vacillations on the reunification issue, he was defeated in elections in January 1959. Foncha, leader of the KNDP, became Premier (Eyongetah and Brain 1974: 133; Le Vine 1964: 207).

The Politics of Reunification

The Ibo Factor In Pre-Unification Southern Cameroons Politics

In the Eastern Region, to which the Southern Cameroons was integrated, the Ibos, who were over seven million, formed a solid bloc. Before World War II, their influence in the Southern Cameroons had been minimal. After 1945, there was, however, an influx of Ibos to the plantation areas of the Southern Cameroons. They also occupied important positions in the Southern Cameroons civil service as teachers, clerks, postmasters, nurses, etc. They controlled commercial businesses and owned shops, buses, taxis and lorries. They were drivers, mechanics, and worked as farmed hands. Their presence is said to have been overwhelming (Nfor 1980: 17; Eyongetah and Brain 1974: 142).

The Ibos were perceived as being industrious, cheerful, gregarious and argumentative, and possessing a flair for trade. Edwin Ardener (1960) points out that Cameroonians saw these qualities in the Ibos as being conceited, brash and untrustworthy.

The injustices suffered by Cameroonians in the hands of Ibo immigrants contributed to the development of the separationist movement in the period between 1953 and 1959. Nigeria became synonymous with the Ibos in the minds of Southern Cameroonians. Politicians like Foncha capitalized on the dislike and fear of the Ibos to whip up the people's demand for separation from Nigeria.[12]

Political parties which advocated for separation from Nigeria capitalized on the prejudice against the Ibos to achieve their aims. Endeley had used the Ibo scare to justify separation from Eastern Nigeria. Foncha and the KNDP were to use the Ibo propaganda against association with Nigeria and in favour of secession and eventual reunification (Nfor 1980: 18; Eyongetah and Brain 1974: 142).

Party Politics and the Reunification Issue in the Southern Cameroons, 1957-1961

Politics in the 1950s in the Southern Cameroons was animated by the questions of seceding from Nigeria and reunifying with French Cameroun. As far back as May 1949, this issue had been raised when Dr. Endeley sponsored a conference of political parties from both the British and French Cameroons in Kumba (Eyongetah and Brain 1974: 128).

This was when Dr. Endeley was leading the struggle to achieve regional status for the Southern Cameroons. This demand for reunification, as noted by Prof. Anomah Ngu,[13] was largely based on sentiment which had an ethnic and linguistic basis, as well as a feeling on the part of a vocal minority, particularly businessmen, that frontier regulations were harmful to trade (Eyongetah and Brain 1974: 151).

In 1951, the Kamerun United National Congress had been formed with Jabea Dibongue as President and Nerius N. Mbile as Secretary General. The main aim of the party, ostensibly, was to demand for reunification of the two Cameroons. Mbile, like Endeley, turned out not to be enthusiastic about reunification, while Dibongue became disenchanted with the *Union des populations du Cameroun's* (UPC) Marxist leanings (Johnson 1970a: 127). As such, attempts at achieving a pan-Kamerun organisation for reunification failed, principally because of the UPC's desire for hegemony and lack of real commitment to the objective amongst Southern Cameroonians. One can safely argue, given the initial reluctance of the Southern Cameroons leadership for reunification, that it was eventually achieved out of the absence of a better alternative.

In 1954, Foncha had broken up with Dr. Endeley's Kamerun National Congress (KNC) over the question of Cameroon's participation in Nigerian politics and Endeley's vacillation on the reunification question. Together with Anthony Ngunjoh and Augustine Jua, Foncha formed the Kamerun National Democratic Party (KNDP), with the declared objective of seceding from Nigeria and ultimately, reunifying with French Cameroon. The grasslands Fons supported Foncha, it has been alleged, because Endeley had intended to curb their political role and influence (Le Vine 1964: 205; Eyongetah and

Brain 1974: 138).

Endeley changed his tone on the issue of reunification when he achieved the separation of the Southern Cameroons from Eastern Nigeria. He now limited his struggle to simply achieving regional status for the Southern Cameroons after 1954. In 1950, Endeley had gone into an alliance with the Kamerun Peoples Party, which was equally committed to association with Nigeria. The KNC had emerged victorious in the 1957 elections, while the KNDP had increased its strength from two to five seats. The elections had been fought by four parties: the KNC, the KNDP, the KPP, and the UPC (Eyongetah and Brain 1974: 143).

When the UPC revolt that occurred in 1955 in French Cameroon was defeated, most of its leadership crossed over to the Southern Cameroons. Their presence and cooperation with the KNDP strengthened the KNDP's resolve to reunite the Cameroons. They were, however, not agreed on the approach to adopt for reunification. The UPC's stand for 'immediate unification and independence' received very little support in the Southern Cameroons. Most of the leadership of the UPC was deported by the British authorities after the 1957 elections (Foncha[14] 1993: 7; Eyongetah and Brain 1974: 143). After the UPC disappeared from the political scene in the Southern Cameroons, a new party, *One Kamerun* (OK) party said to be the UPC in another guise, and led by Ndeh Ntumazah, emerged.[15]

The differences between the KNDP and KNC/KPP alliance became irreconcilable after the two constitutional conferences that preceded the 1958 Constitution. The KNC/KPP felt that the Southern Cameroons stood to gain more economically and financially through continued association with Nigeria and avoiding the political chaos prevailing in French Cameroon (Eyongetah and Brain 1974: 143).

The stand of the leader of the KNC, Dr. Endeley as at May 1958, was, as he stated:

> ... most of us have, at one time or the other, advocated the ultimate unification of the French and the British Cameroons as it was before the 1914-18 war. New events and circumstances have overtaken us, and have removed the question of unification out of the realm of urgency and priority in which we had earlier placed it... (Endeley[16] 1958: 8).

Since popular opinion as represented by the various political parties was divided on the issue, the campaign was carried onto the international scene, as the Southern Cameroons was a trust territory. Foncha and Endeley had gone to speak on their propositions to the trusteeship council and the fourth committee of the UN immediately after the elections in 1959. The UN decided to determine the issue through a plebiscite. In 1959, an all party conference was held in Mamfe. However, they were still unable to reconcile their positions: the KNC-KPP alliance wanted the territory to gain her independence as a region in the Federation of Nigeria. The KNDP wanted the territory to remain a trust territory for a while, gain her independence before reuniting with the Republic of Cameroon; P.M. Kale's Kamerun United Party, after his split with the KNC/KPP was for the independence of the Southern Cameroons as a sovereign state (Eyongetah and Brain 1974: 143; Le Vine, 1964: 205; Ngoh[17] 1990: 8).

The KNDP had made the 'reunification question' an election issue during the 1959 parliamentary elections. Foncha had stated that:

> Secession from the Federation of Nigeria will place the Southern Cameroons in a position to negotiate terms for reunification with the government of any free section of Kamerun which desires it... The question of reunification is now quite clear; it will be accomplished by independent sections rather than dependent ones under British or French (Eyongetah and Brain 1974: 146).

Endeley, who had contested the 1953 elections on the basis of separating the Southern Cameroons from Nigeria, and emerged victorious, in 1959 now felt it was not necessary to:

> ... abandon a secure and floating vessel which offers us sure landing to allow ourselves to drift in an open life-boat because we hope to be picked up by a new and better vessel which we have not even seen on the horizon (Endeley February 23, 1949: Address to the UN).

Foncha barely emerged victorious with 14 out of the 26 elective seats.

At the UN, Foncha maintained the KNDP position that the trusteeship should continue for a while, then independence before reunification (Eyongetah 1974: 154). No adequate explanation is available as to why this position was never adopted as one of the Alternatives, given the fact that the KNDP was the party in power, and, as such, represented the views of the majority of the people in the Southern Cameroons. It would seem that at issue was also the rather inexplicable and problematic contention that trusteeship should continue for an indeterminate period.

Rather, the position of the Cameroon Peoples National Congress (CPNC - the KNC/KPP alliance), and that of the One Kamerun Party was adopted. The third option of independence or continued trusteeship for a little while was not retained.[18]

The plebiscite questions as decided by the UN were:

a) Do you wish to achieve independence by joining independent Federation of Nigeria?

b) Do you wish to achieve independence by joining the independent Republic of Cameroun? (Southern Cameroons Plebiscite, 1961, "The Two Alternatives," 1).

In 1959, the CPNC and the KNDP accepted the UN plebiscite alternatives. Most KNDP members felt betrayed and Foncha faced a leadership challenge from his deputy, Augustine Jua. He only backed down when some members of the KNDP managed to convince him that any reunification with the Republic of Cameroun was going to be based on a loose federation (Ngoh 1990: 8).[19] Growing opinion against the UN alternatives compelled the CPNC, the KNDP and KUP to send delegates to London to request independence as a separate political entity.

The Southern Cameroons delegation received sympathetic hearings in London in November 1960. But the Afro-Asian Bloc at the UN intimated that it will reject the request. This, coupled with the earlier report by Sir Sydney Phillipson, forced Britain to reject the request and reaffirm its support for the UN plebiscite alternatives (Ngoh 1990: 8).

The majority of the electorate in the Southern Cameroons, in spite of the Plebiscite Alternatives, a document published by the British authorities stating the constitutional status of the region by voting to join either Nigeria or the Republic of Cameroun in compliance to UN directives, thought the request of the parties had been granted. Others thought that the Southern Cameroons had been granted a probational period in its reunion with the

Republic of Cameroun, at the end of which if she did not find reunification rewarding, the Southern Cameroons could pullout; if she did, then the 'final document' on reunification would be signed. Under this illusion, the KNDP recorded a landslide victory on February 11, 1961 to reunite with the Republic of Cameroun. Two hundred and thirty-three thousand, five hundred and seventy-one (233,571) votes had been cast in favour of reunification, while 94,741 votes were cast in favour of continued association with Nigeria (Ngoh 1990: 8; Eyongetah and Brain 1974:155; Nfor 1980: 19).

The Foumban Conference and Its Implications for the Constitutional Development of the Southern Cameroons

After the plebiscite, a three-day all party conference was held in Bamenda from June 28 to June 30, 1961. The Bamenda Conference was attended by all the parties in the Southern Cameroons, Native Authority Councils, as well as traditional rulers. Proposals from all shades of opinion attendance were discussed, and a common position was adopted for negotiations with the Republic of Cameroun. The Bamenda Conference agreed, amongst other things, on a loose federation: a clear distinction to be made between the rights of the states and that of the federation in order to secure the greatest degree of autonomy for each state.

In July 1961, delegations of all political parties in both the Southern Cameroons and the Republic of Cameroon - then it was only the Union Camerounaise, as other parties there were not invited - met in Foumban to draw up a constitution for the Federation. The Republic of Cameroun presented the Southern Cameroons delegation a draft constitution for deliberation. Foncha tried to argue for a loose federation. Ahidjo sought to establish a clear preponderance of federal institutions over state institutions. Most of the proposals of the Bamenda Conference were simply ignored.

As far as the Southern Cameroons was concerned, the outcome of the Foumban Constitution was far from meeting her demands. At Foumban, the Southern Cameroonians spent more time bickering amongst themselves over the draft constitution presented to them by Ahidjo. Their contributions to the constitution was limited to making 'observations' and at the most making minor 'suggestions' which changed little, but only consolidated the Gaullist Constitution that had been operating in the Republic of Cameroun since 1960 (Nouck[20] 1992: 10; Le Vine 1964: 213).

This fact can be buttressed with a press release of the Southern Cameroons Information Service[21] on July 24, 1961, that stated:

> ... the Southern Cameroons Delegation continued the examination of the draft Federal Constitution submitted by the Cameroun Republic Delegation, and formulated a certain number of observations...

It is important to point out here that the Conference, albeit coming after a series of meetings between Ahidjo and Foncha, was meant to be only one in a series that will eventually produce a Constitution for Cameroon as could be deduced from the statements of Foncha, Endeley as well as Ahidjo at Foumban.

Foncha, then Premier of the Southern Cameroons, remarked that:

> ... We have done a greater part of the Constitutional proposals if we all can agree upon the points so far produced. I envisage a further meeting, but it will merely be to iron out the few words which might not have been put down here... (Press Release No.1468, July 24, 1961, Buea, SCIS).

Dr. Endeley, leader of the opposition in the Southern Cameroons, on his part noted:

> ... as it is the first conference, and it has succeeded, I am convinced that all other conferences after this will succeed. (Press Release No.1468, July 24, 1961, Buea, SCIS).

Ahidjo agreed with them:

I am very happy to be able to collate our different points of view that we have put forward during these few days in order to give concrete form to the principles of our future constitution. Questions of detail shall be reviewed at the time when the Constitution shall be put into its definite form. (Press - Release NO. 1468, July 24, 1961, Buea: SCIS).

There was never such a general Conference again. Neither the British nor the UN were present at Foumban as should have been the case, as the resolution of the General Assembly of the UN did stipulate.[22]

The Constitution of the Federal Republic was agreed in Yaoundé in August 1961, between Ahidjo and Foncha, pending ratification by the Houses of Assembly of the two states. The West Cameroon House of Assembly, as it was now to be known, never ratified the Constitution (Eyongetah and Brain 1974: 160).

On 1st October, 1961, the Federal Republic of Cameroon came into existence.

Notes and References

1. For a more comprehensive background history to Cameroon's contemporary politics, see Le Vine (1964) *The Cameroons: From Mandate to Independence*, University of California Press, Berkeley.
2. Eyongetah, T. and Brain R. (1974), *A History of Cameroon*, Longman, London.
3. Markovitz, I. Leonard (1977), *Power and Class in Africa: An Introduction to Change and Conflict in African Politics*, Prentice-Hall, Inc. Englewood Cliffs, New Jersey 07632.
4. Nfor, N. Nfor (1980), *Cameroon Reunification: Costs and Problems of National Integration*. MSc thesis (unpublished), ABU, Zaria.
5. Césaire, Aimé (1968), *Discours sur le Colonialisme*, Présence Africaine, Paris.
6. Crowder, Michael (1970), "Indirect Rule - French and British Style" in Markovitz (ed) *African Politics and Society: Basic Issues and Problems of Government and Development*, The Free Press, New York
7. For a more detailed understanding of French colonial policy in Africa, consult: Jean Suret-Canale (1977) *French Colonial Policy in Tropical Africa*, C. Hurst and co, London. M.D. Lewis, "One Hundred Million Frenchmen: The 'Assimilation' Theory in French Colonial Policy" in *Comparative Studies in Society and History IV*, January 1962. Buell, R. Leslie (1928) *The Native Problem in Africa, Vol.II*, Macmillan, New York. Delavignette, Robert (1950) *Freedom and Authority in West Africa*, London. Ndiaye, Jean-Pierre (1969) *Elites Africaines et Culture Occidentale: Assimilation ou Resistance?*, Editions Présence Africaine, Paris.
8. The *Loi Cadre* in the French system established the basic framework for the carrying out of a stipulated policy.
9. For instance, in spite of the well documented advantages of having a common currency, as well as the long established history of a common currency in Francophone Africa, no progress has been made in establishing a common currency in the ECOWAS region that include such English speaking countries like Nigeria, Ghana, Sierra Leone and Liberia.
10. Fonlon, Bernard (1967), "The Language Problem in Cameroon: A Historical Perspective" in *The Search for National Integration in Africa*, by David Smock and Bentsi-Enchill (eds), The Free Press, New York.

11. An analysis of Paul Biya's cabinet (1993) reveals that 95 per cent of all the Francophone members of the cabinet, including the President had studied in France at one time or the other.
12. Interviews with Prof. Victor Anomah Ngu, March 31 1993, Yaoundé; Hon. Peter Ngi Nsakwa, February 25 1993, Nkambe.
13. Interview with Prof. V. Anomah Ngu, March 31, 1993, Yaoundé.
14. Foncha, J.N. (1993) "An Open Letter Addressed to the Government of the Republic of Cameroon on the Operation of Unification: Federal Republic of Cameroon, 1961- 1971," CAM, Bamenda, February.
15. Interview with Albert Mukong, April 22, 1993, Bamenda. He was the Secretary-General of the One Kamerun Party. He confessed that with hindsight, the OK's approach to the reunification issue was wrong.
16. Ngoh, V. Julius (1990), "A Walk Down Memory Lane". Cameroon's Reunification; A Who's Who," *CAMLIFE* Vol.1 No.3, August.
17. Endeley, E.M.L. (1958), "A Statement of Policy made by the Premier of Southern Cameroons," published by the Federal Information Service, Lagos, for the Southern Cameroons Information Service (SCIS), Buea.
18. Interview with Albert Mukong, April 22, 1993, Bamenda.
19. Victor Ngoh in CAMLIFE, 1990, Vol.1, No.3.
20. Nouck, Protus B. (1992) "A Legacy of Slaughtered Sheep and Broken Promises," *CAMLIFE*, Vol. II, No.3, March.
21. Southern Cameroons, Information Service, "Foumban Conference Ends in Complete Agreement on Major Issues" Press Release No. 1468, July 24, 1961, Buea.
22. There is evidence that Resolution 1608 (XV) of the UN General Assembly of 21 April 1961, in particular, paragraph 5 was poorly executed. When Resolution 1608 (XV) is read in conjunction with Articles 3 and 6 of the Trusteeship Agreement for the Territory of Cameroons under British Administration approved by the General Assembly of the United Nations on 13 December 1946, the United Nations General Assembly Resolutions 1352 of 16 October 1959; and the United Nations Trusteeship Council Resolution 2013 (XXIV) of 31 May 1960 and Article 76 (b) of the Charter of the United Nations it is doubtful if the union between the Southern Cameroons and the Republic of Cameroon that took place on 01 October 1961 met the minimum standards set by the United Nations.

Chapter Three

The Impact of Reunification on West Cameroon

"But fear seized all and everyone, as each in his own way tried to make friends with the new lord and tyrant that was taking over from the British Government. At this stage all was lost and we automatically accepted our new status of second class citizens."

Albert Mukong, April 3, 1993.

The French Connection: Cameroon, the Neo-Colonial State Par Excellence

Before we examine the various facets of reunification as it came to be applied, it is important to analyse Franco-Cameroon relations as they have at times been fundamental in determining internal policies. In Chapter Two, we saw how French colonial policy came to influence the outlook of the Francophone-African states. These elite came to assume leadership roles in the various Francophone African states.

The generic term, neo-colonialism, does not adequately convey the intricate, fiscal, political, diplomatic, military, cultural and economic relation that France imposed on her former colonies at the eve of their veneer of independence.[1] Since the various French governments have been very unwilling to extend more than token equality to her former colonies, yet the myth of equality persists mainly because the periphery helps to create France's image of politico-economic and linguo-cultural grandeur (Joseph 1978: 5).

Our main concern here is not with the history of French imperialism. However, we need to understand how Cameroon was brought into the nexus of French imperialism courtesy of World War I, when the Germans were thrown out. As a League of Nations Mandate, under the British and the French, it did not prevent either of the administering authorities to implement patterns of colonial administration already developed in their other colonies (Le Vine 1965: 78; Johnson 1970a: 75; Joseph 1978: 7).

French rule in Cameroon as elsewhere in Africa was characterised by bureaucratic centralism and absolute, as well as arbitrary powers at all levels of the administration. In spite of the facade of sophistication, French colonialism was in fact as exploitative as and more oppressive than that of other colonialists who did not profess such lofty ideals. These goals however served the purpose of co-opting a collaborating stratum amongst the colonised who saw themselves as French, and assisted France in her "sublime mission" (Johnson[2] 1970b: 672; Suret Canale[3] 1971: 22; Azarya[4] 1978: 82).

Cooptation meant that while 'Greater France' was unleashing its firepower on Vietnamese, Algerian, and Cameroonian nationalists, so called African leaders were performing their duties unaffected. They did in fact play a crucial role in the repression as loyal citizens of 'Greater France' (Benjamin 1972: 102; Joseph[5] 1977: 172-173, 258, 274; Joseph 1978: 7; Le Vine 196: 154, 156, 160-161; Johnson 1970a: 254; Johnson 1970b: 672-692).

Our main concern here, however, is how this French colonial tradition has come to affect every facet of contemporary politics in Cameroon. Cameroon, since independence, has been governed not with the constitution but through presidential decrees, reminiscent of the days of the French High Commissioner. In today's Cameroon, the successor to the colonial commandant, the prefets and sous-prefets, together with the gendarmerie, operate within a framework characterised by 'State of emergency' laws, hostility to political initiative, local autonomy of any sort and a system of head and party tax in spite of the restoration of 'multiparty politics' in 1991. Nowhere is this state of affairs more resented than in West Cameroon, where before reunification, the people had been used to a more liberal system of administration. It is this perplexing situation that informed part of their declaration on April 3, 1993 in Buea that:

> ...Our Francophone partners believe in brutalising, torturing and shooting down dissenters ... The hundreds of check points on our roads today seem normal and acceptable to Francophones. They really make this country strange to Anglophones... Before unification we had our individual and civil liberties protected. One could not be arrested and left to languish in prison without a charge. It was unheard of for people's private premises to be searched without a warrant. The police did not carry guns about. We knew nothing of the official night raids called 'kale-kale' ...[6]

What is intriguing here is that with the advent of independence, instead of these obnoxious practices being cast aside, they became more entrenched and intensified within the Cameroonian society. Part of the answer to this phenomenon lies in the nature of decolonisation, and those who became the immediate beneficiaries of the struggle against colonialism. In Cameroon, unlike in Algeria, nationalists were denied victory, in that the colonial regime handed over power to a handpicked surrogate, so as to enable it to retain its grip on the country[7] (Azarya 1978: 132; Joseph 1977: 199, 281, 340-345; Joseph 1978: 13). At independence, France put into place in her colonies, structures which reinforced their dependence on her. She has, as such, been able to emerge in Europe as an economic, military and diplomatic power (Joseph 1978: 14).

The constitutional, administrative and political developments in Francophone Africa have not only been fashioned after that of France, but the structural relationship between France and these colonies have been so woven that the economies of these countries, as well as other relations have been inextricably tied to that of France.[8] In the case of Cameroon, various Accords de Coopération signed between 1960 and 1963 defined such relationships. These agreements, drawn up by French experts, covered every facet of cultural, economic, political and military affairs (Joseph 1978: 16; Markovitz 1977: 79).

In the words of Corbett[9] (1972: 4), the cooperation agreements signed between Yaoundé and Paris included:

> ...a diplomatic convention; a cooperative agreement on economic, monetary and financial matters; a convention regulating relations between the French and Cameroonian treasuries, a general technical cooperation agreement on matters of personnel; a cooperation agreement on matters of civil aviation, aerial navigation, air bases and meteorology; an agreement on military technical assistance; a convention on the role and status of the French military mission in Cameroon; a cultural convention, a consular convention; and a legal convention. The agreement on personnel included three protocols covering military personnel on detached duty in the public service of Cameroon, teaching personnel and judicial personnel put at the disposition of Cameroon.

The full original cooperation agreements, including those revised between 1973 and 1974, have never been published (Joseph 1978: 17). A mutual defence pact was never part of the Accords de Coopération signed between Paris and Yaoundé in 1959, yet at the time of its signature, French troops were suppressing a nationalist uprising in the Cameroon hinterlands. As late as 1971, most senior officers In the Cameroon Army were French men.

All of these agreements were never abrogated, in spite of their abrogation being part of the understanding arrived at with the Southern Cameroons government during negotiations for reunification: Cameroon was not to be neither a member of the commonwealth, nor of the French union, and all agreements signed with foreign countries were to be reviewed. In 1963, Prime Minister Foncha had to remind President Ahidjo that:

> ... all Agreements made between Britain or any other foreign country and the then Southern Cameroons as well as all similar Agreements or treaties made between France or any other foreign power and the then Republic of Cameroon, which were devolved on the Government of the Federal Republic of Cameroon upon Re-unification should now be reviewed...[10]

One of the major pillars of French neocolonialism is the monetary and financial arrangements she has with her former colonies. All former French colonies in Sub Sahara Africa are members of the Franc zone, which guarantees convertibility of these currencies to the French franc. Since 1948, it has stood at a fixed rate of one French franc to 50 francs CFA[11] (Corbett 1972: 116; Joseph 1978: 19). This has been of enormous advantage to France and French firms, who are free to repatriate their local profits back to France. This has meant that when the French franc is devalued, that of her former colonies are automatically devalued, and inflation in France is transferred directly to the periphery, since 80-95 per cent of their imports are from France. As the foreign currency reserves of these countries are held in the French treasury, France has been able to use it to exercise economic, financial and political leverage on them.[12] These funds have been used to shore up France's deficit and ensure she maintains a positive balance of payments vis-à-vis these countries (Corbett 1972: 116).

Commercial banks in Cameroon, after independence, were reorganised in such a way as to leave majority participation in the hands of the Cameroon government. However, this has not reduced the influence of France, which she wields through the Caisse Centrale de la Coopération Économique (CCCE) and other financial institutions of the centre. This is done through leaving the veto power in these banks in the hands of Frenchmen, who oversee French interests in these institutions. In February 1993, in a move largely seen by ordinary Cameroonians as "… the apotheosis of our enslavement to France,"[13] a French man, Emile Finateu was appointed the Director of the Cameroon Treasury.

A lot of the so called 'aid' from France to Cameroon goes into the payment of emoluments to French technical assistants most of whom are drop outs and misfits in France (Benjamin 1972: 136; Corbett 1972: 29). Part of this so called 'aid' is simply used to finance French firms in their economic exploitation of the periphery. Richard Joseph (1978: 21) points out that by 1970, eight large colonial and transnational companies had obtained the Caisse Centrale de la Coopération Économique's 'developmental' credits. After studying the injustices of France's trading relations with her former colonies, Judith Hart[14] insisted on the removal of these disadvantageous practices established under Yaoundé I in 1963 as a precondition of Britain's entry into the EEC (Joseph 1978: 21).

The political economy of Cameroon is not only marked by French domination of Cameroon's monetary and financial policies, but is also characterized by the reciprocal duty-free arrangements that have guaranteed high-priced French goods with a protected market from external and internal competition. In spite of being forced by EEC member countries to abandon these preferential arrangements in the Rome I 1963 agreements, the entrenched network of French firms, banks and various agences de coopération have made sure that the French 'patrimony' remains protected.

Ahidjo's vaunted 'socialist humanism'[15] and later 'planned liberalism' only served as a mechanism of the exploitation of the country by French transnationals. While in 1965 he proclaimed:

> We are… for… planned liberalism… one tempered by regulatory action of the state…

He at the same breath endorsed cut-throat capitalism by stating:

> … We consider that private ownership of productive resources and their utilisation for private profit is an element of progress… (cited in

Joseph 1978: 31)

When Ahidjo on the occasion of his party's congress in Ebolowa on July 4, 1963 timidly declared "... the theme of all our reflections, of all our political, economic and social philosophy is a socialist humanism or, in other words, African socialism.[16] His bosses, the French transnationals like Pechiny-Alucam and Co., summoned him and demanded that he "make his views more precise," and to explain if he intended nationalising companies. Ahidjo had to explain that he has never thought of such an idea (Joseph 1978: 31).

Through FIDES and later on FAC, various French governments invested billions of francs CFA between 1946 and 1966 and thereafter in the economy of Cameroon (Joseph 1978: 33). The first three Five Year Development Plans after reunification relied heavily on foreign public and private capital. This meant heavy loan repayments and repatriation of profits. All this took a heavy toll on government finances and on the economy in general. The problem was compounded by mismanagement and corruption. By January 1993, Cameroon owed France alone a colossal 273 billion FCFA.[17] The net result of this dependence on France is that Cameroonians - Francophones and Anglophones alike - are irked by the high profile takeover of Cameroon's public service institutions by French men. This process of 'recolonisation' came into full gear as from 1990, when Frenchmen were appointed as Liquidators of PAMOL plantations, Cameroon Bank, FONADER and the National Produce Marketing Board. Frenchmen were appointed as Directors of the state-owned Cameroon Airlines, the National Water Corporation (SNEC), the School of Health Sciences (CUSS), the Custom and the Treasury.[18]

The cultural hegemony of the French language in the case of Cameroon, in spite of its sloganeered bilingualism, has served to justify the 'right to rule' to only members of the Francophone professional and bureaucratic class.[19]

The Constitutional Implications of the Foumban Conference for the State of West Cameroon

In 1961, the first bilingual federation in Africa came into being. This brought together peoples whose separate colonial experience and consequently legacies provided marked contrasts not only in language, law, administration and education, but also in such matters as political attitudes and expectations (Le Vine[20] 1976: 273; Benjamin, 1972: ix; Johnson 1970a: 183; West Africa October 19, 1963: 1175).

Ahidjo's masters, the French, were never in support of the reunification idea, but Ahidjo had to embrace it so as to take the wind off the sails of his arch enemies, the UPC, who had made the reunification issue one of the cardinal pillars of their nationalist struggle. So, at Foumban, Ahidjo, with the connivance of the French, did everything to come up with a document that emphasised the role and authority of the central government, contrary to the wishes of the Southern Cameroonians. In this they played into the hands of Ahidjo when the Southern Cameroons delegation proposed that the President be elected by universal suffrage rather than by an electoral college. Their proposal was hinged on the erroneous assumption that the powers of the president will be largely ceremonial (Johnson 1970a: 185; Bayart[21] 1978: 83). Ahidjo knew that given the type of presidential powers he envisaged, having this will simply reinforce them. The constitution made provision for separate legislatures for the East and the West, for separate state executives, for a House of Chiefs in West Cameroon. It established a federal legislature with the right of bloc veto if any of the bills tabled were contrary to the interests of any of the states. There was to be a federal executive with ministers. Ahidjo used the opportunity of the UPC uprising in the East to demand and get wide legislative powers through the use of decrees (Le Vine 1976: 275; Bayart 1978: 83; Interview with Foncha, April 21, 1993). What all these meant is that a federal structure was superimposed on the two systems, leaving them more or less intact. However, there was very little differentiation between the structures of the federation and that of East Cameroon. The loosely worded constitution allowed room for manoeuvring and the president with his powers to legislate by decree put this to good effect at the expense of the West Cameroon state.

The shortcomings of the constitution notwithstanding had there been a semblance of sincerity in its application, the all pervasive feeling of alienation would not have developed to an unaccommodating extent, as it did provide some guarantees for the protection of minority rights. These were entrenched in clauses of Articles 18 and 47. Article 18 stated that:

> Before the law is promulgated, the President of the Federal Republic may request a second reading thereof, either of his own motion or at the

request of either the Prime Ministers of the Federated States. On second reading, the law shall be adopted only if the majority specified in the preceding article comprises of a majority of votes of the deputies of each of the federated states.

While Article 47(I) stated:

> No bill to amend the constitution may be introduced if it tends to impair the unity and integrity of the Federation.[22]

Ahidjo did not, however, have any illusions as to the eventual relationship between the two states. At the Union Camerounaise party Congress just a year after reunification in October 1963 at Ebolowa, he had declared that unification did not necessitate a fundamental change of the constitution of the Republic of Cameroon, but only minor amendments were made so as to bring back West Cameroon to the motherland. His arguments were that:

> ... On the one hand, there was an independent sovereign, enjoying international recognition and jurisdiction, and on the other, a territory without international political status... it is this Republic that has to transform itself into a Federation, taking into account the return of part of its territory with particular characteristics. (Ahidjo 1964: 23; Author's translation from the French).

This was, notwithstanding the assurance he had given to the United Nations in 1959, that East Cameroon will not take advantage of its numerical superiority to absorb West Cameroon.[23]

Having made the West Cameroon leadership to acquiesce to far less than what it had envisaged, given its position at the Bamenda Conference,[24] Ahidjo immediately set about dismantling the administrative structures of the West Cameroon state by absorption. The performance of the West Cameroon leadership at Foumban clearly showed a desire to please Ahidjo. The constitution did not meet the expectations of the West Cameroon leadership, nor its people. However, it is worth pointing out that the initial understanding was that there will be other such conferences before finally coming up with the constitution.

As pointed out earlier in Chapter Two, certain sections of the constitution had been referred to the Southern Cameroons Bar Association for expert advice (Mukong[25] 1990: 15). Instead a delegation of the KNDP met with Ahidjo and his team in Yaoundé in August. The National Assembly of the Republic of Cameroon (East) adopted the constitution. The Southern Cameroons House of Assembly never ratified this constitution. As such, it could be argued that it was an imposed constitution, in spite of the initial participation of Southern Cameroons at Foumban. Since the Southern Cameroons leadership was apparently contented, and still hoped for a revision of the constitution, Ahidjo was never challenged.

What really were the implications of the 1961 constitution for the state of West Cameroon? From 1961, all changes that came as a result of reunification came to affect mainly the State of West Cameroon (Le Vine 1972: 278; Ardener,[26] 1967: 289; Nfor 1980: 98). Article 5 and 6[27] had placed a very comprehensive list of subjects under the federal jurisdiction, and others were to be administered concurrently until such a time that the Federal Government could take them over. By 1967, most of them had come under the exclusive legislation of the federal authorities (Ardener 1967: 309).

Article 38(1) defined the area of state competence as:

> Any subject not listed in Articles 5 and 6, and whose regulation is not specifically entrusted by this constitution to a federal law shall be of exclusive jurisdiction of the Federated States which within those limits, may adopt their own Constitutions.

By 1965, the Federal Government had taken over most of the subjects assumed to fall within the competence of the States. These included the legal and judicial departments; the State Police; Local Government; Community Development; Social Welfare; Archives and Antiquities; Agriculture; Forestry; Cooperatives; Customary Courts; Prisons; Internal Trade; State Public Works; Natural Resources, and Land and Surveys (Ardener 1967: 304; Le Vine: 277).

The powers of the President to legislate by decree meant that in situations where Article 18[28] could be invoked to block federal legislation, he simply by-passed parliament (Ardener 1967: 310; Le Vine 1976: 276).

At reunification on October 1, 1961, Ahidjo issued Decree No. 61-De-

75, dividing Cameroon into six regions under Federal Inspectors. All of West Cameroon constituted one of the regions. The decree brought the local governments effectively under the control of Yaoundé, represented in the regions by the Federal Inspectors. There was a hierarchical bureaucratic channel from the Minister of Territorial Administration who got his orders from the President to the Federal Inspector down to the division, sub-divisional and district levels. This effectively undermined the authority of the state government (Ardener 1967: 327; Nfor 1980: 98, 100). To drive home his point, Ahidjo only appointed Francophones as Federal Inspectors based in Buea, until a new administrative set up was established in 1972 with the abolition of the Federation.

Decree No. 62-DF-442 of December 27, 1963 defined clearly the powers of the Federal Inspector. The police, gendarmerie and the military in the state were placed under his command (Nfor 1980: 101). Appointments, promotions and transfers of the prefects were now done from Yaoundé. All these measures, while effectively stripping the West Cameroon state government of any autonomous administrative structure at the local level, created in the population a sense of bewilderment as to the role of the Prime Minister.

What fundamentally made the 1961 Constitution to be used to effectively undermine state apparatus in West Cameroon was the absence of a revenue allocation formula. It was the inability of the West Cameroon State to control its own finances that made it easier for Ahidjo to do away with federal structures. Revenue from the customs and other fiscal taxation had passed over to the federal authorities at reunification. When the federal government took over these sources of income the already precarious financial situation of the territory worsened. It now had to rely mainly on federal subventions in the absence of a revenue allocation formula (Ardener 1967: 310; Johnson 1970: 219; Benjamin 1972: 82).

The 1961 Constitution ignored completely undertakings given by Ahidjo during deliberations by delegations of equal status. At Foumban, there was no UN representative as had been mandated by resolution A/c4/1.685. The 'Two alternatives', published by Britain as administering authority, spelt out clearly that:

> ... The arrangements would be worked out after the plebiscite by a conference consisting of representative delegations of equal status from

the Republic and the Southern Cameroons. The United Nations and the United Kingdom would also be associated with this conference...[29]

The British government limited her participation in post-plebiscite talks to the Bamenda All Party Conference.

If the February 1960 constitution of the Cameroon Republic was modelled after that of the French Fifth Republic, the federal constitution of 1961 combined parliamentary and presidential forms of government. The constitution was meant to sweep away the government structures that existed in the two states prior to reunification, but because of its wording and the powers that were left in the hands of the president, he was able to manipulate this constitution at the expense of the State of West Cameroon.

West Cameroon had maintained its House of Chiefs, House of Assembly and Ministerial system of collective responsibility. The East retained its institutions unaltered. However, the Constitution created two additional courts: the Federal Court of Justice as the Supreme Court of the land, and the High Court of Justice.

Commenting on the Federal Constitution, Tobie Kuoh, first Secretary General at the Presidency, had this to say:

> ...The Constitution of the country has left a lot of powers in the hands of the President of the country and the National Assembly which in reality, if not an appendage of the executive, is at least its echo. He governs and administers and does not account for his actions to the National Assembly (Akika[30] 1990: 69; Author's translation from French).

It is this absolute power that Ahidjo used to undermine and destroy the state of West Cameroon, with the connivance of over-ambitious self-seeking politicians from West Cameroon.

The Erosion of Anglophone Autonomy: Party Politics and the Consolidation of Federal Authority in West Cameroon, 1961-1970

After reunification, there were a number of forces acting on and against the state of West Cameroon. The nature of party politics in the state after reunification was an integral part of this process. Unlike in East Cameroon where, by 1962, Ahidjo had succeeded in instituting a one party state, in West

Cameroon, multi-party politics retained its vigour. However, the leading figures in West Cameroon politics now understood that the source of power and influence had shifted from Buea to Yaoundé. It was their ability to understand and accommodate to these forces that determined their political fortunes. It was the interplay of these forces that eventually led to the demise of the State of West Cameroon.

It is important to point out here that there was basically no ideological difference amongst the parties of West Cameroon after reunification. Prior to reunification, the main difference was in the approach to independence and reunification. The preoccupation for West Cameroon politicians thereafter was either how to capture or consolidate their hold on power, to the exclusion of all other parties.

This tactical positioning for power and influence found expression in the calls for the formation of a national party. First to appeal for the formation of a national party was Ahidjo in November 1961 (Johnson 1970a: 261). As earlier pointed out, Ahidjo, by 1962, through a process of intimidation, proscription, absorption and bribery, had achieved for the Union Camerounaise in East Cameroon the position of a single party (Le Vine 1964: 220; Ardener 1967: 332; Le Vine 1976: 279 - 280).

At one time or the other, all the parties of West Cameroon were against the idea of a single party, depending on whether by their estimation, it increased or reduced their power and influence, and thereby their ability to bestow patronage (Johnson 1970a: 280). From this perspective, we agree with Kofele-Kale[31] (1987: 137) that the speed with which men long opposed to the single party concept embraced it demonstrated a level of individual greed, ambition, as well as the desire to protect the corporate interests of the emerging Anglophone bourgeoisie.

The debate on the formation of a single party was carried out in West Cameroon at various levels: between the political leaders at the federal level; within the parties at the State level, and within the parties at the local and party congress level (Johnson 1970a: 261).

Dr. E.M.L. Endeley was the first West Cameroon party leader to embrace the idea of a single party. He had openly declared the Conc.'s interest in the formation of a single party on the occasion of Ahidjo's visit in Buea in January 1962 (Johnson 1970a: 261; Bayart 1978: 84). Foncha was less favourably disposed to such an idea but feared that a coalition of the CPNC, the Union Camerounaise and other parties in West Cameroon will undermine his position. To thwart this, the KNDP on April 27, 1962, entered into a working understanding with the UC in the Federal House of Assembly (Bayart 178: 84; Johnson 1970a: 262).

Endeley on his part held that leaders of minority parties were being victimized and could not express their opinion freely for fear of being accused of trying to bring down the government. As such, he argued that:

> … we can operate a one-party system which would certainly guarantee that everybody has the right to express opinions within the party. This would make the best use of talent in the country, and we could evolve a system of agreement without engendering animosity (cited by Johnson, 1970a, p 262).

Foncha, on the other hand in working a modus Vivendi with the Union Camerounaise at the Federal level, was obsessed with the fear of losing his power and prerogatives to the West Cameroon opposition incarnated in Endeley and Mbile (Johnson 1970a: 262). As such, as part of the condition for the formation of a working alliance with the UC, the KNDP demanded and got an agreement that neither of the two parties will try to implant itself in each other's spheres of influence, nor work with any other party.

To most West Cameroonians, the idea of a single national party was very abhorrent. The newspapers, especially the usually pro-government Cameroon Times, wrote editorials and carried letters from their readers denouncing the idea of a single party which they felt, will invariably led to dictatorship (West Africa, July 1, 1966: 479; Johnson 1970a: 264).

Following the UC-KNDP alliance, Endeley felt that rather than limiting it to the two ruling parties, it would be better if all parties in West Cameroon merged, with the view of forming a national party. In an open letter to the KNDP, and published in the Cameroon Champion, he argued:

> … it might have been possible to effect an agreement between our parties of the same nature as you have done with the Union Camerounaise and so prepare the way for the future all-country union… I am sincerely appealing to you to reconsider the possibility of initiating discussion for a common understanding so that we could go forward together from here having resolved our domestic problems before we meet other parties in the East Cameroon to complete a National Party

that will abolish once and for all the bane of multiple mushroom parties (Cameroon Champion, May 15, 1962).

At the annual Conference of the KNDP in June 1962, the idea of merging with other West Cameroon parties was rejected. It was, however, agreed that members of other parties who so wished could join the KNDP. Foncha's strategy must have been informed by two main interlinked factors: Foncha's fear of losing his position as life-President of the KNDP if the parties were to be merged;[32] and the desire to achieve a dominant position in West Cameroon, before negotiating a merger with the UC (Johnson 1970a: 265; Bayart 1978: 84; Kofele-Kale 1987: 162).

In spite of the declared position, the KNDP met with leaders of the CPNC and came out with the following resolution:

1. That after unification there existed no major political ideological differences in Cameroon;

2. That there is a strong need for a National Party in Cameroon;

3. That any further delay will destroy the enthusiasm for unity which President Ahmadu Ahidjo's appeal has aroused;

4. That ways and means should be sought to implement this move for a National Party (Johnson 1970a: 265).

The KNDP developed cold-feet over these initiatives and backtracked, as a follow-up meeting scheduled for August 10 and 11 never took place. The CPNC tried to blackmail the KNDP by issuing a public statement noting that the UC was the largest single party in the country and possessed the best machinery for a national party. Dr. Endeley proposed that as such, both the KNDP and the CPNC should dissolve and join the UC (Johnson 1970a: 265). The KNDP issued a swift riposte, stating that anyone who wished to join the UC in West Cameroon must do so by joining the KNDP. The KNDP declared that there was no question of discussing the formation of a single party with anyone other than members of the UC - KNDP Coordinating Committee (Ardener 1967: 332; Johnson 1907a: 265; Le Vine 1976: 279 - 280; Bayart 1978: 84).

Given the intransigence of the KNDP on the issue of a national party, the CPNC seized the occasion of a presidential visit to West Cameroon, and with the apparent encouragement from Yaoundé, issued an ultimatum published in the Cameroon Champion[33] to the KNDP to dissolve itself and join the UC by January 1, 1963. The veiled threat was that if the KNDP did not initiate the move, the CPNC will negotiate with the UC (Johnson 1970a: 266; Bayart 1978: 85; Kofele-Kale 1987: 162). During Ahidjo's visit, the Cameroon Champion[34] carried an editorial:

> Tribalism is at its peak (here); nepotism in the civil service is a creed of a political party (KNDP); political warfare and rivalry is the order of the day; malice, hatred, and enmity the pinnacle of sectional desires... Please come to our aid... You have to issue directives as to the form our contribution will take.

This was the view maintained by Justice (rtd) Samuel Endeley, brother to the CPNC leader, Dr Endeley. He argued that it was necessary then to abolish multiparty politics in West Cameroon as:

> ... The one party system removed a number of ills which plagued the English-speaking part of Cameroon. And had we continued the way we were doing after the plebiscite... because the situation was intolerable, nepotism which was going on and biases against a set of people on this side of the country, led to some people to be virtually forced out of the country... (Interview, March 9, 1993).

In February 1963, the CPNC tabled a motion in the West Cameroon House of Assembly to the effect that Ahidjo:

> ... intervene in order that all persons interested take immediately the proper measures to insure the realization of a single party through the absorption of all existing parties in one single one[35] (cited in Johnson: 1970: 266).

The embarrassed KNDP amended the motion, giving its support to the principle of a national party.

It was during this time that the schism in the KNDP that will eventually precipitate the formation of a single national party began to develop. This intra-party feuding was provoked by disillusionment with the fruits of reunification, personality clashes and personal ambitions, resentment over the influence of ethnic and regional loyalties, and disillusionment with Foncha's leadership (Ardener 1967: 85; Johnson 1970a: 267; Bayart 1978: 85; Kofele-Kale 1987: 137).

What fuelled the feud was the imminent vacancy of the office of the Prime Minister of West Cameroon occasioned by Dr. Foncha's departure to Yaoundé as Vice-President, as required by the Constitution. At a secret meeting held at Isongo before the August 1963 Bamenda convention of the KNDP, Foncha was advised to retain the Premiership. As he did not make any categorical decision on the matter, camps began to develop around the two most powerful men in the party after Foncha, Augustine N. Jua and S.T. Muna (Johnson 1970a: 267)

The immediate issue was the election of the party's Vice-President and Secretary-General. It was assumed that whoever was elected the party's Vice-President will automatically become Prime Minister when Foncha moved to Yaoundé. Augustine Jua and Nzo Ekhah-Nghaky were standing for the posts, against S.T. Muna and Tabi Egbe respectively.

Jua's strength lay with the party's rank and file who saw him as forceful, shrewd, and although more complicated than Foncha, was more likely to defend state interests against the Federal Government. Both Jua and Ekhah-Nghaky cultivated the image of being determined to brook no nonsense on matters of West Cameroon interests (Muna Documents; Ardener 1967: 333; Johnson 1970a: 269). The party leadership however felt Jua was hot headed and impetuous, and although less tribalistic than Foncha, will arouse fears in Yaoundé (Johnson 1970a: 269).

Muna was generally perceived as being foxy, talented and sophisticated. As a politician, he had a lot of prestige for being one of the very few West Cameroonians to have served as Minister as far back as 1951 in the Nigerian Government (Interview with Akere Muna, March 30, 1993; Johnson 1970a: 269). He enjoyed a lot of support with the party's top shots but was regarded by the party's rank and file, in spite of his popularity as a 'federation man'. It has been alleged that one of the reasons for making Foncha life-president of the party at the Mamfe Convention was the fear that Muna might try to displace him. This could equally be said of Jua, who on several occasions had challenged Foncha's leadership of the party. Muna was known to be an opportunist, as he had been a political ally to all important political leaders in West Cameroon, depending on the ebb and tide of the politics of the day. He claimed to have the support of both Foncha and Ahidjo in his bid for the Premiership (Ardener 1967: 333; Johnson 1970a: 269).

It was at the August 1963 Bamenda Convention that the Foncha-Muna-Egbe camp met with the first of several defeats in the bid to move Muna into the Prime Minister's office.[36] At the Convention, Jua exploited the general dissatisfaction with Foncha's leadership in the state, especially in the civil service. There were complaints of orchestrated KNDP political victimisation characterised by arbitrary dismissals from the civil service on the basis of association with opposition party members. Ironically, support for Muna was equally based on the perceived tribalistic practices of the Foncha regime. The Jua camp emerged victorious. Johanes Bokwe was elected second Vice-President, while E.T. Egbe got the less distinguished post of Legal Adviser (Johnson 1970a: 271).

Muna and Egbe resorted to constitutional and legalistic arguments to carry out their campaign with the firm belief that they had the support of the party's parliamentary wing and president. Jua and Ekhah-Nghaky now emphasized party discipline. Foncha, caught in between the warring factions, wavered.

During the party's annual convention at Kumba in November 1964, Jua and his supporters sought to consolidate their bid for the Premiership by having the party constitution amended to read: "Where the leader of the KNDP is an elected member in the West Cameroon House of Assembly, he shall be the Party leader of the Parliamentary wing, and where the KNDP is the majority party he shall be recommended to become the Prime Minister" (cited by Johnson 1970a: 273). Vaguely worded, it made Foncha's role ambiguous. There was already talk of getting him removed as the party's life president.[37] Foncha disapproved of the amendment but was no longer sure of Muna's standing amongst members of the Western House of Assembly.

It was during this time that Dr. Fonlon began to write a series of very popular articles on the political situation in West Cameroon.[38] He focused on the inept leadership of the KNDP and the State. He wrote "... For trained minds will hardly submit to a clumsy, bungling muddle-headed leadership which even with all the good will in the World, they cannot sincerely bring themselves to respect..."

Fonlon's activism stemmed from the general frustration of West

Cameroonians in and out of government and who yearned for an articulate spokesman, which the political class had failed to provide. From his base as Federal Deputy and Deputy Minister of Foreign Affairs, after the 1964 parliamentary elections, he initiated in September a KNDP-UC close door meeting of top leaders (Johnson 1970a: 309).

The major grievances of the KNDP leadership was centred around the inequality of treatment of the West Cameroon State in the Federation, especially in the formulation of policy at the federal level and of a constitutional review, with a view to restoring some of the authority of the States had lost to the Federal Government (Johnson 1970a: 309).

The disillusionment with the fruits of the federation was borne in the fact that the West Cameroon leaders had expected to win a degree of influence and participation in the governing of the federation, almost equal to that of Eastern leaders. Johnson (1970a: 312) states that although they never expected to play as powerful a role in the Federation as their East Cameroon counterparts, they at least assumed that they would enjoy the freedom of ruling themselves as they so pleased and to retain a sense of moral equality of the two States as the dual embodiment of the Cameroon nation.

The 'higher national mission' Fonlon proposed as an attempt to re-assert moral equality with East Cameroon and re-open the constitutional question (Johnson 1970a: 312). Fonlon asserted that the materials to be used in building the new Cameroon had to be:

> ...the two historic geographical entities, East and West Cameroon... and the principal cultures that have met in this federation ... Since we came together, the KNDP has done hardly more than stand by and look on. For talking sincerely, can we name one single policy in any field - economics, education, internal affairs, external affairs - that has been worked out jointly by the two parties? Can we point a finger at one idea that took birth in the KNDP and was welcome and implemented by this government? There has been disillusionment, discontent and frustration are sinking and spreading... this desperation can become explosive. The KNDP demands to take a genuine part in the making of this country (Fonlon, ABBIA, 1965).

The KNDP made six demands, that:

1. A general framework policy covering all major fields of government activity, together with a specific plan for its implementation should be established through joint UC-KNDP efforts.
2. The KNDP should enjoy effective participation in the conception, elaboration and implementation of all government policy.
3. Permanent committees of representatives from both parties should be established to elaborate government policy on a continuing basis.
4. The constitution should be revised; government policy decisions should be taken in a Council of Ministers.
5. Ad Hoc Committees should be established immediately to work out the details of these proposals.
6. These changes should be put into effect before the April 1965 presidential elections (Johnson 1970a: 314)

These demands were resisted by the Eastern delegates who could not see how party agreements could supersede and interfere with the constitutional freedom and responsibility of the president to decide executive policies and procedures. The eastern position, as Johnson (1970a: 314) points out, was an assertion of the primacy of the State over the party.

At the end of the meeting, Foncha and Ahidjo announced that a 17-member national working committee will be set up to "reinforce their collaboration and to better their methods of work, notably in the relationship between the two parties" (Johnson 1970a: 316). When the committee eventually met in October, they were more concerned with the problem of merging the two parties.

Foncha and Jua did express their hope of a constitutional review in 1965. No such review ever took place, as the West Cameroon leaders were instead embroiled in the struggle for positions at the expense of the interest o f the West Cameroon State. The 1964 Parliamentary Elections were followed in 1965 by Presidential Elections. Ahidjo and Foncha were returned to power unopposed respectively as President and Vice-President. As the constitution required, Foncha had to relinquish his post as Prime Minister of West Cameroon.

In the ensuing intraparty rivalry over the post between Augustine Jua and S.T. Muna, Muna lost.[39] While the majority of the KNDP parliamentarians in the state House of Assembly supported Jua, Muna was supported by Foncha, most of the West Cameroon parliamentarians in the Federal House of Assembly, and he claimed to have the blessings of Ahidjo. Foncha convened a meeting of State and Parliamentary delegations so as to find out who will command the most respect in the House between Jua and Muna. In an open vote, Jua had the support of 23 of the party's thirty assembly men. Foncha asked Muna to stand down, but Muna insisted his name be submitted alongside Jua's to Ahidjo. Muna was accused of challenging the party. He retorted by accusing Foncha of being the party's 'number one devil', while Ekhah Nghaky was the party's 'number two devil' and that the President was going to appoint him anyway (Muna Documents: Files No. 98(72), p 2; 98(106), p 1; Interview with Foncha, April 21, 1993; Ardener 1967: 334; Johnson 1970a: 274; Bayart 1978: 85; Kofele-Kale 1987: 161).

After Jua's appointment as Prime Minister, Muna's staunch supporters were expelled from the party. They were E. T. Egbe, W.N.O. Effiom, J.M. Bokwe, M.N. Ndoke, Sam Mofor, L.I. Omenjoh, M. Fusi, Ntaribo Tataw, B.T. Sakah (Muna Ducuments, File N0. 98(78J). Muna resigned before his suspension could be turned into expulsion. Jua and his supporters came out of the struggle with the party completely under their control. Foncha lost complete control of the party.[40]

Muna and his supporters formed a new party, the Cameroon United Congress (CUC). The CUC, rather than offering an alternative form of government to that in West Cameroon , her manifesto simply focused on the alleged injustices and lack of democracy in the KNDP. It was the formation of the CUC that precipitated the formation of a single party (Ardener 1967: 334; Johnson 1970a: 274, Bayart 1978: 87).

The CUC was generally seen in West Cameroon as an extension of the Union Camerounaise.[41] Stark (1980: 118) has argued that the CUC's policies and initials were aimed at reflecting Ahidjo's ideas and in obtaining his favour. The Muna saga showed that his faction of the West Cameroon leadership was far ahead of the others in understanding in whose hands political power was and in the struggle to better position themselves for the 'spoils of office' the greatest casualty became the state of West Cameroon. Those who did not understand this were soon pushed aside.

After the split in the KNDP, Jua sought to strengthen his position in West Cameroon by negotiating the CPNC opposition. Initially, he enticed CPNC members like F.N. Ajebe-Sone whom he made Secretary for Finance and Hon. Tamfu[42] whom he made Secretary of State attached to the Prime Minister's office to join the KNDP.[43]

The KNDP finally formed a coalition government with the CPNC in August 1965 (West Africa, February 19, 1966: 202). N.N. Mbile was made Secretary of State for Public Works and Transport. A special post was created for the CPNC leader, Dr. Endeley. He was made the leader of Government Business (Johnson 1970a: 277; Bayart 1978: 86), a post that had been abolished when the Southern Cameroons got autonomy from Nigeria. Foncha was not in support of the KNDP-CPNC coalition. There was talk of forming a new party, made up of KNDP and CPNC members, and in this way by-pass Foncha as the life-president of the KNDP (West Africa, July 1, 1966: 479). The willingness of the KNDP to form a coalition government showed how she had been weakened by the intra-party feuding and the formation of the CUC. Before now, she had all along refused to bring in members of the opposition into the government, unless they resign from their party.

The Formation of a Single National Party and the Demise of the State of West Cameroon

Contrary to the view that now obtains in West Cameroon, the single party was not imposed on the State. As pointed out earlier, each of the major political parties in West Cameroon did at one time or the other oppose or support the idea of a single national party, depending on how it was going to affect their political fortunes. Moreover, events in West Cameroon did create the conditions and the excuse for Ahidjo to intervene in its internal politics.

With the reduction of the political strength of the CPNC at reunification, its leader had realised he could revive his political fortunes only through championing the course of a single national party. In the process the CPNC became "... the principal advocate in West Cameroon of the idea of a single party for the nation" (Interview with S.M.L. Endeley, March 9, 1993; Johnson 1970a: 265 - 267; Kofele-Kale 1987: 162).

Most politically conscious West Cameroonians were generally opposed to the idea of a single national party. Amongst the elite, especially West Cameroon intellectuals, voices were raised against it. It is however the political class that became principal collaborators in the process.

After the formation of a coalition government in West Cameroon, the two leading political parties, the KNDP and CPNC on August 19, 1965 pledged "... to work for the preservation of their existing parliamentary system and political institutions in West Cameroon" (Kofele-Kale 1987: 160).

On June 11, 1966, Ahidjo called an all party conference, and there, it was agreed that the other parties dissolve themselves, and together with the UC, form a national party (Ardener 1967: 335; Johnson 1970a: 284; Bayart 1978: 87). Fonlon, in spite of his declared distaste for the one-party system, together with E.T. Egbe, S.M.L. Endeley and Nzo Ekhah-Ngahky, all leading Anglophone intellectuals, were part of the twelve-man committee set up to draw the statutes of the new party (Johnson 1970a: 284; Bayart 1978: 89; Kofele-Kale 1987: 161).

When the provisional committee of the new party was set up, Dr. Fonlon together with Tabi Egbe, Nzo Ekhah-Ngahky, Foncha, Elangwe, W.N. Effiom, Jua and Dr. Emmanuel Endeley were all members. The UC had an overwhelming presence with twenty-two members. The new party, the Cameroon National Union, was launched on September 1, 1966. The inability Of West Cameroon political leaders to settle their differences meant they had to rely increasingly on Ahidjo, and thereby playing into his hands. The minority parties felt that through clustering around the UC will facilitate their return to positions of influence and authority (Johnson 1970a: 262; Bayart 1978: 86).

At the formation of the national party, Dr. Endeley declared:

> His Excellency, the President of the Federal Republic with his usual generosity, candour and love of fair play, has come one step towards warring West Cameroonians and volunteered to dissolve his large and well established party, the UC, so that we may meet him halfway and together build up the CNU on a stable basis of equality with no advantage or privilege to anyone, big or small (cited in Johnson 1970a: 285).

Given the role of leading West Cameroon politicians in the formation of a single party, we have to agree with Kofele-Kale (1987: 162), that "... their support for the single party was not predicated on ideology but more upon a careful calculation of the profits to be derived from it. The views of the Anglophone masses whom these politicians purportedly represented were ignored."

With the formation of a single national party, it was only a matter of time before the federal arrangement will be discarded. The elimination of the Anglophone political parties marked an end to political pluralism in Cameroon for decades to come. It was only with the new wave of 'democratic reawakening" in Africa that, against government opposition, a new political party, the Social Democratic Front, was launched in Bamenda, West Cameroon.[44]

The Abolition of the Federation, 1972

With the formation of a single national party, Ahidjo began taking steps to bring his 'federalist' supporters into positions of power, so as to consolidate his hold on West Cameroon. Nelson[45] (1974: 148) argues rightly, and as we have pointed out that with the establishment of a single party, there was a "gradual erosion of the power of regional interest and the growth of the forces of national unity." These forces expressed themselves in several ways, but mainly through administrative and political transformation of existing structures.

The Federal Government accelerated the process of taking over functions in which the state and federal jurisdictions overlapped, such as education, local government, and internal security. There was equally an increasing demand by state civil servants and departments to be 'federalised' since federal civil servants enjoyed higher salaries and better conditions of service[46] (Kofele-Kale 1987: 89).

At the political level, with the establishment of a single Party, and through the single list system, Ahidjo was able to influence the election of candidates for the legislative elections of 1967. A number of staunch Jua supporters were left out (Johnson 1970a: 278; Bayart 1978: 88).

Jua's popularity had diminished as a result of the politico-financial scandals that came to light during his tenure as Prime Minister, and his continued persecution of civil servants who did not support his party. As such, when Ahidjo, on 11 January, 1968 appointed S.T. Muna as Prime Minister of the State of West Cameroon, this met with little opposition (Johnson 1970a: 278; Bayart 1978: 88). Muna's supporter, W.N.O. Effiom, became speaker of the West Cameroon House of Assembly. Fonlon was made Federal Minister of Transport, Post and Telegraph, and Foncha maintained his position as Vice- President. The 'autonomists' now firmly weeded out were feebly represented within the organs of the single party and state (Bayart 1978: 89).

Ahidjo, on the eve of presidential elections in 1970, had the constitution amended to make it possible for one person to cumulate the functions of federal Vice-President and Prime Minister of West Cameroon. Foncha was elbowed out of the political scene, although he remained the Vice-President of the CNU, as Muna became Vice-President.

There was no protest from Foncha when he was thrown out. Foncha was a simple, modest, honest gentleman, who became enamoured with Ahidjo's strong personality.[47] He was weak, soft and too naive to deal with someone of Ahidjo's cunning. He clearly lacked the ability to live up to the challenges of the time. He was never meant to be a politician. After Foumban, he never knew what he wanted. Foumban sealed his political fate, but he trudged on (Nfor 1980: 89), propelled forward by events and circumstances of which he was not in control.[48] His personal success was in becoming the Vice-President of the Federal Republic of Cameroon.

Ahidjo now played his master card: On May 2, 1972, he made his intentions of abolishing the federation known to the Political Bureau of the CNU. On May 6, he announced to an astounded National Assembly that a referendum will be held on May 20 to consult the population on the abolition of the federal system. His excuse, to the National Assembly, was that this is going to do away with the expensive federal structure, as:

> ... although most services have been federalised the budget of the State of West Cameroon is still experiencing difficulties in spite of a balancing subsidy from the federation totalling more than 2,000 million francs CFA, that is to say an amount equivalent to almost three quarters of the budget... the federal structures were adopted at the time of reunification above all to give our fellow citizens of West Cameroon the assurance that the heritage which they were contributing after more than fifty years of separation would only not be ignored but would be taken into consideration within the framework of a bilingual pluricultural state (Camnews, May 19, 1972).

On May 20, 1972, Cameroonians went to cast their votes of either 'Yes' or 'No' on the question:

Do you approve, with a view to consolidating National Unity and accelerating the economic, social and cultural development of the nation, the draft Constitution submitted to the people of Cameroon by the President of the Federal Republic of Cameroon instituting a Republic one and indivisible, to be style the United Republic of Cameroon?

Of the 85 per cent of the country's 3, 326, 280 voters who went to the polls, 99.9% voted 'Yes', while 176 people said 'No' (Eyonetah and Brain 1974: 178). It was conveniently forgotten that it was only West Cameroonians who had participated in the February 11, 1961 plebiscite, and as such, were the only ones who should have decided on the abolition of the federation or otherwise.

On June 2, 1972, Presidential Decree No. 72-270 instituted the United Republic of Cameroon. There is no doubt that one of the reasons why the centre found it easy to undermine the federal structures was the absence of a revenue allocation formula. The lack of independent sources of revenue generation for the state of West Cameroon meant it came to increasingly rely on federal 'benevolence'. Ahidjo made sure that in spite of the abolition of the federation, the assimilative process was not so fast as to push West Cameroonians to revolt. The cultural identity of the people symbolised in the English language, educational as well as legal systems were for the time being left intact.

Why was there very little protest from the Anglophone political class to the abolition of the federation which was generally perceived as an embodiment of the highest ideals of reunification? Kofele-Kale (1987: 137) has argued that the Anglophone elite desired a federation only as long as they were allowed to exercise control over the state of West Cameroon, and as their influence over the State structures began to be whittled down, the federal arrangement no longer suited their designs. As such, its survival was only important as long as they thought it served their personal and collective class interests. Since they felt they were getting less and less from the federal arrangement[49] and as the leadership had given up all hope of any political autonomy for the region, it was pointless continuing the arrangement. As Justice Endeley observed[50] "... we played into the hands of this people because we were enjoying certain positions as individuals and under the one party system... an opposing voice would have been treated as sedition..."

Congratulating the president was a way of adapting to an evolving political situation, and as such, the Fako section President of the CNU, Dr. E.M.L. Endeley at the party's second congress in Douala in 1975, congratulated the President for declaring a unitary state. The section President for Mezam, Fon Angwafor, went further and stated:

> ... The glorious revolution of May 20, 1972 is the result of a wave of change which began in 1966... This peaceful revolution is the first stage toward pan-African unity (cited by Kofele-Kale 1987: 163).

The 1972 constitution established Ahidjo as the sole repository of authority and absolute power. His power to legislate by decree was renewed for twelve months (Bayart 1978: 89). Legislation by presidential decree has continued to date. The post of Vice-President was abolished and Muna who had replaced Foncha in 1970 as Vice-President became Speaker of the largely ceremonial National Assembly.

The country was carved up into seven provinces, each headed by a Governor appointed by the President and directly responsible to him through the Minister of territorial administration.[51] West Cameroon was divided into two provinces, the North-West and South West Provinces, with capitals Bamenda and Buea respectively (Eyongetah and Brain 1974: 180; Le vine 1976: 279).

At the 1975 CNU party congress in Douala, Ahidjo caused the post of Prime Minister to be inserted in the constitution. Paul Biya, a Francophone, was appointed Prime Minister. Ahidjo never successfully masked his intentions for the State of West Cameroon. He did not encourage the State's particularism, nor did he see the integrative process in Cameroon as one of cultural accommodation, but rather as a process of cultural assimilation (Johnson 1970a: 289). As such, since the federal arrangement for Ahidjo and his associates was only a temporary expedient, and as Jean Marie Bonnier, a French diplomat and close adviser to the regime said in 1963, they accepted "... the federal arrangement only as marking a period of transition... their real aim and expectation is to assimilate the West into patterns of government being developed in East Cameroon" (cited by Johnson 1970a: 290). It could therefore be argued that the first phase of the process of assimilating West Cameroonians came to its conclusion with the abolition of the federal system in 1972 by Ahidjo.

For the Anglophones, the abolition of the federal system meant an end to the commitment to create a socio-political system capable of balancing the entrenched differences resulting from the country's dual colonial heritage. It was this difference that had justified the separate existence of two states.

For the Anglophone political class, it was time to consolidate old gains and acquire new ones. So it was that 63 per cent of Anglophone Parliamentarians in the post-unitary National Assembly were former parliamentarians in the abolished West Cameroon House of Assembly (Kofele-Kale 1987: 164). They were equally strongly represented in the post-referendum cabinet, and of the seven cabinet members, only three: Chongwan Awunti, Christian Bongwa and Achidi Achu[52] had not held previous political office. Of the others, Tabi Egbe and S.T. Muna had been members of the cabinet since 1961, while Luma and Elangwe were Secretaries of State in the former West Cameroon. These were the immediate beneficiaries of the Unitary State. Their strong representation in the cabinet did not mean they enjoyed the powers and authority commensurate to their high ministerial positions.

Table 3. 1: Distribution of Ministers and Vice Ministers by Region in the 1972 Cabinet

Region	Population[a]	%	No. of Ministers	Percentage
North	2,333,957	29.1	6	20.7
West Cameroon	1,601,046	20.9	7	24.2
South Central	1,491,945	19.5	8	27.6
West	1,035,597	13.5	6	20.7
East	366,235	4.8	1	3.4
Littoral	935,166	12.2	1	3.4
Total	7,633,946	100	29	100

ᵃThe population figures are based on the 1976 census.

Sources: Irving L. Markovitz (Ed) 1987, Studies in Power and Class in Africa, OUP, Oxford, p 152. Emmanuel Akika (collectif), "Changer le Cameroun" (1992) Le Cameroun Eclaté? Anthologie Commentée des Revendications Ethniques, Éditions C3, Yaoundé.

The apparent strong representation of West Cameroon in the 1972 cabinet belies the fact that the Ministers wield little power and authority which they could use to positively influence the lives of the population of West Cameroon.

The Socio-Cultural Impact of Reunification on the State of West Cameroon

Reunification had been achieved on the understanding that inherited colonial differences in language and institutions would be respected and creatively integrated into a new collective national experience. There was the fear on the part of West Cameroonians that they will be swamped not only culturally, given the overwhelming numerical superiority of their Francophone compatriots, but equally in other aspects of life. The stakes for West Cameroonians as such, went beyond the status of English in the federation. It was a question of sharing the spoils of office which was tied to their share of natural resources and power, as all these were linked to the 'foreign language' used for official purposes (Johnson 1970a: 294).

In Cameroon, the commitment to the French language was well ingrained in the Francophone psyche, not only because of the nature of French cultural imperialism, but equally because many more of them were well educated. In the early years after reunification, most French speaking officials in the federal government demonstrated a degree of imperiousness by refusing to learn or speak English even though most of them had some schooling in it (Johnson 1970a: 294).

Contacts between peoples from the two states tended to be perceived through the cultural prism of 'English' and 'French' stereotypes (Ardener 1967: 329). This attitude was captured graphically by Mbassi Manga, when as far back as 1964 he wrote that the French are said to be, "... sophisticated, talkative, artistic, passionate and wily, while the English are known to be "...

sportsmanlike, reserved, trade-loving, conventional, intelligent, courteous, honest, extremely nationalistic and humourless" (Mbassi Manga, ABBIA, March 1964).[53] These metropolitan stereotypes are applied liberally by Cameroonians to each other. This cultural and psychological chasm is even more acute today than during the early years of reunification. As Victor Epie Ngome[54] stated in 1993, "Anglophones see Francophones as fundamentally fraudulent, superficial and given to bending rules: cheating at exams, jumping queues, rigging elections..." The Francophones on the other hand see the Anglophones as being imbued with an "air of self-righteousness and intellectual superiority."

Ahidjo seemed to have been well aware of this cultural factor as an impediment to 'nation-building'. He thus advocated that:

As far as culture is concerned, we must in fact refrain from any blind and narrow nationalism and avoid any complex when absorbing the learning of other countries... we have followed the path of bilingualism since we consider... that it is in our interests to develop these two world-wide languages...

...Our goal... consists firstly, both in and out of school, of gradually creating a civilisation which, whilst being based on our African heritage, will also draw its inspiration from what is best and most valuable in the cultures imposed on us...[55]

It is however, very debatable as to how seriously Ahidjo took this, since even in the constitution, in spite of French and English being recognised as the official languages (Article 1:4), only the French text of documents were authentic (Article 44), until this clause was eventually dropped after protests.

The problem of cultural pluralism and the fear of assimilation occupied the minds of most educated West Cameroonians in the early days of the Federation.[56] They proposed various strategies of tackling the issue.

In the early years of the federation, the official policy, as is still the case today, was to get all educated Cameroonians to be bilingual in English and French. To this end, experimental bilingual Grammar schools were opened at Man O War Bay in 1963 - this was later transferred to Buea and in Yaoundé. The first set of 90 students at the Man O War Bay - 45 West Cameroonians and 45 East Cameroonians - received their lessons in French and English, and at the end of their course, wrote both the French BEPC and GCE

Ordinary Levels[57] (Ardener 1967: 329; Nfor 1980: 148). Eventually, classes were organized for senior civil servants in English or French, depending as the case may be, on their first official language.

Yet, as Chumbow[58] (1980: 298) has pointed out,

> ... by far more Anglophone... efforts achieved a respectable degree of bilingualism than Francophone. This obviously retrogressive ascendancy of French over English as a result of the population factor and in part to the "Frenchification" effect of the French colonial policy which presented the French language to all its colonies as the language of civilization "par excellence". Since French has a de facto popularity and superiority (despite a de jure equality with English), Francophones have a less natural urge or stimulus towards acquiring English.

Anglophone reaction to this strong attachment to the French language and culture by their Francophone compatriots has been in two ways, mainly: a tiny minority is involved in a kind of 'francophonisation'. This involves the exclusive use of the French language even amongst Anglophones, change of names to French ones, usually with the false notion that power and privilege are monopolised by Francophones and that Francophones are the 'in crowd' while Anglophones are the 'outsiders' (Kofele-Kale 1987: 165).

To a far greater number of Anglophones, as Chumbow (1980: 299) points out, language loyalty has taken on the same significance as nationalism does for nationality. That is, a state of mind, in which language (like nationality) has assumed a high position that has to be defended.

Linked closely to this language issue is the type of educational system that obtains in West Cameroon, and which Anglophones want for their children. Here, we equally look at the development of the system of education. At the time of reunification, the literacy rate of West Cameroon was still very low compared to East Cameroon. Ahidjo felt leaving education under the control of the state government would strengthen regional loyalties, and as such, while primary education was left in the hands of the state, post-primary education was brought under the charge of the federal government (Johnson 1970a: 300; 1980: 141).

At reunification, there were moves to harmonise the educational system. The school year in West Cameroon was made to match that of East Cameroon, and to run from September to June. The years to be spent in primary school were reduced from eight to seven, with a view to bringing it to six, as in East Cameroon. But it has remained at seven to date.[59] The Francophone *probatoire* was supposed to be brought down to five years, so as to maintain the same number of years as the GCE 'O' levels, while the *BEPC* was to be abolished; but this has never been achieved.

There was an immediate increase in primary school enrolment during the first three years after reunification. Primary school attendance increased by 34 per cent and the number of primary schools increased by 29 per cent. This was largely as a result of the efforts of the state governments that made the first four years of primary education free (Johnson 1970a: 320; Nfor 1980: 144).

Table 3. 2: East and West Cameroon Primary School Enrolment 1958-1961

Year	West	East	Total
1958	54,900	294,221	349,121
1959	64,000	330,983	394,983
1960	73,400	377,089	450,489
1961	86,200	330,393	416,593

Source: Wilfred Ndonkgo (1975), Planning for Economic Development in a Federal State: The Case of Cameroon, 1960-1971, Weltforum Verlag Munchen, p 72.

Education, however, remained largely in the hands of lay and mission organisations that by 1967 still controlled 85 per cent of schools in West Cameroon. In 1960, West Cameroon had a total of 460 primary schools with 73,400 pupils. By 1965, there were 689 primary schools with 124,254 pupils. By 1973, only 26.72 per cent of primary schools were owned by the government, whereas in East Cameroon, the percentage was as high as 77.37 per cent (Nfor 1980: 146). This lopsided development of education was a carryover from the colonial period where, whereas the French invested in education, the British were not interested in educational development and as such, left it in the hands of the missions. In spite of government, efforts after reunification, the gap remained wide between the two regions.

Table 3. 3: The Development of Primary Education in Cameroon. 1960 – 1977

PRIMARY	East Cameroon								West Cameroon							
	1960		1965 - 66		1972 - 73		1976 - 77		1960		1965 - 66		1972 – 73		1976 - 77	
	NO. OF SCHS	ENROLLMENT	NO. OF SCHS	ENROLLMENT	NO. OF SCHS	ENROLLMENT	NO. OF SCHS	ENROLLMENT	NO. OF SCHS	ENROLLMENT	NO. OF SCHS	ENROLLMENT	NO. OF SCHS	ENROLLMENT	NO. OF SCHS	ENROLLMENT
PUBLIC	821	107 795	1 471	275 683	2 056	454 670	2 446	590 769	n.a.	n.a.	n.a.	n.a.	186	570 29	230	917 50
CATHOLIC	111	138 184	197	216 305	812	212 269	755	215 448	n.a.	n.a.	n.a.	n.a.	226	610 78	224	611 00
PRESBYTERIAN	663	739 37	780	107 493	630	631 78	526	850 26	427	640 76	n.a.	n.a.	279	708 67	273	695 32
OTHERS	455	828 5	51 4	990 46	86	183 77	129	333 61	n.a.	n.a.	n.a.	n.a.	n.a.	n.a.	n.a.	n.a.

| TO TAL | 2 05 4 | 328 201 8 | 3 3 | 609 463 0 | 3 5 8 4 | 778 494 8 | 3 8 5 6 | 924 604 7 | 4 2 | 640 76 | n .a . | n.a. | 6 9 1 | 188 974 | 7 2 7 | 222 382 |

n.a. : Not Available

Source: Nfor N. Nfor (1980). "Cameroon Reunification: Costs and Problems of National Integration." M.Sc. Thesis (Unpublished), Ahmadu Bello University, Zaria, Nigeria

In 1958, there were only three secondary schools in the Southern Cameroons, all owned by the missions. There were equally two vocational schools. However, from 1962, government established a bilingual grammar school at Man O War Bay in Victoria and this was later moved to Molyko in Buea. A high school, CCAST Kumba was opened, and in 1964, was transferred to Bambili (Nfor 1980: 148).

Federal officials, mainly Francophones, were posted to supervise secondary schools and technical education, but because of staff shortage, State officials continued to be involved. The division of educational control between the state and federal authorities posed a lot of difficulties. A case in point was the status of CCAST Bambili, which as a pre-university institution, was under federal authority, but the State proposed to add an 'agricultural terminal component'. The federal government felt this was not necessary (Johnson 1970a: 303). Initially, CCAST was set up to eventually develop as a full flesh university, but the federal government never permitted it to take off.[60]

Over the years, commercial students in West Cameroon have been writing London Examinations Board assessments like "RSA," "City and Guilds" in the absence of Cameroonian equivalents. These examinations were handled in Cameroon by the Ministry of National Education. Candidates for the examinations paid their registration fees to the Ministry, who after deducting handling charges, was supposed to forward the rest to London. But over the years, the ministry had not been forwarding the money, in spite of charging students exorbitant sums when they register. London, in reaction, sent examination papers and results intermittently, and this led to a situation in which students who sat for these examinations whenever they did come, had to wait for years for their results.

No other section of education suffered from the obnoxious policy of assimilation in the guise of harmonisation more than technical education. It is important to point out here that technical education, generally, is the most neglected aspect of education in Cameroon. For instance, during the academic year 1986/87, while there were 291, 842 students pursuing general secondary education, only 90,666 students were in technical schools, and of this number, 66,646 were in private technical schools.[61]

In 1969, the Certificat d'Aptitude Professionnelle (CAP), a Francophone examination, was introduced into West Cameroon. As a purely Francophone examination, the result was that about 90 per cent of teachers of technical schools in West Cameroon were Francophones, who delivered lectures in French and in most cases in Pidgin English, to students who had no previous knowledge of French. Examinations were set in French and then translated into unintelligible English. The consequence was that Anglophone students recorded catastrophic results at the CAP and Baccalaureate, which are purely Francophone examinations. All of this led to the complete destruction of technical education in West Cameroon.

West Cameroon had a longer tradition of 'Teachers Training' than East Cameroon. By 1969, as such, she had established a better pedagogy for preparing teachers to take care of nursery and primary education. However, in 1978, a decree was enacted that made the teaching pedagogy uniform in the whole country.[62] The consequence has been a complete disruption of teaching pedagogy in West Cameroon.

With the declaration of a unitary state in 1972, government began to neglect the educational sector, in that subsidy to schools which were run mainly by missionary organisations and individuals were reduced. The result of this was that in the lay private institutions with very few or no qualified staff, teaching was poorly done and the students, living mainly in rented quarters, suffered the negative effect. The result of government neglect of education is that the responsibility passed on solely to parents, who under the auspices of the various 'Parents-Teachers Associations' (PTAs), employed teachers, constructed classrooms and equipped them.

In 1962, a federal bilingual university was established in Yaoundé. Like those established in most Francophone African countries at the time, it was modelled after the metropolitan system, and had a strong French input in both administrative and academic staffing. The university's bilingualism began and ended at its profession, as 95 per cent of the lecturers were either

Frenchmen or Francophones. Anglophone students who had no previous knowledge of French were compelled to follow lessons in French (Johnson 1970a: 305; Nfor 1980: 154).

The first Head of the English department was a Frenchman, and was only replaced when this met with protest. Little was done to make the university bilingual. As recently as 1983, an economics lecturer was replaced for teaching his course in English.[63] It was only in 1974 that an Anglophone, Prof. Victor Anomah Ngu, became the Deputy Vice-Chancellor. As of 1993, no Anglophone had been dean in any of the faculties, and of the seven affiliated institutes, it was only in the late seventies that an Anglophone became Deputy Director of the University Centre for Health Sciences.[64]

Table 3. 4: Staff Distribution At Yaoundé University: 1977/1978 (Anglophone/Francophone Compared)

Faculty/Institution	Francophone		Anglophone	
	No. of Staff	%	No. of Staff	%
Law	28	87.50	4	12.50
Letters	63	74.12	23	25.88
Science	78	87.64	11	12.36
ENS	60	88.24	8	11.76
ENSA	52	100	-	0
ESIJ	28	87.24	4	12.50
IRIC	10	66.24	5	33.33
ENSP	35	94.59	2	5.41
CUSS	41	77.36	12	22.64
IAE	4	80.00	1	20.00
TOTAL	364	83.87	70	16.3

ENS = Higher Teachers Training College
ENSA = Higher School of Agronomy
ESIJ = Higher International School of Journalism

IRIC = Institute of International Relations in Cameroon.
ENSP = Higher National Polytechnic
CUSS = University Centre for Health Sciences
IAE = Institute of Business Studies
All abbreviations are in French.

Source: Nfor (1980), Cameroon Reunification: Costs and Problems of National Integration, p 155.

With such conditions, students of Anglophone background found it rather extremely difficult to cope in the university. In a study conducted in 1974,[65] Dr. Nfor Gwei (1975: 435-447) found out that in the university of Yaoundé, Anglophone students between 1964 and 1974 averaged only 6 per cent of the total student population. They were not only outnumbered by their Francophone counterparts, but in the specialised institutions such as the Higher National Polytechnic, there were hardly any Anglophone matriculations.

With over 95 per cent of lectures being conducted in French, many Anglophone students were discouraged from attending the University of Yaoundé. This led to an exodus of West Cameroonians to English speaking countries for education. They could be found in their thousands in countries like Nigeria, the USA, Britain, and Canada. The situation led Nfor Gwei (1975: 446-447) to point out that:

> Because the English-speaking students form a tiny minority, the language of instruction, the teaching methods, the educational programmes, the examination system and the social atmosphere at the university do not tend to favour them but the French-speaking majority... unless steps are taken to protect the interests of the minority, the tendency is often to ignore them and their own interests and aspirations. The reaction of members of the minority groups to problems which weigh heavily on them would be either one of submission or protest.

This has been the case, as over the years, the Anglophone students in the University of Yaoundé, in spite of the repressiveness of the regime, have refused to submit to the status quo. One of such encounters was in November 1983, when the then Minister of National Education, Rene Ze

Nguele, proposed new examination methods which will make the study of both English and French mandatory, and make the GCE in general look similar to the Francophone examinations.[66] This sparked off a boycott of classes by Anglophone students in the university, and led to a wave of demonstrations in the two English-speaking provinces, until the reforms were abandoned.

The Economic Impact of Reunification on the State of West Cameroon

One of the reasons that were advanced for reunification on the part of West Cameroon was its alleged inability to sustain itself economically. As such, West Cameroon politicians hoped reunification was going to take the region out of its economic backwardness, and enable it achieve financial stability. What was the actual impact of reunification on the economy of West Cameroon?

In no other sector was the impact of reunification felt as much as in the economic field. The financial situation of West Cameroon had always been very precarious. This situation was further confirmed to the West Cameroon authorities by the Phillipson, Anderson and Berril reports[67] (Ardener 1967: 311; Johnson 1970a: 107; Nfor 1980: 164; Kofele-Kale 1987: 159).

The Phillipson report,[68] prepared between July and October 1959, found that the revenue of a separate Southern Cameroons might just be sufficient to enable it maintain and even modestly expand its recurrent services. The Berril report[69] did not differ much from the Phillipson report. The Anderson report,[70] prepared with reunification in mind, considered the various administrative, trade and financial problems envisaged. It considered three currency options:

i) That of keeping two currencies for the two States; the pound and franc for West and East respectively;

ii) Allowing the two currencies to circulate in the two states; and

iii) Changing from pound to the franc in West Cameroon (Ardener 1967: 311)

Andersen's recommendation that the pound be replaced with the CFA franc was eventually adopted and on April 2, 1962, a presidential decree established the CFA franc as the sole legal tender in the Federal Republic of

Cameroon. Three months were given for the people of West Cameroon to change their pounds for the CFA at the rate of 1 pound for 692 CFA francs to end by June 30 (West Africa, October 26, 1963: 1213; Ardener 1967: 314; Johnson 1970a: 325; Nfor 1980: 167). The currency conversion brought home to most ordinary West Cameroonians the impact of the integration of the two states. It brought a lot of confusion, and traders initially refused the new money. It also led to a lot of inflation as prices of certain goods doubled.[71] The currency conversion meant West Cameroon left the sterling zone. The entry of West Cameroon into the franc zone meant strict currency regulations. Offices of the department of foreign trade and foreign exchange control were established at Victoria in June 1962. This reduced the flow of currency and caused a lot of difficulties for business companies (Ardener 1967: 318; Johnson 1970a: 332).

The imposition of exchange control meant trade with the sterling zone was limited to a part of the needs of importers, who had difficulties in obtaining suitable non sterling supplies. Prior to reunification, goods could be obtained into the Southern Cameroons from anywhere without restrictions, except the need for a licence for imports from the Eastern bloc countries. In the Cameroon Republic, no restrictions were imposed on goods from France and other franc zone countries. Imports from other countries were subject to a licence (Ardener 1967: 318).

Like the new Import Licensing and Exchange Control Regulations, in a bid to reorient the commercial life of West Cameroon from sterling to the franc zone, a customs barrier was established with Nigeria. This meant that trade with Nigeria now shifted towards East Cameroon. As a result, revenue from taxes on things like beer and cigarettes dropped, since these things were now coming in but from East Cameroon (West Africa, November 2, 1963, 1241; Ardener 1967: 317; Nfor 1980: 167). The federal government made subventions to offset this loss. By 1964 - 1965, the subvention accounted for two thirds of the estimated West Cameroon revenue of 3 million pounds. The flow of cheap food stuffs from West Cameroon to the East contributed to inflation in the West in that prices of staples like plantains and coco yams went up.

By 1962, West Cameroon was spending about 313 million CFA francs in purchases from East Cameroon. Of her total imports in 1964, 10 per cent came from East Cameroon. This trade was unidirectional, as apart from agricultural products, West Cameroon produced virtually nothing. Exchange with East Cameroon was limited to foodstuffs, and this amounted to only about one per cent of her external trade (Nfor 1980: 171).

Another immediate consequence of reunification was that West Cameroon was obliged to leave the Commonwealth. This meant she had to lose the 15 per cent Commonwealth preference on bananas, as well as various percentages of preferences on her exports. The 15 per cent preference was however maintained until July 1963 (Ardener 1967: 315; Johnson 1970a: 327).

The Cameroon Development Corporation forfeited her right to a £3 million loan from the Commonwealth Development Corporation in 1961. Only £1 million was remitted to the corporation (West Africa, April 23, 1966: 563; Nfor 1980: 173). This was because the Commonwealth Development Corporation was prohibited from lending outside of the commonwealth.

The Cameroon Development Corporation had serious financial problems.[72] It needed vast sums of money to rehabilitate old plantations, develop new ones and maintain trees to maturity. Such maintenance was costing £ 400, 000 per annum by the end of 1964, or 30 per cent of recurrent expenditure. The profit the Corporation made was far too small to provide necessary capital. The Corporation was obliged to borrow 1 million pounds repayable in 18 annuities as from 1970 from Nigeria. As the loans acquired were inadequate, instead of improvement in production, the situation deteriorated. There were losses in some years including 1964. This situation led to a lot of retrenchment. From the 1954 peak of 24,000, by 1963, the labour force reduced to 13,000 (West Africa, April 23, 1966: 563; Nfor 1980: 174).

By 1960, income from banana exports had fallen off from its 1958 peak. It now formed only 36 per cent of total export earnings. After joining the franc zone, the value of banana exports fell further and by 1964, they provided only 21 per cent of total export earnings. This amounted only to 39 per cent of the 1958 figure. The value of other main West Cameroon exports also declined. They had reached their peak in 1960. In 1964, they fell to 72 per cent of their value in 1957. The effects of the cancellation of Commonwealth preference was characterised by a general export decline from the boom years before 1960 (Ardener 1967: 317).

Table 3. 5A: CDC Production Statistics: 1959-1964 (In Metric Tons)

Production	1959	1960	1961	1962	1963	1964	1965
Bananas	34,842	35,153	34,365	32,716	24,874	17,200	16,783
Rubber	2,622	2,267	3,831	4,239	5,080	4,859	6,377
Palm Oil	4,234	4,824	6,329	4,928	7,253	5,918	8,177
Palm Kernels	2,162	2,184	2,438	1,979	2,532	1,935	2,671
Cocoa	200	217	157	124	110	171	162
Tea	23	45	82	101	148	197	318
Pepper	33	28	35	35	28	44	33
Area Under Cultivation (Hectares)							
Bananas	5,445	5,025	4,359	3,884	2,305	2,164	1,300
Rubber	7,613	8,371	9,800	10,682	11,629	12,040	12,190
Oil Palm	7,712	8,054	8,285	8,251	8,222	8,363	8,221
Cocoa	505	539	554	554	593	505	503
Tea	136	217	298	337	344	344	320
Pepper	17	17	17	17	25	27	27

Source: Nfor N. Nfor (1980), Cameroon Reunification: Costs and Problems of National Integration.

The table shows an enormous decline in the production of bananas. Between 1959 and 1965, production was 48.17 per cent. This was not unconnected with the loss of commonwealth preference and the British market. Between 1960 and 1965, the production of cocoa dropped by 25.35 per cent. In 1965, pepper dropped to its 1959 production.

However, tea, rubber and palm oil witnessed remarkable increases, but this could not compensate for the losses for bananas.

Table 3.5B: Comparative Table of the Principal Produce Exported from West Cameroon for the Years 1965 and 1966

Produce	Tonnage	
	1965	1966
Bananas	54,455	18,520
Cocoa	8,262	7,336
Coffee	6,305	7,826
Palm Oil	12,911	11,427
Rubber	6,392	7,379
Timber	19,249	23,733
Tea	542	140
Palm Kernels	5,556	5,683

Source: National Archives, Buea, File No. Qb/a 1966/14: "Note on the Economic Situation in West Cameroon during the Year 1966."

The overall increase in exports, unlike in table 3.5A, where only the production of the CDC is shown, the export figures include that of peasant farmers, which was far higher than that of the CDC.

Another fallout of reunification for the state of West Cameroon was the harmonisation of the tariffs and the complete lifting of internal customs barriers between the two states. These contributed to the stagnation and decline the West Cameroon economy witnessed during this period. Cameroon's entry into the Equatorial Africa Customs Union (UDEAC) required that the West Cameroon tariff system be aligned to that of East Cameroon (West Africa, April 23, 1966: 447). This treaty came into force on January 1, 1966.[73]

In the old West Cameroon system, a common tariff was levied on goods regardless of where they came from. The new higher tariffs were more complicated and came with the imposition of four categories of duties:

(a) A straight forward import duty;

(b) A common external tariff on all goods from non-EEC and OCAM (Organization of Afro-Malagasy Countries) countries;

(c) A common import turnover tax; and

(d) A supplementary tax (West Africa, April 23, 1966: 447; Nfor 1980: 173).

These measures brought a lot of difficulties to traders. Many large firms found it easier to switch over to EEC goods. But as these goods were more expensive, this led to a general increase in prices and consequently, a steep rise in the cost of living. The combined effect of import licensing, exchange control regulations, and tariff harmonisation was that a lot of firms preferred folding up. Firms like United Africa Company (UTC), John Holt, Kingsway, Cadbury and Fry, Printania and Emen Textiles International folded up (West Africa, April 22: 1966; Ardener 1967: 323; Johnson, 1970a: 322; Nfor 1980: 174; Ngwafor 1989: 62).

Another feature of reunification was that since there was no provision for revenue allocation in the constitution, and as revenue generating departments like the customs were federalised, the West Cameroon state came to depend on the financial 'benevolence' of the federal government. Federal subsidies for the first five years rose from FCFA 2 billion (USD 4 Million) in 1962-1963 to FCFA 4 billion (USD 8 Million) in 1966-1967. This accounted for about 70 per cent of the budget of West Cameroon in the financial year, 1966-1967 (Johnson 1970a: 318). Subsidies for West Cameroon were at times larger than those granted to East Cameroon. But without advance knowledge of federal subsidy, economic planning became a very hazardous affair. Besides, subsidies were not adequate to offset the cost of adjusting to East Cameroon's financial, economic and trade practices, nor were investments made so as to rectify the lopsided development which was very unfavourable to West Cameroon.[74]

Worried over economic stagnation, the West Cameroon government tried to redress the situation. The West Cameroon Development Agency undertook several joint ventures. In 1963, a trading corporation (UCTC) was set up in collaboration with the Swiss Union Trading Company. The Cameroon Commercial Corporation was established as a distributor, meant to stem the tide of retail trade shrinkage.[75] Most attempts at establishing small scale industries failed. The most successful government venture was the setting up of the West Cameroon State Lottery with technical assistance from Israel (Ardener 1967: 320).

Clearly, in spite of institutional appearances, the West Cameroon government had no control over the economy.

Communications and Road Infrastructural Development and the Decline of the West Cameroon Economy

As in the colonial days, there has been a very negligible improvement in road infrastructure in West Cameroon. In instances, where the central authority has paid attention, this has been in the development of infrastructure to further make West Cameroon physically and psychologically dependent on East Cameroon. This has been achieved by crippling land, rail, air and sea transportation within the region and externally with the rest of the world unless when it is through East Cameroon.

Immediately after reunification, the federal government set about looking for ways to integrate the economy of West Cameroon to that of East Cameroon. A number of studies were commissioned to look into ways of integrating the economies so as to make them mutually beneficial. A World Bank study recommended that since the capacity of the Douala estuarine port was limited, and needed to be constantly dredged of silt, the port of Victoria should be enlarged and linked via Tiko to Douala by road (Ardener 1967: 323). This would cut off the 200kms detour through Kumba and reduce the journey to 35 kms. Studies by Société Générale d'Exploitations Industrielles and a Stanford Research Institute team[76] made similar recommendations that the Bota/Victoria port could be constructed to serve "Cameroon and probably the landlocked republics to the north and west" (Ardener 1967: 323). The road was constructed and in 1969, it was inaugurated by president Ahidjo. No attempt was made to improve the facilities in Victoria.

Linked to the design of crippling the Victoria and Tiko ports was the construction of the Kumba - Mbanga rail line. Apart from the CDC narrow gauge rail system used in its plantations for internal transportation of produce to the port of Tiko, the Kumba -Mbanga line happens to be the only rail construction in West Cameroon meant to link it with the port of Douala. This was used to divert farmers produce such as cocoa, coffee and timber from the Victoria port to Douala.

The federal authorities maintained a differential in port fees between Douala and Victoria in favour of Douala. They then clandestinely required ships to call only at the Douala port.[77] This had the effect of reducing the number of ships that anchored at Tiko and Victoria. In1960, they accounted for 10.16 per cent of the total cargo loaded at the 10 ports of Nigeria. In 1977, they accounted for a negligible 2.35 per cent of cargo loaded at the ports of Cameroon in spite of their capacity. This was as a direct result of their closure by presidential decree in 1973 (Ardener 1967: 323; Nfor 1980: 196). Since Douala was decreed the sole shipping port for Cameroon's produce, cocoa, rubber, bananas, timber and pepper are transported to Douala for export at great operational cost to the farmers, the CDC and Produce Marketing Board. Victoria was maintained only for export of palm oil and kernel, and this was because of the heavy equipment installed there by the CDC. This accounts for its meagre percentage of maritime transport. It was only with the construction of the oil refinery at Bota that more ships began using the Victoria port. But this is still comparatively very negligible.

In the 1976 - 1981 Development Plan, 18,426 million francs (USD 75.2 millions) was allocated for both Tiko and Victoria ports. Between 1982 and 1992, 4.2 Billion francs CFA (USD 1.7 billions) was used in dredging the port of Douala.[78]

Douala handled about 92 per cent of maritime trade and traffic, and this meant port associated activities in Victoria and Tiko moved to Douala. It also meant enterprises that depended entirely on the ports for their activities either had to fold up, or moved to Douala. These and other central authority initiated policies led to the depopulation of most principal towns in West Cameroon.

Table 3.6: Population of the Principal Towns of the United Republic of Cameroon as at 1976

S/NO	Town	1967	1970-71	1976	% Increase 1971-76
01	Douala	200,000	250,000	458,426	83.37
02	Yaoundé	98,000	178,000	313,706	76.24
03	Kumba[a]	40,000	50,000	44,175	-11.65
04	Nkongsamba	39,800	71,000	71,298	.42
05	Garoua	30,000	28,000	63,900	128
06	Tiko[a]	15-20,000	11,000	—	—
07	Maroua	18,000	24,000	67,187	179.95
08	Foumban	18,000	n.a	33,944	—
09	Victoria[a]	15,000	32,000	27,016	-15.58
10	Ngaoundere	15,000	20,000	38,992	94.96
11	Bamenda	10,000	24,000	48,111	100.46
12	Bafoussam	8,6000	n.a	62,493	—
13	Edea	6,000	23,000	25,493	10.84
14	Buea	5,000	13,000	24,493	84.62
15	Mbalmayo	5,000	n.a	22,106	—

[a]Notice that the three towns that registered negative growth: Kumba, Victoria and Tiko are all in West Cameroon. In the 1967-1971 estimates, Kumba was the third largest town in Cameroon.

Source: Nfor (1980), Cameroon Reunification: Costs and Problems of National Integration.

Another major highway that was constructed was the 22 km road linking the North West Province of West Cameroon to East Cameroon via the Western Province. All other roads within West Cameroon have been neglected. This included the Kumba –Mamfe - Bamenda road which links the major towns of West Cameroon without passing through East Cameroon. This road was projected to be tarred in the 1955 -1960 Economic Programme of the government of the federation of Nigeria, but because of separationist agitations by West Cameroon (then known as the Southern Cameroons), it was shelved (Nfor 1980: 189). In 1965, the US Government granted the Cameroon government aid and loans amounting to FCFA 4,1 billion ($8.2 million) for the construction of the Kumba - Mamfe road. In 1975, when Ahidjo was seeking a fourth mandate, he went and inaugurated an unconstructed Kumba - Mamfe road (Ardener 1967: 322; Nfor 1980: 189). The Bamenda – Mamfe - Ekok road which links West Cameroon to Nigeria, and happens to be part of the Trans-African Highway, as of 1993 is worse than it was 32 years prior. Because it has been neglected, it is impassable during most of the very heavy wet season in this region.[79]

The nature of the roads within the provinces has greatly impeded economic development. In the North West province, of the seven divisions, six of the Divisional Headquarters are linked by the ring-road. In spite of numerous petitions for this road to be constructed, government has not done anything. Instead, it has frustrated attempts by the British government who provided a grant for its construction by not contributing its 15 per cent share. In fact, because of the lack of repairs, during the wet season, these divisions are virtually cut off from the provincial headquarters, Bamenda. At times, for instance, it takes 7 hours to travel the 96 km distance from Bamenda to Kumbo.

Since these areas are primarily agricultural, this makes evacuation of produce hazardous and very expensive. The complete inadequacy of the road network in the Northwest Province was highlighted when during the Lake Nyos disaster of August 21, 1986, in which 1, 746 people lost their lives in an alleged natural gas leak, relief agencies discovered the only means of getting supplies to the affected area was only through airlifting them from Bamenda by helicopter (Cameroun 1982-1992: 139; Susungi 1992: 97).[80] The entire North West province has 37 km of bituminized road.

In the South West province, the situation is even worse, as parts of the province, such as Akwaya District and parts of Ndian Division, are completely cut off from the rest of the country. In fact, the inhabitants of these areas find it easier to communicate and do business with the Cross River State in Nigeria instead. Ndian Division, which happens to be where most of the country's proven oil reserves are to be found, like Akwaya, are places in Cameroon where the use of fuel from Nigeria is not prohibited. Government officials when visiting Akwaya, have to go through Nigeria, and journey the rest of the distance on foot. This is despite the fact that Akwaya is supposed to be linked to the rest of Manyu and Menchum division by road, as stated in the 1976-1981 fourth Five Development Plan.[81] It is only after the oil refinery was opened in Victoria in 1981, that a few kilometres of roads within the town and the Victoria – Idenau road, which leads to oil fields, were tarred.

Table 3.7: General Summary of Tarred Road Network in Cameroon (in Km) as at 1991

Provinces	National Highways	Provincial Highways	Divisional Roads	Total
Far North	521	100	–	621
North	307	46	83	436
Adamawa	309	–	–	309
Northwest	51	–	–	51
Southwest	227	–	–	227
West	281	83	17	381
Littoral	358	119	37	514
Centre	650	106	139	895
South	187	36	132	355
East	92	–	–	92
Total	2,983	490	408	3,881

Source: Fieldwork: Provided by Akonji Atekwana; Jeune Afrique Economie (1998) Special Edition, May.

To conclude, it is rather too simplistic to present the problem of exploitation as being carried out by Francophones against Anglophones. Of course, in the process of infrastructural development and participation in political development, regions of East Cameroon have equally been neglected. What is at issue is figuring out what role West Cameroon and key political and economic personalities from the region have played in the development of the Republic of Cameroon since reunification. More importantly is the role key political personalities played in undermining the political economy of West Cameroon and its influence on national affairs. Since reunification as understood by leading political figures in West Cameroon was premised on equality, albeit one in which the overwhelming dominance of East Cameroon in all spheres was recognised, little has been done to bridge the gap. Instead, it has widened. In as much as the failure to get a respectable degree of equity from the East Cameroon controlled central authority reflects a calculated institutionalised attempt at undermining the principle within which West Cameroon got into the union, the failure is equally the fault of the West Cameroon political class to demand and get fair treatment, either because of corporate self-interests, or simply because of the lack of a purposeful leadership.

Notes and References

1. Joseph, Richard (1978), *Gaullist Africa: Cameroon under Ahmadou Ahidjo*. Fourth Dimension Publishers, Enugu, Nigeria. A more recent term that has been used to capture the relationship between France and its satellite states in Africa, and coined by François-Xavier Verschave, is *françafrique*.
2. Johnson, Willard (1970b). "The Union des Populations du Cameroun in Rebellion: The Integrative Backlash of Insurgency," pp 671-692 in *Protest and Power in Black Africa* by Robert I. Rotberg and Ali A. Mazrui (eds), OUP, New York.
3. Suret-Canale, Jean (1971), *French Colonialism in Tropical Africa*, C. Hurst and Co., London.
4. Azarya, Victor (1978), *Aristocrats Facing Change: The Fulbe in Guinea, Nigeria and Cameroon*, University of Chicago Press, Chicago, USA.
5. Joseph, Richard (1977), *Radical Nationalism in Cameroon: Social Origins of the UPC Rebellion*, OUP, Oxford
6. The author attended the *All Anglophone Conference* between April 2 - 3, 1993 in Buea, the former capital of West Cameroon.
7. Le Vine (1986: 28) points out that in the last three years before independence, the government of Cameroon which came about as a result of France's last two statutes on Cameroon after the *Loi Cadre*, provided for a kind of diarchy in which the executive and a Cameroonian legislature shared power with the High Commissioner. The statutes created allowance for the High Commissioner to intervene to affect the composition and policy direction of the executive council. It was this prerogative that Jean Ramadier exercised to elbow out Andre Marie Mbida, Cameroon's first colonial Prime Minister in 1958, in favour of the more compliant Ahidjo.

    Mongo Beti, on his part, wrote this of Ahidjo (1972) *Main Basse sur le Cameroun: autopsie d'une decolonization* (Francois Maspero, Paris):

    > ... As for Gaullism, it was particularly on the lookout for vassals on whom it could perch to enhance its international status. For reasons of convenience, as well as 'social weight', it allied with the colonial lobby in providing a cover for the local initiatives of colonial administrators... In these undertakings... it was necessary

> to lead along this man, Ahidjo, by the arm. Here was an African leader one had well in hand and who, on the Cameroon scene, and easily presented himself as a national leader without equal…
>
> … beginning in 1960, the date of the accession of Cameroon to full political sovereignty, the little Peul was no longer able to disguise himself. He had to endorse because of his lack of troops the intensification of French military operations during which the guerrillas were pitilessly hounded, villages razed, and the people bombed with napalm…

This supports the view point, as substantiated by numerous authors and eye witness accounts, of the cooptation of a collaborating stratum, which helped France in doing her dirty job in Cameroon.

8. Most constitutions of the emerging independent Francophone African countries in the early 1960s were modelled after that of Gaullist France. In a move to shortchange the Southern Cameroons, France swiftly 'granted' independence to the Republic of Cameroon in January 1960 without a constitution, so as to strengthen her position in negotiations for reunification. She only got a constitution in February of 1960.

9. Corbett, Edward (1972), *The French Presence in Black Africa*, Black Orpheus Press, Washington, DC

10. Personal Library of Hon. S.T. Muna (Documents) Ngenmbo, File No. 98(57) *KNDP Correspondence*, Ref. LPG.l/l, September 14, 1963, p 3. Prime Minister of West Cameroon, and Vice President of the Federal Republic, Hon. John Ngu Foncha.

11. Following the devaluation of the FCFA in 1993, it is now pegged at 100 FCFA for each French franc and after France joined the European Community's Euro zone at a fixed rate of 6.65957 French francs to one Euro, the FCFA rate to the Euro was fixed at FCFA 665,957 to each Euro, maintaining the 100 to 1 ratio. It is important to note that it is the responsibility of the French Treasury to guarantee the convertibility of the FCFA to the Euro.

12. Part of the reason as to why it has been rather very difficult to reach a decision on the development of a common currency amongst ECOWAS countries is because France knows this will be politically and economically disadvantageous to her, and as such, has seen to it that the Francophone member countries of ECOWAS abort the move.

13. The article by Hilary Kebila then editor of the popular weekly *Le_Messager*, in his column "The Gospel" on February 10, 1993 captured the mood of Cameroonians on the controversial appointment of Emile Finateu as the Director of Treasury in Cameroon.

14   Judith Hart was part of the team that negotiated Britain's entry into the EEC.

15   It is believed when Ahidjo declared his socialist sympathies at Ebolowa on July 4, 1962, it was only to try and place himself in the ranks of popular leaders at the time such as Sekou Toure and Kwame Nkrumah, who expounded such a philosophy. After being asked to explain himself by his French masters, Ahidjo assured them that he did not intend to nationalise French investments. Thereafter, he seized every opportunity to condemn socialism.

16   Ahidjo, Ahmadu (1964), *Contribution a la Construction National*, Présence Africaine, Paris.

17   Le Messager, February 10, 1993, p5

18   Cameroon Post, February 22, 1993, p 14.

19   It is generally believed in Cameroon that the French cannot allow an Anglophone Cameroonian to become President. France does not hide its meddling in Cameroon's politics. During the first ever contested presidential elections in Cameroon on October 11, 1992, France did not hide it from the charismatic and nationwide popular opposition leader of Anglophone origin that he could not be allowed to become president of Cameroon. In spite of the fact that he eventually won the elections, as acknowledged by the Supreme Court President's declaration that the elections were characterised by irregularities but that the Supreme Court had no authority to annul the elections.

20   Le Vine, Victor (1976), "Political Integration and the United Republic of Cameroon," pp 270 - 284 in David Smock and Kwabena Bentsi Enchill (eds), *The Search for National Integration in Africa*, Free Press, New York.

21   Bayart, J.F. (1978). "The Neutralisation of Anglophone Cameroon," in Richard Joseph (ed), op cit, pp 45-65.

22   The Constitution of the Federal Republic of Cameroon, 1961.

23   Ahidjo at the special 4th Committee of the United Nations on the reunification of the Southern Cameroons in New York in 1959 had declared, inter alia: "we do not wish to bring the weight of our population to bear on our British brothers. We are not annexationists..."

24   The Bamenda All Party Conference's position was for a loose Federation with minimum federal interference in state matters. This Conference was held between June 26 and 28, 1961.

25   Mukong, Albert (ed) (1990), *The Case for the Southern Cameroons*, CAMFECO, Washington DC, USA.

26   Ardener, Edwin (1967), "The Nature of the Reunification of Cameroon" pp 285 -337, in *African Integration and Disintegration: Case Studies in Economic and Political Union*, edited by Arthur Hazlewood, OUP, London.

27   Articles 5 and 6 of the 1961 Constitution read:

"5. The following subjects shall be of federal jurisdiction-

(1) Nationality; (2) Status of aliens; (3) Rules governing the conflict of laws; (4) National Defence; (5) Foreign affairs; (6) Internal and External Security of the Federal State, and Immigration and Emigration; (7) Planning, Guidance of the Economy, Statistical Services, Supervision and Regulation of Credit, Foreign Economic Regulations, in particular Trade Agreements; (8) Currency, the Federal Budget, Taxation and other Revenue to meet federal expenditure; (9) Higher Education and Scientific Research; (10) Press and Broadcasting; (11) Foreign Technical and Financial Assistance; (12) Aviation and Meteorology, Mines and Geological Research; Geographical Survey; (13) Conditions of service of Federal Civil Servants, Members of the Bench and Legal officers (14) Regulation as to procedure and otherwise of the Federal Court of Justice; (15) Border between the Federated States; (16) Regulation of services dealing with the above subjects.

"6 (1) The following subjects shall be of federal jurisdiction -
(a) Human Rights; (b) Law of Persons and Property; (c) Law of Civil and Commercial Obligations and Contracts; (d) Administration of Justice, including Rules of Procedures in and Jurisdiction of all Courts (but not the Customary Courts of West Cameroon except for appeals from their decisions); (e) Criminal Law; (1) Means of Transport of federal concern (roads, railways, inland waterways, sea and airports); (g) Prison Administration (h) Law of Public Property; (i) Labour Law; (j) Public Health; (k) Secondary and Technical Education; (l) Regulation of Territorial Administration; (m) Weights and Measures.
(2) The Federal States may continue to legislate on the subjects listed in this Article, and to run the corresponding administrative services until the Federal National Assembly or the President of the Federal Republic in its or his field shall have determined to exercise the jurisdiction by this Article conferred.
(3) The executive or legislative authorities as the case may be of the Federal States shall cease to have jurisdiction over any such subject of which the Federal authorities shall have taken charge.
Article 18 read:
> "Before promulgating any bill, the President of the Federal Republic may of his own accord or on request by the Prime Minister of either State, request a second reading, at which the law may not be passed unless the

	majority required by the last preceding Article shall include a majority of the votes of the members from each Federal State."
29	'The Two Alternatives,' a document published by the British Authorities setting out the status to be enjoyed by the Southern Cameroons, if it opted to either stay within the Federation of Nigeria or reunite with the Republic of Cameroon.
30	Akika, Emmanuel (ed) (1990), Changer Le Cameroun : Pourqoui Pas ?, Collectif, Yaoundé.
31	Kofele-Kale, Ndiva (1987), "Class, Status and Power in Post reunification Cameroon: The Rise of an Anglophone Bourgeoisie 1961-1980," pp 135-169 in Irvin Leonard Markovitz (ed) (1987) *Studies in Power and Class in Africa*, Oxford University Press, Oxford.
32	At the Mamfe KNDP party Conference in 1959, Foncha had been made life President of the party. In an interview on March 30, 1993 with Akere Muna, he was of the opinion that this was to make sure that his father, S.T. Muna, a more astute politician than Foncha, did not challenge him for the leadership of the party. In anger, S. T. Muna had refused to stand for any elective position in the party.
33	*Cameroon Champion*, December 7, 1962.
34	*Cameroon Champion*, January 11, 1963.
35	The motion was introduced by the CPNC's Hon. Tamfu, who, after carpet-crossing to join the KNDP, later, was rewarded with a Secretary-ship in the Government.
36	In spite of Foncha's support at the convention, Muna failed to win the post of vice president of the party. This was pointed out to him by Boniface Nforbin in a write-up, "Muna in a Fix," that his quest for premiership was simply fuelled by his inordinate ambition (Muna Documents, File No. 98(160).
37	Muna Documents, File No. 98 (27), "The KNDP Bamenda NEC meeting," p 7, July 17-20, 1965.
38	Some of these articles were serialised in the *Cameroon Times* and later published in the journal *ABBIA*. One of such articles tagged "Under the Sign of the Rising Sun," being the symbol which Ahidjo and Foncha used in their 1965 presidential campaign was particularly vitriolic in its criticism of the KNDP leadership.
39	Muna Documents, File No. 98(78), "Circular No. HQ 34/119, to all KNDP constituencies and Executive committees. Appointment of the New Prime Minister," issued by John Ngu Foncha, President of the KNDP.
40	Muna Documents, File No. 98(27), "Summary Report on the KNDP Bamenda NEC Meeting," July 17-20, 1965, pp 8 and 9.
41	At the All Anglophone Conference on April 3, 1993, and during an interview with the author on April 21, 1993 in Bamenda, Foncha revealed that Ahidjo laughed at him when he threatened to walk out on him with his men, and told

him that he had already got all those he is calling his men. Foncha felt they had all been offered financial inducements and positions. Justice Samuel Endeley expressed a similar view in an interview with the author on March 9, 1993.

42. It was Hon. Tamfu, who as a member of the CPNC, tabled the motion in the West Cameroon House of Assembly in February 1963 to the embarrassment of the KNDP, for the formation of a single national party with the *Union Camerounaise.*

43. Hon. E.T. Egbe outlined these KNDP strategies in a brief to Muna. Muna Documents, File No. 98(27), p 8.

44. The ruling Cameroon People's Democratic Movement (CPDM) had organised parades across the country against multiparty politics, and did not grant authorisation for the new party to be launched. At its launch on May 26, 1990, six young people were shot dead when troops drafted into Bamenda to prevent the launch opened fire on the jubilating population.

45. Nelson, Harold D., Robert, Gordon, McDonald C., McLaughlin, James, Marvin, Barbara and Moeller, W. Philip (1974), *Handbook for the United Republic of Cameroon*, US Government Printing Office, Washington DC.

46. This was also pointed out at the *All Anglophone Conference* that was held in Buea on April 2 and 3, 1993.

47. African politics cannot be divorced from the personalities of individuals. In an interview with Akere Muna on March 30, 1993 in Yaoundé, as well as with many others, the general opinion of Foncha was that he was a simple, modest and honest man, and rather too naive, who could not resist Ahidjo's strong personality.

48. The Rev. Prof. Bame Bame in an interview with the author in Yaoundé on March 26, 1993, was of the opinion that West Cameroon never really had leaders, as most of those who were there merely served their personal interests. Most of those interviewed were *of* the opinion that Muna, unlike Foncha, was extremely cunning, although he was dynamic, pushful and capable of successfully fighting back when his personal interests were at stake.

49. The federation was marked by a general frustration of West Cameroonians on their inability to contribute meaningfully to nation building. Thus, Fonlon's outburst at the UC-KNDP 1964 meeting, in which he demanded for a constitutional review and an increase in the participation of West Cameroonians in policy formulation and decision making.

50. Interview with Justice (rtd) S.M.L. Endeley on March 9, 1993.

51. After Biya became President he enacted Presidential Decree No. 83/930 of August 22, 1983, creating five new provinces by carving up the former Northern Province into three and dividing the Centre-South into two, thus bringing the number of provinces to ten.

52. Achidi Achu became Prime Minister in 1992. It was the first time for an Anglophone to hold such high office. For the first time, too, Deputy Prime

	Ministers with specific duties were appointed, as well as a Secretary-General at the Presidency, thus effectively making the post of Prime Minister a ceremonial one.
53	Mbassi-Manga, Francis (1964), "Cameroon: A Marriage of Three Cultures," *ABBIA*, No. 5, pp 131-144, Yaoundé (March).
54	Epie Ngome, Victor (1993), "Cameroon: Anglophobia" in *FOCUS ON AFRICA MAGAZINE*, pp 27-29, Vol. 4, No.3 (July - September)
55	Ahidjo Ahmadou (1964), "The President Speaks on Culture," *ABBIA*, No. 7, p 4 (October)
56	Prof. Bernard Fonlon and other young West Cameroonians wrote extensively on this issue, especially in the Cultural Review, *ABBIA*.
57	*West Africa*, October 26, 1963, p 1213, Claude Welch, in a series of articles in *West Africa*, starting on October 19, 1963, titled "Cameroon since reunification," looked at the various aspects and challenges of reunification in Cameroon, and how these were being tackled.
58	Chumbow, Sammy Beban (1980), "Language and Language Policy in Cameroon," pp 281-311 in Kofele-Kale (ed) *An African Experiment in Nation Building: The Bilingual Cameroon Republic Since Reunification*, Westview Press, Boulder, Colorado.
59	John Ngu Foncha (1985), "A memorandum Addressed to His Excellency, Paul Biya, President of the Republic of Cameroon on a University of Arts, Science and Technology in Bambili," 14th November, p 3.
60	John Ngu Foncha, ibid, p 2.
61	Akika, Emmanuel (1990), *Changer le Cameroun: Pourquoi pas?* Livre Blanc par un groupe d'intellectuels (Octobre) Yaoundé, p 281.
62	"Cameroon Calling," *Radio Cameroon*, Yaoundé, August 8, 1993.
63	This is one of the issues Anglophone students of the University of Yaoundé raised in an appeal titled, "Open Letter to All English-speaking Parents of Cameroon from the English-speaking students of the North West and South West Provinces," on August 20, 1985. Apparently, the course of Dr. Bisong, and economics lecturer had been suspended because Francophone students complained about his teaching the course in a 'foreign language' that is, English.
64	It is important to note that since the mid 1990s and subsequent to the Higher Education reforms in 1993 that created six universities in the country, at least three Cameroonians originating from the North West and South West provinces have been Rectors (Vice-Chancellors) of the initial lone University of Yaoundé. However, this work covers the period prior to and until 1993.
65	Gwei, Solornon Nfor (1975), "Education in Cameroon: Western Pre-colonial and Colonial Antecedents and the Development of Higher Education," PhD dissertation, Department of Education, University of Michigan.
66	Accusations of assimilation over the years have usually tended to be centred on educational issues. As such, the English-speaking West Cameroonians

have come to see the GCE examination as the last bastion of their cultural heritage, and have sought to maintain it as is against all reforms, which they have very often regarded with deep suspicion. This question of the GCE proposed reforms was one of the issues the Anglophone Yaoundé University students raised in their August 20, 1985 letter (see Appendix II).

67 Muna Documents, File No. 98, 14th June 1965, p 2. This was an address delivered to Hons. S.T. Muna and E.T. Egbe on the political crisis provoked by Muna's Prime Ministerial ambitions. One of these issues which Mr. William Nkinen raised was the reason as to why it had not been possible for the Southern Cameroons to gain independence as a sovereign state.

68 Philippson, Sir Sydney (1959), "Report on the Financial, Economic and Administrative Consequences to Southern Cameroons of Separation from the Federation of Nigeria," Prime Minister's Office, Southern Cameroons.

69 Berril, K.: "The Economy of the Southern Cameroons under United Kingdom Trusteeship," Mimeo, Buea, August 1960.

70 Andersen, Kjell, "Report on the Economic Aspects of a Possible Reunification of the British Cameroons with the Republic of Cameroon," Mimeo, Yaoundé, 1961.

71 National Archives, Buea, File No. ab/a 1966/14. "The Economic Situation of West Cameroon."

72 The CDC plays a central role in the economy of West Cameroon, and is the largest employer in Cameroon, after the state.

73 A lot of information on this can be found in the National Archives, Buea, File No. Qb/a 1964/10 "The Harmonisation of Economic system of East and West Cameroon, 1964," and in File No. Qb/1966/14,"The Economic situation of West Cameroon."

74 A good summary table of Government revenues for recurrent and capital budgets from 1960/61 through to 1965/66 is to be found in Willard Johnson (1970a), *The Cameroon Federation: Political Integration in a Fragmentary Society*.

75 Ngwafor, Ephraim N. (1989), *May Former Victoria Smile Again*, Institute of Third World Art and Literature, London.

76 Turner, Frank L., et al (1965), "The Economic Potential of West Cameroon" in 9 volumes, Stanford Research Institute, Palo Alto.

77 National Archives, Buea, File No. Qb/a 1966/14, "Note on the Economic Situation in West Cameroon," by Vincent C. Nchami, April 13, 1971.

78 Cameroun 1982-1992, *Des faits et Des chiffres, le Bilan de la Décennie Biya*, Imprimerie Saint-Paul, Yaoundé, Septembre.

79 The situation is not very different now.

80 Susungi, N. Nfor (1992), *The Crisis of Unity and Democracy in Cameroon*.

81 Fourth Five-year Development Plan, 1976-1981, Planning and Regional Development, Yaoundé.

Chapter Four

The Failure of National Integration: An Analysis of the Biya Regime, 1982-1993

Surely these people are not born merely in order to serve the whims of people like themselves. Who gave this pernicious right to some people to enslave the will of other beings like themselves, to take away their sacred treasure - freedom? Who permits them to abuse the rights of nature and mankind?... Merciful Lord, Father of all men, tell me: is it your wise hand that brought into the world these serpents, these crocodiles, these tigers who feed upon the bones and flesh of their kin and drink their blood and tears like water?

V.G. Belinsky

The Nature of the State in Cameroon Under Biya

Biya's succession to Ahidjo followed Ahidjo's plan. In 1977, he had caused the constitution to be amended, making the Prime Minister the constitutional successor to the President. However, soon after the November 1982 peaceful transfer of power to Biya by Ahidjo, relations between the two deteriorated. Ahidjo had remained head of the single national party, the CNU, and had tried to assert the supremacy of the party over the state. Let us, however, briefly examine the nature of absolute power in the politics of Cameroon.

As had been demonstrated in Chapter Three, in Cameroon, before the accession of president Biya to power, and thereafter, the structure of power altered very little. This is not to say there were no fundamental institutional/constitutional changes. It should be noted that all the changes went to reinforce the powers of the Head of State. It is these powers that have made the various rulers - Ahidjo until 1982, and Biya thereafter - to be the main initiators of policy, and personnel change within what could be described as a bureaucratic-military oligarchy.

What we are concerned with here is the structure of political power, and consequently, the character of the political elite. The 1960 Gaullist constitution of the Republic of Cameroon provided a very strong Presidency, and as such, political power emanated from him. It is this structure, erected by the French, and which Ahidjo through his own ability thereafter, by creating varying aggregations of elite support eventually transferred to Biya. It is this absolute power that Biya was referring to, when in a television interview, he told a journalist that he can with a nod of his head (coup de tête), dismiss him as the "Editor-in-chief" of Cameroon Television, without justifying this to anybody.

As earlier pointed out, Cameroon's post-reunification federal constitution reinforced the powers of the executive presidency, characterised by a centralised bureaucracy. As Le Vine[1] (1986: 23) points out, independence in 1960 and reunification in 1961 enabled Ahidjo to embark on a series of elite-building exercises culminating in the formation of a single party in 1966, of which the abolition of the federation in 1972 was the logical conclusion. As such, in spite of Ahidjo's dominant role in the country's structure of power, support for him was never absolute, as he had to rely on a personal supportive network and coalitions that included in varying combinations, important Anglophone politicians, former opponents, leaders of major Southern and Western ethnic groups, his own northern allies, businessmen, traditional chiefs and members of the country's intelligentsia. In this process, there was a gradual institutionalisation of ethno-regional balancing.

This process went down the whole administrative hierarchy from top to bottom. The process affected mainly the top and intermediate politico-bureaucratic class from the presidency, vice presidents, prime ministers, national assembly, cabinet ministers, a retinue of aides, members of the Political Bureau and Central Committee of the single party. Anglophones were very present in this set-up. However, their leaders seemed to lack the courage to defend their interests.

After Biya became president, there was some sort of continuity in policies and the people who were in charge of them. However, as Ahidjo was not prepared to take a backseat, and tried to control state machinery by asserting the supremacy of the party, which he had remained the chairman, over the state headed by Paul Biya. As the challenge and threat from Ahidjo developed between January 1983 and April 1984, so too did Biya become increasingly assertive.

The stand-off culminated in a failed assassination attempt in August 1983, and bloody coup attempt in April 1984 allegedly instigated by Ahidjo. After the resignation of Ahidjo as party Chairman in 1983, Biya became chairman of the single party as well as Head of State. After the failed coup attempt, he seized the opportunity in the purges that followed to bring in his own men into government.[2]

It can therefore be argued that it was the issuing struggle between Ahidjo and Biya that enabled the latter to change the composition and character of the national leadership and to strengthen his grip on power. In the process he came to rely more on men from his own region. As such, after 1984, Biya's top hierarchy tended to reflect a regional disequilibrium in favour of men from his region. So it was that after the July 7, 1984 cabinet reshuffle, half of those occupying top administrative and political positions were from the Centre and South Provinces, Biya's ethnic region. From 1984 to 1993, of the one hundred and thirty-three personalities that held ministerial and affiliated positions in the cabinet, presidency and prime ministry, at least fifty-six have been from the same ethnic group. This quota represents a proportion far in excess of their demographic weight in Cameroon's geo-ethnic and political landscape.

In the early years after 1984, Biya's selective purge was thorough. These changes affected top personalities in the ruling party, the CNU, which after 1985, became the "Cameroon People's Democratic Movement" (CPDM), state-owned enterprises as well as the administration. The extent to which these changes initially affected leading Anglophones showed the degree of power and influence they wielded. As these changes hardly affected top Anglophones, it could be argued that their participation in the actual process of decision-making was at best marginal.

President Biya and the Intensification of the Alienation of the Anglophones

By the time of Biya's accession to power, leading Anglophone politicians and senior civil servants had become adept at shifting the blame for the plight of West Cameroonians on what came to be cynically known as "the system," rather than on their inability to protect the interests of the region. Granted the system had been systematically undermined by the Francophone leadership. It was a system where job opportunities and career advancement depended on political patronage, and as such, anyone who wanted to advance his career prospects had to toe the party line. "The system" was built on the denigration of everything from West Cameroon, and in which West

Cameroonians, frustrated by their inability for career advancement, unleashed this frustration on their fellow West Cameroonians in various ways.

This was largely possible, and as has been pointed out, because Ahidjo came to represent the state. Consequently, the rigidly centralised system developed through executive legislation (by decree), meant that provincial delegations had no authority to initiate programmes and as every employment and appointment decision came to be made in Yaoundé, an inefficient and very corrupt bureaucracy developed. It was common then, as it is now, in spite of the highly restricted press freedom, to read articles in the English edition of the official newspaper, The Cameroon Tribune, deploring the situation, and as one of such articles graphically described:

> ... Workers are recruited but instead of processing their dossiers as early as possible, those charged with this responsibility prefer to wait until these recruits leave the extreme ends of the republic to follow (sic) their dossiers in Yaoundé. Going to Yaoundé for this purpose you must be armed with 'dash' to tip at every table the dossiers are to be processed (quoted in Nfor 1980: 114 - 115).

Compiling documents for integration or for examinations into professional schools (such as Teachers' Training Colleges, Nursing Schools, Agricultural Colleges, etc) required travelling to Yaoundé. These documents which at times numbered about 15 separate ones, usually included: birth certificates, certificate of attestation of 'true copies of original certificates', certificate of non-conviction, etc, all of which required that expensive fiscal stamps be affixed on. A single document may require up to five of such stamps, each of which was not less than 500 francs CFA, and each of these documents had to be countersigned by the district officer, and the commissioner of police. After compiling these documents and having them processed in Yaoundé, there was no guarantee that you will soon start receiving your salary.

The psychological frustrations of the people having to travel to Yaoundé for every small government document have caused untold hardship. It is difficult to capture the experience of the older generation of English-speaking Cameroonians, especially who never having learned French, nor never had to undergo through all these processes during the days of the West Cameroon government, now had to suffer indignities in the hands of

Francophone bureaucrats, or even, fellow Anglophones, who will not pay attention to them, when they present their problem in English (Susungi 1992: 91). It is very common to hear radio announcements of fatal accidents involving civil servants on their way to follow up their documents in Yaoundé.

As has been pointed out, West Cameroonians to an extent played a role in the development of such a system. Those who were in positions of authority and influence - with very few exceptions, like the irrepressible Dr. Bernard Fonlon could only in private voice their frustrations at the way things have turned out, but it did not disturb them from benefitting from the situation. Leading Anglophones remained part of the privileged class whom Markovitz (1977: 208) described as

... a combined ruling group consisting of the top political leaders and bureaucrats, the traditional rulers and their descendants, and the leading members of the liberal professions and the rising business bourgeoisie. Top members of the military and police forces are also part of this bureaucratic bourgeoisie. They are located in agencies that enable them to derive their livelihood from the "national income" from the productive efforts of others.

Kofele-Kale (1987: 155) ably demonstrates the presence of this Anglophone petty bourgeoisie: firstly, as a bureaucratic elite of governors, secretary-generals, senior divisional officers, district officers, senior military officers, directors, and then as top party leaders, ministers, vice ministers, parliamentarians and leading traditional rulers.[3]

Kofele-Kale (1987: 152-154) draws attention to the very "strong" Anglophone presence in all branches of the single party and government. As such, rather than being passive observers, the West Cameroon elite has been active participants in the process of the marginalisation of West Cameroon. In this case, it is important to distinguish between the Anglophone elite that enjoyed the fruits – albeit not proportional- of the exploitation and oppression of not only the Anglophones, but equally the ordinary Francophone. While paying lip service to the upliftment of the ordinary Anglophone, the privileged Anglophone class, together with their Francophone counterparts, serves as sounding boards to presidential initiatives and play a central role in the visible structures of legitimation and national support for Ahidjo and his policies, and to Biya thereafter (Le Vine 1986: 25). It is on this Anglophone mass discontent that they fall back to exploit, when they "loss" their privileged positions so as to further their corporate interests.

The ideological basis for the creation of such a system found expression in the need for national unity. The official calls for national unity, thus served as a mirage for suppressing political pluralism and dissent. This state of affairs, given the oppressive nature of state apparatus led to a situation of collective acquiescence, and individual frustration borne out of alienation, and the suppression of group aspirations.

The Biya Regime: Raised Hopes and Broken Promises

At the advent of Biya, the fears of the Anglophones could be summarised in Dr. Fonlon's 1980 petition to Ahidjo, which read inter alia:

> ... There is a deep seated feeling of apprehension amongst the Anglophones. This fear is because after almost 18 years of unification they still have this impression of being kept away from certain aspects of national life. Some Cameroonians do not hide it from them that they are regarded as second class citizens. Hence, the generally held view (which in others has become a firm conviction) that Anglophones can in the best of cases be only assistants, in no matter which ministry.
>
> ... If the Anglophones who are so placed under Francophones were less qualified and less experienced than the latter, this situation could easily have been understood. But this is not always the case. Mr. President, Sir, you will understand, as such, why I speak of a deep feeling of frustration amongst the Anglophones. (Akika 1992: 265 - 266. Author's translation from French).

When Biya became president in 1982, and during his maiden visit to the Northwest Province, he tried to dispel the fears of the Anglophones. He addressed them in the English language. It was the first time the population will hear their President address them in a language which they understand. Then he equally raised the issues which were closest to the hearts of Anglophones: that is, decentralisation, and the lack of infrastructural facilities in the region. He promised to immediately find solutions to them. In Buea, he made similar promises.

At his inaugural, Paul Biya had proposed to the Cameroonian people a

"New Deal". The main policy guidelines for this "New Deal," just as Ahidjo's "national unity ," was to be "national integration" and "rigour and moralisation". This meant the development of a nation-state with no regional/ethnic particularisms. The "New Deal," with its components of rigour and moralisation was meant to bring about a judicious and stringent management of public affairs, coupled with transparency and public accountability by government officials. However, as Cameroonians soon came to realise these professed policies were mere slogans as public life soon degenerated to being the affair of an ethnic cabal.

"National integration" was soon reduced to an ideological justification for the exclusion of lingua-regional interests with a negative backlash on the development of a nation-state. In practice, this meant an attempt at effacing the cultural legacy of the British in Cameroon and thereby completely assimilating the Anglophones. So it was that in 1983, the name of the seaside town Victoria was changed to Limbe. There was no parallel change of names of French origin in the Francophone region. Hence, names like l'avenue Charles de Gaulle, Lycée Leclerc, Centre Jamot, etc have remained unchanged. Then on February 4, 1984, Paul Biya carried out his coup de grace, by enacting Law No. L 84-001, reverting to the name which the Francophone territory was known with before reunification, the Republic of Cameroun, by deleting the word united from it. The country had been named the United Republic of Cameroon after Ahidjo's 1972 subterfuge in the name of a referendum.

National integration, as such, became the new catch-phrase for the complete marginalisation of the Anglophone region. With the installation of what one observer termed a "tribal aristocracy" by Biya, after the 1984 botched coup d'état, national integration came to be perceived cynically by English speaking Cameroonians especially, as a demagogic expression of primitive accumulation of individual and corporate interests to the exclusion of other groups.

This state of affairs has been the subject of several petitions, memoranda and other acts of dissension by the Anglophone elite since 1984. No less a personality than Hon. Tandeng Muna highlighted the failure of national integration and consequently nation building when in January 1984, as Speaker of the National Assembly and at the time constitutional second in command, he addressed a memorandum to the Head of State, titled " Some Points of Social Justice." It is worth recalling that Hon. Muna was instrumental in undermining the federal institutions when as Prime Minister of West Cameroon and Vice President of the Republic, he collaborated with Ahidjo in dismantling the federal structures. In his memorandum, he wrote:

> ... virtually every Anglo-Saxon qualification is inferior to French ones, and so Anglo-Saxon standards are supposed to be inferior to French ones. This gives an idea of the frustrations which English-speaking citizens' face virtually at all levels in the University, in the public service and in state corporations with regard to their progress.[4]

As national integration came to be interpreted as a complete eradication of the Anglo-Saxon legacy of the Anglophones, and as the fate of the linguo-cultural minority came to increasingly depend entirely on the ever more assertive Francophone majority, there was a perception by the Anglophones of what to them, was a "systematic and creeping Frenchification".

In June 1985, self-styled elite of West Cameroon origin residing in Douala and who had been consistent in their demands for the restoration of Anglophone autonomy wrote one of several memoranda to Biya, pointing out:

> ... The humiliating and revolting colonial status that is gradually but systematically being imposed upon the English speaking Cameroonian by the administration ...

> ... We have over the years watched with increasing alarm the various unilateral manipulations of the constitution to the extent that the English speaking region of Cameroon is now being treated by the administration either as a conquered territory or as a buffer zone, and its citizens as foreigners.[5]

If West Cameroonians differ in their ideological orientations, one point in which they all seem to agree on is the question of the marginalisation of the region, and as this extract from a memorandum by members of parliament and senior civil servants who are generally regarded as being pro-establishment submitted to President Biya on June 11, 1985, indicates:

...the Northwest and Southwest Provinces, peculiar in nature because of historical, cultural and linguistic factors...

...These problems many of which are genuine and inherited from the former regime are political, economic, socio-cultural and administrative.

Among the political problems raised are some related to the status of Anglophone Cameroonians in the Unitary State, the protection of their rights and interests and even the legality of our existing political institutions ...

Appeal to the president and his government more than ever before to leave no stone unturned in the quest for solutions to problems specific to Anglophone Cameroonians among which are justice and democracy, preconditions for peace and progress.[6]

The students (see Appendix II) were not left out in this questioning of the nature and structure of state institutions, and of what was seen as the overwhelmingly "francophone" character of a supposedly, officially 'bilingual' state.

Few Cameroonians who claim to be objective could deny that Anglophone grievances were not genuine. With the accession of Biya, the Anglophone Community had hoped that her situation was going to ameliorate. Instead, Anglophones found themselves completely at the sidelines. Apart from Prof. Victor Anomah Ngu, who was Minister of Health between February 1984 and May 1988, Anglophones continued to occupy the marginal "traditional anglophone" ministries like transport and mines and energy, where care had been taken to devolve real decision-making to the Directors of State Corporations under these Ministries.

In the case of the Ministry of Transport, four such autonomous state corporations: the Cameroon Airlines, Cameroon Shipping Lines, National Railway Corporation and the Urban Transport Corporation existed. In the Ministry of Mines and Energy Resources, these included the National Electricity Corporation (SONEL), the National Water Corporation (SNEC), the National Hydrocarbons Corporation (SNH) and the National Refinery Company (SONARA).

The heads of these corporations are appointed by the Head of State to whom they are directly responsible through their Boards. To the Anglophones, this explains why at Mines and Energy, as of 1993, there had been a succession of Anglophones for nineteen years.

Government response to these appeals was to step up repression. Under the name of maintaining internal security, the government through various departments of the Ministry of Territorial Administration (MINAT) such as the National Police, the National Intelligence Service (CENER), the Gendarmerie, Military Mobile Mixed Brigade (BMM) and even the Presidential Security, stepped up repression, as this editorial of the Cameroon Monitor[7] indicates:

> 1986 looks set to follow the trend of the preceding years under the government of President Paul Biya, with the arrests and detention of over 500 people without charge in Cameroon. Among the several hundred arrested are many intellectuals and professionals. Those arrested have been put in camps in various parts of the country and reliable sources stated that many are facing torture by the paramilitary Mobile Mixed Brigade (BMM) which is responsible for the interrogation of political opponents...

In December 1986[8] the Cameroon Monitor highlighted the "Anglophone problem" thus:

> The Lake Nyos disaster in August has exposed the chronic lack of infrastructure and development that pertains in English speaking West Cameroon.

The affected region approximately 200 miles from Yaoundé has been without proper roads and communications for years. To travel from one part of West Cameroon to the other has proved impossible without first travelling to the Francophone area and then back to West Cameroon. This is one example of the overall strategy of denying regional development to the Anglophone minority by the Francophone government of Paul Biya and his predecessor Ahmadu Ahidjo.

> ... the reason for the lack of development in West Cameroon has been political. Ever since the installation of the Ahidjo regime by the French in 1960, Cameroon had been presented to the world as a Francophone country than a bilingual one...

> ... the dissolution of the Federation deprived West Cameroonians of their regional status and their cultural identity as an English-speaking people... as well as suffering, like all Cameroonians, from the barbaric rule of Ahidjo, they were relegated to the role of second class citizens in their own country.
>
> ... This second class citizenship has continued under Paul Biya, and coupled with the nation-wide oppression that already exists, is fuelling a very tense situation in the country... (cited in Mukong 1990: 53 - 54).

Repressive laws passed during the early years of Ahidjo's totalitarian regime were not repealed. Decree No. 5 of October 4, 1961, while arrogating the right for the declaration of a state of emergency to the President, also introduced detention camps known as les Centres d'Internment Administratif, where the government send persons considered "dangerous to public security" for indefinite periods of detention (Mukong 1990: 48).

Decree No. 62-18 of March 12, 1962 instituted censorship and prosecution of the author of any publication that criticizes any politician or senior civil servant, even if the allegations were true. In 1988, Mr. Albert Mukong, a famous political prisoner and Human Rights activist was once again detained for expressing his views on the Biya regime over the BBC. He was released only after spending a year in detention. In February 1990, he was picked up again along with Yondo Black, lawyer and former President of the Cameroon Bar Association, and others allegedly for planning to form a political party. The international publicity given to the trial and the mobilisation of the Cameroon Bar Association led to the release of Mukong and others in April, after they had faced a military tribunal. However, Yondo Black and Ekane Anicet spent some time in jail for allegedly insulting the President.

In May 1990, after a Radio Cameroon programme, "Cameroon Calling' in which participants advocated for political pluralism highlighted in multi-parties, nine journalists, together with the three university lecturers who took part In the debate were arrested. It was only after students took to the streets to protest that they were released. However, this did not stop the government from sending the nine journalists on disciplinary transfers.[9]

Ethnicity and Regionalism in the Politics of the Biya Regime

Prior to the accession of Biya to power, there was a false perception that the country was divided between the largely Moslem North and the Christian South; then in the South, between the Francophones and the Anglophone minority. The main focus here is not with these arbitrary divisions, which gloss over ethnic rivalries that is actually at the thrust of politics in Cameroon. The situation was further exacerbated with the imposition of a single party for over twenty-four years. By accentuating the use of state machinery to further ethnic interests, the Biya regime brought to the fore ethnic differences which in turn, created a lot of tensions.

Since the main focus is the fate of the West Cameroon region and its people, vis-à-vis the Francophone-led regime, the instrumentalisation of ethnicity in politics and governance in Cameroon is not central to the analysis. It is sufficient to point out that admission into professional schools, award of grants; appointments into public office, etc, have always been done based supposedly on some form of ethno-regional calculation. The main criterion for this, as has always been claimed by the regime, is based on the population of a province/region, while taking into consideration the literacy rate in any given region. As one of the various ethno-regional quota allocations a public service, Ministerial Order of October 4, 1982 provided for the following quotas:[10]

North Province		30 %
Centre South Province		19 %
Western Province		13 %
Littoral Province		12 %
Northwest Province}	West	
South West Province}	Cameroon	8 %
East Province		4 %

Former Soldiers	2 %

The arbitrary allocation of quotas has given rise to all sorts of manipulation of census figures to justify the quotas. This has made it difficult to arrive at a true population figure for the various provinces in Cameroon. The figures of the 1987 census, published in 1991, four years after they were carried out, were as follows:

Table 4. 1A: Population of the Various Provinces (Regions) in Cameroon Based on the 1987 Census

Province/Region	Population	Percentage
Northern Region	3,183,045	30.3%
Centre-South	2,025,398	19.3%
Western Province	1,339,791	12.8%
West Cameroon	2,075,990	19.8%
Littoral Province	1,352,833	12.9%
East Province	517,198	4.9%
Total	10,494,225	100.0%

Source: Akika, Emmanuel (ed) (1992), Le Cameroon Eclaté?, p. 540.

If this is compared with the 1976 census figures, then it becomes clear that there has been very little change in the percentage figures. While there was a slight overall increase in the population of all the regions, when the percentages are taken into consideration, it is noticeable that for West Cameroon, it declined from 20.9% (cf Table 4.1B) to 19.8%.

Table 4.1B: Population Figures of the 1976 Census in Cameroon

Province/Region	Population	Percentage
Northern Region	2,233, 957	29.1%
Centre-South	1,491,945	19.5%
Western Province	1,035,597	13.5%
West Cameroon	1,601,046	20.9%
Littoral Province	935,166	12.2%
East Province	366,235	4.8%
Total	7,663,946	100.0%

Source: Akika, Emmanuel (ed) (1992), Le Cameroon Eclaté? p. 540

In spite of the distortion and manipulation of census figures, when the quota arithmetic is being worked out, consideration is not given to internal migration. Whilst, for instance, the populations of the Littoral and Centre-South regions have been substantially increased by people from other regions, as a result of the concentration of commercial, industrial and administrative affairs in these regions, when ethno-regional quota is being applied, people are referred back to the region of origin of their parents.

Moreover, the true population of West Cameroon has never been ascertained since reunification. It has always been arbitrarily fixed to conform to the designs to which the government intends to use them. While for instance, as of 1993, the actual percentage was about 25 per cent of the total population of Cameroon, or 3,500,000, officially it oscillated at about 20 per cent. Besides, this ethno-regional quota is usually not adhered to, and when appointments are being made based on government's geo-ethnic calculation,

West Cameroon is treated as an ethnic grouping. Merit has never been one of the considerations for such appointments.

After 1984, there was an overwhelming ethnic tilt in favour of the Betis; the ethnic group of the President, from top to bottom on all appointments. So it is that as of April 1991, twenty of Cameroon's most important state corporations were headed by people from the same ethnic group. Since 1983, there has been a succession of Betis in the strategic ministries in Cameroon, such as Defence, Territorial Administration, Finance, Public Health - apart from the brief tenure of Prof. Anomah Ngu - Commerce and Industry, Plan and Stabilization, etc.

By May 1991, of the 49 Divisional Officers in Cameroon, 21 were Betis, and of the ten Governors in Cameroon as of February 1993, four, that is 40% of them, were Betis. This has given rise to what is generally perceived as the development and entrenchment of an ethnic aristocracy under Biya. This not surprisingly has led to an increase in ethnic tensions.

It should be noted that in spite of the overwhelmingly ethnic feature of Biya's rule, the exploitation of Cameroonians have not been the preserve of the elite of a single ethnic group. Others, including Anglophones, have been co-opted into this cabal.

However, there is no doubt that there is a deliberate policy of excluding Anglophones from positions of real authority and influence. A glaring example which has been pointed out previously is that when an Anglophone was appointed Prime Minister after the March 1992 parliamentary elections, most of his functions were transferred to the presidency. Then the post of secretary-general at the presidency was reinstated, and given additional authority over certain functions that previously fell under the remit of the Prime Minister. Also, for the first time, the posts of Deputy Prime Ministers were created and charged with specific functions. A Beti, Remy Ze Meka, was made secretary-general at the Prime Minister's office and controlled practically all the activities left within the Prime Ministry. This has made the post of Prime Minister largely devoid of the authority and influence it previously exerted.

During the Ahidjo era, in spite of his demonstrated bias for the North in various ways, he did maintain some degree of ethno-regional equilibrium both within the single party and in government. With the perception that the Biya regime in spite of the arbitrary quota formula had tilted the ethno-regional equilibrium overwhelmingly in favour of his ethnic group, there is a resurgence of ethnic polarisation.

It is within this context, that members of government of Beti origin make attempts at manipulating ethnicity, with varying degrees of success, to subvert the democratic struggle by inciting the Betis through tracts, extreme rightwing papers, such as Le Patriote, Le Globe, Le courier, that appeal to the Betis to rise up and protect "their power". This has led to the formation of numerous extreme rightwing, shadowy, paramilitary organisations, such as Auto Defense and Action Directe, which consistently, carry out violent attacks against Anglophones and Bamilekes as well as on their property. This has come to complicate the general, institutionalised state discrimination that has been carried out against the Anglophones over the years.

As has been pointed out, Anglophones as well as Francophones have been responsible in varying degrees for the "anglophone predicament". This is not meant to play down the role of the Francophone – led regime, exercised largely because of numerical strength, and the all pervasive French imperialist influence in Cameroon. As the various Francophone regimes have always subtly co-opted unqualified and incompetent Anglophones, they have as such, not had the moral authority to defend the interests of Anglophones.

A brief analysis of personnel distribution in government departments along linguo-cultural lines follows.

The Ministry of Defence[11]

Before the February 5, 1993 promotion of senior officers in the Armed Forces, there were seven generals in the Cameroon Army of whom Brigadier-General James Tataw was the lone Anglophone. If retired at the age of sixty in 1993, this means that there will no longer be an Anglophone who is general in the Armed Forces. The only other Anglophone who should have qualified for the rank of General before the year 2000, as per regulations of the Armed Forces, is Lt. Col. George Fomundam.

The only full Anglophone Colonel in the Gendarmerie, Col. Gaius Fomusoh, was due to be retired as from 1993. None of the ten Gendarmerie provincial legions were commanded by an Anglophone. Three of these legions were being commanded by officers from the Lekie Division in the Centre Province, as of April 1992. In the Army, the only Anglophone commanding a Battalion at the time was Lt. Col. Fomundam. For the first time, an Anglophone, Lt. Col. Ngafor, was appointed early in 1993 to head the Combined Military Academy (EMIA).

On February 5, 1993, eight new generals were appointed in the Armed Forces. This brought to fifteen the number of Generals in the Army. Major General James Tataw, who was promoted with his mates in 1983, was not promoted ostensibly because of his age. There was speculation that the appointment of new Generals at a time when salaries of civil servants were reduced because of the economic crisis seemed to have been meant as a reward for the role they had been playing in suppressing the struggle for democracy.[12]

Of the 15 Generals, at least six were of the same ethnic group as President Biya. Evidence seem to demonstrate that although a substantial number of Anglophone officers are academically and militarily more qualified, they are discriminated against in terms of recruitment, promotions and appointments.

Table 4. 2A: Distribution of Senior Personnel at the Ministry of Defence and at the Secretariat of State for Defence (1990 – 1991)

RRegion	Superior Commands		Region Commanders		Inspectors		Dir. & Tech. Advisers		Legion Commanders		Sector Commanders		Total	
Of Origin	NUMBER OF PERSONNEL	%	NUMBER OF PERSONNEL	%	NUMBER OF PERSONNEL	%	NUMBER OF PERSONNEL	%	NUMBER OF PERSONNEL	%	NUMBER OF PERSONNEL	%	NUMBER OF PERSONNEL	%
ACentre South	8	53.33	5	41.67	4	33.33	9	28.13	5	50.00	0	0.00	31	34.07
BThe Northern	1	6.67	0	0.00	0	0.00	2	6.25	1	10.00	2	100	7	7.69

125

Region														
Western Province	1	6.67	1	8.33	5	41.67	9	28.13	1	10.00	0	0.00	20	21.98
West Cameroon	2	13.33	3	25.00	1	0.33	4	12.50	0	0.00	0	0.00	10	10.99
Littoral	1	6.67	3	25.00	2	16.67	8	25.00	3	30.00	0	0.00	20	21.98
Eastern Province	2	13.33	0	0.00	1	0.00	0	0.00	0	0.00	0	0.00	3	3.33
TOTAL	15	100	12	100	12	100	32	100	10	100	2	100	91	100

A = This is made up of two provinces with a total population of 2,025,398, according to the 1987 census figures, constituting 19.32 of the total population of Cameroon. However, given how the ethnic –regional quotas are formulated, it is important to note that the population of the region has been boosted by the large number of non-indigene .residents in the region.

B = The Northern Region is made up of three provinces: The North, Far North, and Adamawa.

SOURCE: Emmanuel Akika (ed) 1992, Le Cameroun Eclaté? Anthologie Commentée Des Revendications Ethniques, p. 548

Table 4.2B: Distribution of the Officer Corps in the Armed Forces: Francophones and Anglophones Compared (March 1992)

CATEGORY OF PERSONNEL	GENERALS		COLONELS		LT. COLONELS		MAJORS		CAPTAINS		LIEUTENANTS		SECOND LIEUTENANTS	
	FRANCO	ANGLO	FRANCO	ANGLO	FRANCO	ANGLO	FRANCO	ANGLO	FRANCO	ANGLO	FRANCO	ANGLO	FRANCO	ANGLO
Infantry	10[A]	1	30	2	33	1	66	9	142	16	227	18	55	2
Air Force	-	-	2	-	20	-	10	-	67	2	129	2	23	-
Gendarmerie	4	-	19	1	16	2	24	9	65	12	113	10	25	3
Navy	-	-	1	-	1	-	12	-	35	1	46	1	15	2
Medical Corps	-	-	8	-	15	-	9	5	10	2	-	-	-	1
TOTAL	14	1	60[3]	3	85	3	121	23	219	33	515	31	118	7
PERCENTAGE	93.3	6.67	96	4	95.5	3.5	81	19	85	15	94	6	94	6

A = In February 1993, eight officers were promoted to the rank of Brigadier General or equivalent. None was Anglophone.

B = The figure is about 62 after the February 1993 promotions.

Source: Compiled based on initial field research undertaken by Mr. Akonji Atekwana

Table 4. 3: Distribution of Posts of Responsibility in the Republic of Cameroon: Francophone/Anglophone Compared (March 1992)

CATEGORY	MINS & ASSIMILATED		VICE-MINS & ASSIMILATED		SEC-GENS & ASSIMILATED		DIR-GENS GROUP 1 CO		DIR-GENS GROUP 2–4 CO		DIRECTORS CENTRAL ADMIN		TOTAL		GRAND TOTAL	PERCENTAGE	
	FRANCO	ANGLO	FRANCO	ANGLO	FRANCO	ANGLO	FRANCO	ANGLO	FRANCO	ANGLO	FRANCO	ANGLO	FRANCO	ANGLO		FRANCO	ANGLO
residency: S.G	5	2			2						5		9		8	9.77	0.23

128

residency: Others	9	2								4		7	8.89	1.11
at. Sec	-	-							0		2	1	8.05	1.95

urity											
at. Assembly	-	-					4	6	3	9.57	0.43
rime Ministry	-	1	2				8	3	1	0.49	9.51
COSO	-	-								5.00	5.00

C.in. of Defence	1	-						70		81		90	5.26	.21
err. Admin.	1	-						25	8	38	1	79	5.31	4.69
gricultu	-	1				0	2	8		5	6	1	3.77	6.23

re														
oc. Affairs	1	-							3		6	1	3.87	6.13
in. of Fin.	1	-			4	5	39		74		83		5.08	.91
in of P&T	1	-							0	1	8	1	9	4.06	5.94
	2	5												

i n . o f E / R e l .	5			8	3				6	3	39	1	0	1.76	8.24
i n . o f J u s t i c e	1	-		1					5		8	1	8	4.06	5.94
i n . o f L	1	-							9		9		6	7.5	2.5

/Stock														
in. of H/Educ & Sci. Res.	1	-						6	4	4	7	1	6.06	3.94
in.	1	-							8		9	8	6.76	3.24

of Health in.	1	-						6	1		6		0.77	9.23
of Labour														
rade & Ind.	1	-						3	4		6		5.655	.55
u	1	-						6	0		3		0.9	.0

blic Serv.											0	9
INPAT	1	-					5	1	5	2.73	.27
in. of Inf. & Cultur	1	-					8	4	2	0.95	9.05

e & T/P	1	-						9	6	3	6.79	3.21
/Works & Trans.	1	-			0			5	6	3	6.79	3.21
in. of Touris	-	1						7	8	3	8.26	1.74

m in. of Youth & Sports	1	-						3		6	1	3.87	6.13
in. of Nat. E	1	-						30	9	35	0	55	7.09	2.91

d.														
in. of Mines & Energy	-	1						0		0	1	1	8.43	1.57
res. Of the	1	-											00.00	

Rep.												
res. Nat. Ass.												00.00
res. ECOSOC	-	-										00.00
rime	-	-										00.00

Min.													
RAND TOTAL		8	2	7	69	0	2	0	0	,416	14	,785	78	,063

Presidency of the Republic

At the Presidency, the few Anglophones present were confided to inconsequential positions. Given that all powers in the Republic are concentrated at the Presidency, this means they are effectively kept away from any positions of real decision-making, and are at best confided to ceremonial positions. By March 1992, Hon. Tabi Egbe occupied the post of Roving Ambassador; Effiom was Chancellor of National Orders, while John Ebong Ngolle took over from Ogork Ebot Ntui as Minister in Charge of Missions in April 1992. So it is that in over ten years, of the 25 people who had occupied the position of Secretary-General or Assistant Secretary-General at the Presidency, only one Anglophone, had been appointed to the position of Assistant Secretary-General.

The Mass-Media and Bi-Culturalism in Cameroon

Very few people can doubt the role which education and the mass media play in transmitting a people's culture. In Chapter Three, an analysis of the various ways by which the various Francophone-led regimes have tried to destroy the "Anglo-'Saxon' nature of the system of education in West

Cameroon, was made.

No one can underestimate the educational and cultural roles of the radio and the television in any given society. In Cameroon, the editorial policy and contents of the official media: the press, as well as the radio and television have always been determined by the state. This situation was dramatized in 1990 when after the launching of the Social Democratic Front (SDF) in Bamenda, the government compelled journalists to tell outright lies on radio and on television. This led to a situation whereby some journalists wrote an open letter to the then Minister of Information and Culture, Henri Bandolo, accusing him of forcing them to tell lies to the public.

Since this analysis focuses on radio and television, it will suffice to mention that as of 1993, the government owned press organ, the Cameroon Tribune published five times a week in the French language, and twice a week in the English language. Before 1990, there were very few independent papers and fewer still that published in the English language. A vibrant; English language press developed with the advent of multi-party politics in 1990, but the government has sought through various means to muzzle the press.

The Development of Television in Cameroon[13]

Television broadcast began in Cameroon in 1985. Then the television unit was known as Cameroon Television, and programmes were screened twice weekly during weekends. Although the programmes were initially devoid of any real substance, it would seem, the public savoured them.

However, an analysis of Cameroon Radio and Television (CRTV) as of 1993 leaves no doubt that there seem to have been a concerted effort to dissipate the "bicultural" identity of Cameroon, of which this was best incarnated in its bilingualism. After the CRTV was reorganised, a lot of English language programmes were cancelled. English language journalists appealed but without success that CRTV return to its former programming.

Table 4.4: English Language Programmes that Have Disappeared Without Replacement

1. Minute by Minute
2. Tel-A-Word
3. Cooking Time
4. Thinking Time
5. Looking Back
6. News Drill
7. Headline
8. Franc View
9. Provincial Spotlight
10. Sports Parade: a programme conceived and produced in English but which soon became completely a French language programme,
11. Tam-Tam Weekend: This programme was initially produced in English, but practically soon had very little aspect in English.

Source: Ntemfac Ofege et al (1990) "Memorandum to the Director-General of CRTV".

On September 8, 1989, the CRTV was reorganised and this effectively brought to the forefront the thorny problem of the bilingual nature of programming, as Anglophones were effectively kept out of the decision-making process. As Table 4.5 indicates, the distribution of strategic posts left decision-making at all levels in the hands of only Francophones, who occupy all posts of responsibility.

Table 4.5: The Distribution of Posts in the Cameroon Radio and Television Corporation (1989-1990)

Post Of Responsibility	Francophones	PERCENTAGE	Anglophones	PERCENTAGE	Total
Directors General	2	100	0	0.00	2
Editors-in-Chief	2	100	0	0.00	2
Directors	3	75	1	25	4
Assistant Directors	3	75	1	25	4
Deputy	17	77.27	5	22.73	22

Directors					
Heads of Department	72	87.80	10	12.20	82
Asst. Heads of Dept.	86	78.18	24	21.81	110
TOTAL	185		41		226

Source: NTEMFAC, Ofege et al (1990) "Internal Memorandum by the English-speaking Staff of CRTV to the Director-General."

As of 1993, the central administration was headed by Francophones. All "Editors-in-Chief" and all those attached to the Central Administration like the Head of the Special Unit, as well as all Public Relations Officers were Francophones.

One of the Directors - the Technical Director - amongst four is an Anglophone, and of the four Assistant Directors only one was an Anglophone, whose role was to coordinate the news in English. This meant that all decisions concerning information, production and programming were taken only by Francophones.

Of the twenty two Deputy Directors, only five were Anglophones, and of these only two were with the Central Administration, and had responsibilities of little importance. Out of the eighty-two Service Heads, only ten were Anglophones, and of one hundred and ten Assistant Heads, only twenty-four were Anglophones. The strategic positions of gathering information were all occupied by Francophones. The situation has since degenerated with the appointments of Francophones who had undertaken higher education in English to fill a number of operational and management positions.

Is the Television Audience Embarrassed by the English Language?

When the first episode of the American soap opera, "DALLAS" was screened, the announcers presented excuses to the tele-viewers as it was in English. However, furious tele-viewers did not stop harassing the CRTV with phone calls as to why the American soap opera was being screened in the English language at the end of each episode, in spite of the fact that another American soap opera, "DYNASTY" was being screened during that period in the French language.

The televised news analysed this phenomenon and a decision was made during the regular morning meetings that the television audience be reminded that the English language was one of the official languages, and that bilingualism as a policy was practised on television. However, this decision was applied only by the English language news. During the televised news in the French language, the Directorate on the contrary decided instead to appeal to tele-viewers to be patient, as the programme was just for an hour of a screening day.

On September 7, 1989, the last episode of the West German series "DERRICK" was screened. The series began in English then continued in French. Then it was decided that the French language version be set aside, so that the series could continue in the English language. Instead, the English language version was set aside, in favour of the one in French, the language in which the series ended. After the last episode, "DERRICK" was supposed to be replaced by another German series, "THE OLD MAN" which was screened in the French language, but this time, during an hour allotted for programmes in the English language.

Taken individually, these incidents do not present the true picture of the encroachment on English language programmes on the Radio and on Television. It is not sufficient to present the global situation of the intention of the Francophone management to marginalise the English language on radio as well as on television.

There's wide perception that the management of CRTV regarded Anglophones as rabble rousers. It was also common knowledge that the services attached to the Directorate had written a report to the General Manager against the courageous manner with which Anglophone journalists report events, and which they claimed, was responsible for the dismissal of the previous General Manager.

Thus there seem to be overwhelming evidence to demonstrate that there was a concerted effort to eradicate the English language on television, and to culturally prejudice the minds of young Anglophones by obliging them to watch programmes only in the French language.

Television Programmes in the English Language

As the prevailing situation in 1989 depicts, in spite of the apparent onslaught, some English language programmes managed to survive. Initially, during this period, the national television transmitted a total of 39 hours, 30 minutes each week, from Wednesday to Sunday, divided as follows:

Wednesday -	18:00 – 23:15	5 hrs 15 minutes
Thursday -	18:00 – 23:15	5 hrs 15 minutes
Friday -	18:00 – 23:45	5 hrs 45 minutes
Saturday -	15:00 – 23:45	8 hrs 45 minutes
Sunday -	09:30 – 24:00	14 hrs 30 minutes

The only English language programmes on television were "SESAME STREET" for children which usually came up every Saturday, and "DALLAS" screened every Wednesday.

This meant that an adult Anglophone could comfortably watch television only once week: on Wednesdays. For the Anglophone child, since the only opportunity for him to watch television in a language which he understands was once a week, and since the rest of children's programmes were in the French language, this left him with a negative impression of the English language, which normally he should be proud of.

On at least five days of transmission in the month of October 1989, the only English language programme was "The News".

Thursday	October 5	Only	"The 7:30 News"
Friday	October 6	Only	"The 7:30 News"
Thursday	October 12	Only	"The 7:30 News"
Friday	October 20	Only	"The 7:30 News"
Thursday	October 26	Only	"The 7:30 News"

During the three other days, apart from "The News," English language programmes lasted only for 30 minutes.

Saturday   October 7   "Sesame Street" and "The News"
Thursday   October 19   "Agriscope" and "The News"
Saturday   October 28   "Sesame Street" and "The News"

Distribution of Transmission Time between French and English Language Programmes on Television

From a detailed analysis of the programmes schedule, the conclusion is that of a total of 156 hours of television transmission for the month of October 1989, only 28 hours and 45 minutes were allotted to programmes in the English language, that is, 18.2 per cent of the total, while French language programmes were transmitted for 127 hours 30 minutes, that is 81.8 per cent.

Table 4. 6A: The Distribution of Transmission Time on Television Between French and English Language Programmes for the Month of October, 1989

Division Of Transmission Time	Wednesday	Thursday	Fridays	Saturdays	Sundays	Total	% %
Total transmission time	26 hrs 15 min	26hrs 15 min	29 hrs 45 min	41 hrs 15 min	73 hrs 30 min	156 hrs 30 min	1100
Total time for English language programmes	8 hrs 30 min	2 hrs 30 min	4 hrs	4 hrs 45 min	9 hrs	28 hrs 45 min	118.2

Total time for French language programmes	17 hrs 45 min	13 hrs 45 min	25 hrs 45 min	37 hrs 30 min	63 hrs 30 min	127 hrs 15 min	881
Total time for the News in English	2 hrs	2 hrs	2 hrs	2 hrs	6 hrs	14 hrs	550

Source: Ntemfac, Ofege et al, "Internal Memorandum by the English-speaking staff of CRTV to the General Manager".

More than 50 per cent (14hrs, 30 minutes) of the 28hours, 45 minutes of programmes in the English language was devoted to "The 7:30 News" and other current events programmes: "The World This Week," "Flashback," and "The Presidency"

From Table 4.6A, we realise that there was a total transmission time of 26 hours, 15 minutes on Thursdays for the month of October. Programmes in the English language were allotted only 2 hours 30 minutes, of which 2 hours were devoted to "The news".

For the four Sundays during the month of October, there was a total transmission time of 72 hours 30 minutes. Only nine hours of these were allotted to programmes in the English language, and of these, 66% (that is, 6 hours 30 minutes) were devoted to current events programmes.

During all the Saturdays in October, there was a total transmission time of 41 hours and 45 minutes, and only 4 hours and 45 minutes of these were programmes in the English language. Thus as far as the Anglophone audience is concerned, the role of the television as a medium of entertainment is completely neglected.

During this period, the CRTV signed a contract with CANAL FRANCE INTERNATIONAL. This simply exacerbated an already precarious situation for English language tele-viewers. The programmes of CFI were meant for Francophone African countries and not "bilingual" countries and broadcast 4 hours of news and entertainment seven days a week. This implied an increase of 28 hours of transmission per week, amounting to 102 hours a month.

The impact of this was devastating, especially on Anglophone children who were obliged to watch these programmes simply because they did not have another choice. Table 4.6B brings out clearly the true picture of the situation. This also doubled CRTV transmission time from 156 hours to 258 hours each month.

Two hundred and twenty-nine (229) hours of the 258 hours of transmission time were devoted to French language programmes. That is, 88.7 per cent of the total time. English language programmes remained at 28 hours 30 minutes, or 11.3 per cent of the total time.

Table 4.6B: Distribution of Time Between English and French Language Including CFI Programmes

Distribution Of Time	For CRTV	For CFI	Total	Percentage
Total	156 hrs	102 hrs	258 hrs	100
Total for French Language Programmes	127 hrs 30 min	102 hrs	229 hrs	88.7
Total for English Language Programmes	28 hrs 45 min	-	28 hrs 45 min	11.3

Source: NTEMFAC, Ofege et al (1991), "Internal Memorandum by the English-speaking Staff of CRTV to the General Manager".

Although the agreement with CFI brought a blend of very interesting programmes to those who understood French, as for televiewers of English expression who do pay a "Television Tax," as well, like everyone else, they had nowhere to turn to, since the CRTV did not bother considering proposals made to her by the "AMERICAN CABLE TELEVISION NETWORK, CNN" in 1988.

English Language Programmes on the Radio

On Monday, October 2, 1989, at 2.00 pm, faithful listeners to the English language programme, "Luncheon Date" waited patiently for the signal tune. But "Cameroun Magazine," a French language programme which had been on the airwaves since 12h00 continued. Listeners, most of whom were not aware of the shift in time of the programme, were worried as to what had happened to it. There had been instances like this when other programmes had not been on the air at the usual time, and soon simply disappeared without explanation. Thirty minutes later, when "Cameroun Magazine" had finished, "Luncheon Date" came onto the airwaves. Listeners soon learned that there was a new schedule being put into place, and that accounted for the shift of the time for "Luncheon Date".

To have shifted the programme "LUNCHEON DATE" from 2.00 pm to 2.30 pm meant abandoning a tradition that had been established for over 25 years. Over the years, the signal tune for this programme had conditioned the behaviour of many Cameroonians. In the Francophone provinces, it had become the signal to return to the office. The flimsy excuse for this, as it was claimed, was that it was meant to correspond with the working hours in the English-speaking provinces. The real intention, as it became apparent, was to do away with a tradition, and denigrate the interests of English-speaking listeners who work in Francophone provinces.

The treatment that was meted to "LUNCHEON DATE" is in effect a generalised practise of the Radio Service of the CRTV, and often times this meant the suppression of an English language programme in favour of one in the French language in a medium which is already oversaturated with French language programmes (70% of air time), against only 30% for programmes in the English language, as demonstrated by Table 4.7.

Table 4. 7: Distribution of Air-Time Between French and English Language Programmes on the National Radio and Television

Time	Programme	Language
5:50 am – 6:25 am	Rhythm at Dawn	English
6:25 am - 9:00 am	Antenne Matinale	French
9:00 am – 11:00 am	Variety Programmes	English
11:00 am – 12:00 noon	Roue Libre	French
12:00 pm – 2:30 pm	Cameroun Magazine	French
2:30 pm – 4:30 pm	Luncheon Date	English
4:30 pm – 5:40 pm	Antenne Jeunesse	French
5:40 pm – 7:30 pm	Variety Programmes	English
7:30 pm – 9:45 pm	Divers	French
9:45 pm – 10:15 pm	Variety Programmes	English
10:15 pm – 1:00 am	Service de nuit	French

Total Broadcast Time per Day = 19hrs30 mins
Total Time for English Language Programmes = 6hrs 30 mins
Total Time for French Language Programmes = 13 hrs
Percentage of English Language Programmes = 30%
Percentage of French Language programmes = 70%

Source: NTEMFAC, et al (1990).

The focus on The CRTV is not only because of the importance of the mass media in shaping the attitudes of people, but equally because the treatment which matters of Anglophone interests and Anglophones received at the CRTV is replicated in almost all government departments and state corporations.

Multipartism, the Emergence of West Cameroon "Liberation" Movements, and the Implications of the October 11, 1992 Presidential Elections for the Stability of the State

The rebirth of multiparty politics in Cameroon with the launching of the Social Democratic Front on May 26, 1990, in spite of very strong government resistance, had been inextricably linked to the desire of Anglophones for freedom. This helps to explain why they have been very active in the pro-democracy movement in Cameroon. The advent of multiparty politics was stimulated by a favourable international political climate, occasioned by the collapse of authoritarian regimes in Eastern Europe, and the subsequent insistence by Western democracies that African governments liberalise as a pre-requisite for continued economic assistance.

In Cameroon, an economic mismanagement and corruption provoked economic crisis meant that people were more willing to challenge the established order. It is under such conditions that the Anglophone elite, after realising that they were completely left out in the scheme of things and condemned to play the role of "eternal seconds" made it easier for the veteran activist, Mr. Albert Mukong, to persuade a number of them to join him in organising a political party.[14]

In February 1990, Mukong, along with the former president of the Cameroon Bar Association, Yondo Black, and about a dozen other people, were arrested for planning to organize a political party. After CPDM orchestrated marches in the provinces against "precipitated multipartism," Mukong and the others were tried by a military tribunal on April 19, 1990. While the others were released, Yondo Black and Ekane Anicet were each given a year's sentence by the military tribunal "for insulting the president".

Meanwhile, on March 16, 1990, Mr. John Fru Ndi had deposited documents for the formation of a new party, the Social Democratic Front (SDF) in Bamenda. At the launching of the party on May 26, 1990, government troops that had been deployed in Bamenda to prevent the launching, shot six young people, who were jubilating. Official government propaganda presented the launching of the SDF as a secessionist bid by the Anglophone minority, sponsored by Britain and Nigeria. It was common after the launching to hear top government officials and CPDM party stalwarts refer to Anglophones as les ennemis dans la maison, that is, "enemies in the house" and with a touch of sarcasm announce that those who were not satisfied with their lot qu'ils aillent ailleurs, that is, they could go elsewhere.[15]

With the advent of political pluralism, the hitherto disorganised and underground Anglophone political and civic organisations, most of which advocate for some form of regional autonomy surfaced. Some of these organisations included the shadowy extreme left movement, "The Patriotic Front Alliance," "The Free West Cameroon Movement," which advocates for outright secession, "The South West Elite Association," initially sponsored by CPDM party stalwarts from the South West Province, and whose primary objective is to protect the interests of people of the South West Province, and as such has been unsuccessful against a common West Cameroon front. The "Cameroon Anglophone Movement" advocates as a basis for the renegotiation of any form of union with East Cameroon, the October 1961 Foumban Accord. Thus, almost all of these groups in varying degrees advocate some form of a federation but differ in the strategies of achieving this.

The proliferation of 'liberation' movements led to an intense debate amongst the Anglophone political class and activists. Invariably the consensus that seemed to have emerged was that the best approach to achieving a federation was in first attaining Anglophone unity. As such, there were increasing calls for "Anglophone solidarity," which as Bisong Etahoben (Campost, April 4, 1991) puts it:

> ... we have been unanimous in one thing, and that is the fact that the Francophone has been so overbearing on us because having bigger population than us, he always feels he holds the trump cards...
>
> ... What I have tried to say all along is that it is not the SDF, nor the LDP nor the CPDM that will help solve the Anglophone problem. They can only have their way and say in this country if they present a united front...
>
> ... before the Anglophone join the chorus in demanding for the holding of a national conference, they should first hold their own conference... and give our future generations a new birth hope...

It was such repeated calls for a "common Anglophone platform" that led the Anglophone members of the "Constitution Drafting Committee" set up after the 1991 Yaoundé "Tripartite Talks"[16] to convene an "All Anglophone

Conference" in Buea. The All Anglophone Conference, held between April 2 and 3, 1993, brought together all shades of opinion in West Cameroon, including the "liberation" movements. The Conference declared:

> ... That all Cameroonians of English speaking heritage are henceforth committed to, and will work towards the restoration of a Federal Constitution which takes cognisance of the bicultural nature of Cameroon and which will protect the citizens against such violations...[17]

It is probably the resolve of the Anglophones to adopt a common stance on the political destiny of the region that Biya's "national debate, ... announced in March 1993, principally to undermine the "Union for Change's"[18] principled stand against the results of the October 11, 1992 presidential election, had been limited to the publication of a highly authoritarian unitary constitution. The "Anglophone Supreme Council," a sixty-five man body elected during the All Anglophone Conference, published an alternative federal constitution, which the government indicated, it will not consider.

In spite of the return to multiparty politics, and apparent liberalization of the political space, the government became increasingly more repressive. Civil servants of different political persuasion were arbitrarily victimised. Between 1990 and early 1993 not less than 690 persons lost their lives, either through being shot by government troops during demonstrations, political assassinations and government manipulated ethnic clashes.

The government organised parliamentary elections in March 1992, after the seven months trial of strength in 1991 with opposition parties grouped under the "National Coordination Committee of Opposition Parties". It was the March 1992 parliamentary elections that split the opposition parties, as those in favour of participation in the elections were described by those not in favour, as simply out to capture the instruments of state power (as opposed to the parties which wanted a fundamental change in the structure and system) decided to join the CPDM in the elections.

The opposition was thus split into two diametrically opposed camps. What came to be known as the radical opposition or "The Alliance for the Reconstruction of Cameroon through a Sovereign National Conference" argued rightly that there could be no free and fair elections without first dismantling the structures of the monolithic one-party state. Of the 70 legalised parties in Cameroon by March 1, 1992, 32 went for the Elections and four eventually got into the parliament. As a result of the boycott of the elections by the radical opposition, the CPDM emerged with 94 seats and was forced to form a coalition government with the Movement for the Defence of the Republic (MDR), which had six seats. Meanwhile, demonstrations organised by CAM, one of the pro-federation movements on February 11, 1992 were brutally repressed.

President Biya in order to regain some semblance of legitimacy decided to organise presidential elections on October 11, 1992. As the Supreme Court President, Justice Alexis Dipanda Mouelle acknowledged while announcing the election results, the CPDM together with the Ministry of Territorial Administration, rigged the election. He, however, added that the Supreme Court had no authority to annul the election results. The "Union for Change" led by the SDF, main opponent to the CPDM, claimed it had won the election by 38.57 per cent against 36.86 per cent for the CPDM. The CPDM government claimed to have won the election by 39.98 per cent against 35.97 per cent for its closest rival, the SDF. Following post-election violence, a state of emergency was declared in the North West Province, notwithstanding that there had been violence in the South Province too, where a systematic "ethnic cleansing" against Anglophones and Bamilekes took place. The State of emergency was only lifted after a lot of international pressure during the last days of December 1992.

Whatever figures that are used - that of the government or the opposition - an analysis of the October 11 presidential elections demonstrated that contrary to the widely held view, Cameroonians - Francophones and Anglophones alike - are prepared to accept any person irrespective of his linguistic background, as president. The inability of the President-elect to take over stemmed largely from the support the National Union for Democracy and Progress (UNDP) whose leader, Bello Bouba Maigari, came third in the elections with 18.6 per cent of the votes, gave to Paul Biya, while Biya with the complicity of France refused to hand over.

The ignoble role of France here stems largely from the fear that an Anglophone as president will bring to an end France's privileged relationship with Cameroon. Biya was able to successfully manipulate the October 11 presidential election, largely because he had complete control of the electoral machinery: the judiciary, complete control of the Ministry of Territorial Administration, which conducted the election, and violated with impunity the very laws the government made. In spite of his indisputable incompetence, France preferred to maintain him, rather than have an Anglophone who has already been questioning her role publicly in the country, as president.

Another factor that militated against the opposition was the division within its ranks. Bouba Bello preferred to ally with Biya, rather than with Fru Ndi while Adamu Ndam Njoya did not see himself standing down, in favour of an Anglophone.

France had unsuccessfully tried through media propaganda to present the SDF as an Anglophone regional party sponsored by Britain, Nigeria and the USA. Yvon Omnes who was France's ambassador to Cameroon until 1992 and notorious for his constant appeals to the SDF to renounce violence, while supplying funds to the internal security boss, Jean Forchive, and the Minister of Territorial Administration to repress the democratic struggle, in the name of "fighting for democracy" after completing his tour of duty was brought back to the Presidency of Cameroon as special adviser to Paul Biya.

The struggle for democracy in Cameroon has as such become a struggle to liberate Cameroon from the economic grip of France and her political meddlesomeness. In the struggle, France has powerful allies in the privileged Francophone elite who have been in power since 1958 and who are afraid of losing their privileges. This is why the Anglophone factor becomes very crucial: as there is the perception that Anglophones tend to be more independent minded, and since they have been rather at the fringes of power, most of the Anglophone political leaders do not seem to have been involved sordid deeds which France can use to blackmail them to do its bidding. It was this factor that also contributed to the opposition's inability to present a single candidate as most of the other presidential candidates: Bouba Bello Maigari, Adamu Ndam Njoya, and Samuel Eboua, were all closely linked to the ancien regime.

The October 11 presidential elections eroded whatever little credibility the Biya regime had. Consequently, the population had refused to pay taxes and continued with other forms of civil disobedience against a government they considered to be illegitimate. As France had come to be seen as the main impediment to change, there was a general campaign against French products. All these increased the government's inability to meet with its financial obligations, including the payment of the salaries of civil servants.

The government sought to dissipate the population's resolve through various strategies: it became more repressive, as troops constantly shot at demonstrators; political assassinations, kidnappings, etc. Also the government co-opted the parliamentary opposition with ministerial appointments and thereby reducing it to an appendage of the CPDM and the government. As such, all the parties in parliament at the time were also part of the government. These included the MDR, UPC and the UNDP.

To further divide the opposition's principled resolve on respecting the verdict of the October 11 presidential elections, the government in March 1993 announced what it called grand débat national, meant to provide Cameroon with a new constitution. As pointed out, the purpose of this was two-fold: to confer legitimacy to the government, and if the radical opposition accepted such a debate, to take off some of the internal as well as international pressure on it. Meanwhile, the Anglophone provinces, as well as the Western and Littoral Provinces remained virtually under an undeclared state of emergency.

The government limited the "national debate" to the publication of a unitary and strongly authoritarian constitution. The alternative "federal constitution" submitted to the government's technical committee by its Anglophone members was not given consideration.

The "federal constitution" proposed allowed for a degree of regional autonomy and took into consideration the bilingual and bicultural nature of Cameroon. It made allowance for the carving out of new states within the two regions. This proposed draft constitution by and large met the demands of the Anglophone community, but the government insisted that it be not considered.

This attitude stemmed largely from the fundamental difference in the legated traditions of the two linguistic groups: the Francophones following the Napoleonic tradition tends to be very centrist, and as such, look at ideas of federalism with considerable suspicion. The Anglophones on their part have tried to explain that federation is not synonymous to secession. Rather, it is a way of uniting peoples with diverse cultures and political traditions.

To sum up, "liberalisation" of political life in Cameroon did not only bring to the fore the "Anglophone problem" but also opened up ethno-regional grievances which if not addressed will remain a destabilising factor in the body politic. The authority and legitimacy of the regime will continue to be challenged on the streets, as long as it continues to remain intransigent on the Anglophone issue. This may push radical elements within the Anglophone community to declare a sovereign state. Apparently, this seems to be the preferred position of France, rather than allow a federal Cameroon with an Anglophone president since this will have serious consequences in the Central African region, as the various francophone countries will follow suit, with a negative backlash effect on the interests of the French in the region.

Notes and References

1. Le Vine, Victor (1986), "Leadership and Regime changes in Perspective," pp 20 - 51 in *The Political Economy of Cameroon* by M.G. Schatzberg and I.W. Zartman (eds). Praeger Publishers, New York, USA.
2. Sengat Kuo, once a very close collaborator to both Ahidjo and Biya, affirmed this view in an interview with *Le Messager*, Vol.11, No.21, June 9, 1992.
3. Pierre Flambeau Ngayap's work (1983), *Cameroun: Qui gouverne? D'Ahidjo à Biya. L'Heritage et L'enjeu*, L'Harmattan, Paris, provides a very insightful analysis of Cameroon's ruling class.
4. Muna, S. T. (1984) "Some Points of Social Justice." A Memorandum Presented to H.E. Paul Biya, President of the Republic of Cameroon by S.T. Muna, president of the national assembly.
5. "Memorandum submitted to His Excellency Paul Biya, Head of State, Head of Government and National Chairman of the CPDM Party by a joint committee of the elites of the North West and South West Provinces resident in the Littoral Province," June 1985.
6. "Memorandum submitted to His Excellency Paul Biya, Head of State, Head of Government and National Chairman of the CPDM Party by a joint committee of the elites of the North West Province resident in Yaoundé and parliamentarians from this province attending the 1985/1986 budgetary session."
7. This is an organ of the London based "Committee for Human Rights in Cameroon," *Cameroon Monitor*, Vol.1, No.1, February 1986.
8. *Cameroon Monitor*, Vol. 1, No.3, December 1986, "Tragedy and Betrayal."
9. When analysing the role of the media in a Bicultural society, we realise it is a common government practice to send journalists and other civil servants on disciplinary transfers, when they do not play by the rules and present a view contrary to what the government will prefer the population to believe.
10. cf Akika, Emmanuel (ed) (1992) *Le Cameroun Eclaté? Anthologie Commenté Des Revendications Ethniques*. Editions C3, Yaoundé, p 27.
11. Most of the information used in this section is drawn from research carried out on behalf of the Cameroon Anglophone Movement by Mr. Akonji Atekwana, a retired civil servant and at the time, Coordinator of the Social Democratic Front in the Centre Province.

12 *Jeune Afrique economie*, No. 165, March 1993, p 118.
13 This section is largely developed from the French version of a report prepared by Boh Herbert and Ntemfac Ofege and signed by sixty-three English-speaking journalists of the Cameroon Radio-Television (CRTV) and titled "Mono Cultural Cameroon Radio Television at the Service of Bi-cultural Cameroon". It is used here with the kind permission of Ntemfac Ofege.
14 Mr. Albert Mukong narrates his central role in the formation of the Social Democratic Front in his book entitled, *My Stewardship in the Cameroon Struggle*, 1992.
15 Noted for such pronouncements were Emah Basil, the then Government Delegate for Yaoundé Metropolitan Council, and a CPDM party stalwart and Andze Tsoungui, at the time Deputy Prime Minister in charge of Territorial Administration.
16 The November 1991 "Tripartite Talks" in Yaoundé brought together opposition parties, the government, and prominent "independent" Cameroonians. It was meant essentially to resolve the political impasse occasioned by the opposition led civil disobedience campaign, whose aim was to make government agree to a Sovereign National Conference.
17 The Buea Declaration, 3rd April, 1993, see Appendix III.
18 A coalition of opposition parties led by the Social Democratic Front that had contested the October 11, 1992 presidential election, and who claimed that its presidential candidate; John Fru Ndi had won the election.

Chapter Five

Summary and Conclusion

In times like these, we need hearts that can crystallize the flames of social injustice into the forces of social harmony. The era of laying blames on our ancestors while we blind ourselves with daily obsessions that posterity will vindicate us from our overt complacency and tacit complicity is gone. When the bells of injustice toll, they chime in every heart, when the waves of oppression rise, they sink beneath them every soul. As we continue our charted course let us be conscious of the stumbling blocks from within our very own ranks and narrow bends from without. Yet we can overcome these stumbling blocks with startling hope and negotiate these narrow bends with broad minds.

George Ngwane, April 1993

Summary

Chapter One, examined the role of the various forces that came to be determining factors in the politics of contemporary Cameroon. The plight of Anglophone Cameroon as a minority in the Republic of Cameroon has come to be the major contradiction and point of conflict in the well publicised policy of national integration. The "Anglophone problem" could be summed up as one of systematic institutionalised discrimination and shunting to the margins of the political process. This has been exacerbated by the issue of unbalanced regional development policies that have been pursued over the years by the various Francophone led regimes.

The phenomena of discrimination and alienation do raise a number of questions relating to the different perspectives in which the Anglophone/Francophone dichotomy could be perceived. The assumptions here are hinged on the nature of constitutional guarantees (or the lack thereof) to the rights of minorities, the effect of French colonial assimilationist policies in Africa, the class character of the Cameroon state, and the nature of the Anglophone leadership.

The theoretical framework is constructed on what system of government is best suited to symmetrical nation building in multicultural societies? The argument is advanced for the adoption of federalism not just because it is an intrinsically better system of managing diversity in multicultural societies but equally because it is inherently more democratic. As such, it is a viable system that can lead to national integration and nation-building, without leading to perceptions and accusations, of institutionalised discrimination.

Chapter Two focussed on the role of colonisation in the development of modern political institutions in the Cameroons. As such, we analysed the nature of both British and French colonial policies in Cameroon and their role in the development of modern political institutions. We pointed out that since their approach to colonialism was fundamentally different; this led to the development of different and opposing attitudinal and behavioural patterns of the peoples in British and French Cameroons. Consequently, Cameroonians in these two regions differ in their approach to administration, law and politics.

We examined constitutional developments in the British Cameroons before 1960 and dwelled on the struggle in the British Cameroons to detach the territory from the Eastern Region of Nigeria. Since the British Cameroons was perceived to be dominated by the Ibos, the nationalist struggle in the territory also took the form of an anti-Ibo xenophobia. As such calls for reunification also became a way of liberating the territory from the perceived grip of the Ibos.

We brought out the role played by the various political parties in the territory: the KPP, KNC, KNDP, CPNC in the struggle for either reunification with French Cameroon or integration into Nigeria, as well as the role of the UN. We pointed out that the KNDP eventually won the UN organised plebiscite. This led to constitutional talks with the independent Republic of Cameroon and that ushered in reunification as a federation on October 1, 1961, with the country being known as the Federal Republic of Cameroon.

Chapter three opened with an examination of the role of France in Cameroon since independence. We concluded that given France's privileged position in its relations with Cameroon, characterised by her intricate web of economic, financial, political and military interference in Cameroon's internal and external policies, one could hardly claim that Cameroon is truly a sovereign country.

We analysed the Foumban Conference of August 1961 which resulted in the formation of the Federal Republic of Cameroon. We pointed out that the

Foumban Conference was never conclusive and its resolutions were never ratified by the Southern Cameroons House of Assembly, and as such the constitution that was drawn up after the conference was an imposition on the state of West Cameroon.

An analysis of the nature of party politics in West Cameroon after reunification brought out the fact that with reunification there was no longer any major ideological differences between the parties in West Cameroon. However, as those who had championed the cause for integration with Nigeria felt left out in the new dispensation, they sought to work their way back to political relevance through collaborating with those perceived to wield power. As such, they felt that the only way in which they could continue to play any meaningful role in the political landscape of Cameroon and share in the 'spoils of office' was to champion the cause of national unity, which they felt could only be achieved through a single national party.

The situation was not helped by intra-party fighting within the KNDP which led to splits that precipitated the formation of a single national party, the CNU in 1966. With the formation of the single national party, the stage was set for abolishing the federation and absorbing the state of West Cameroon in 1972 when the United Republic of Cameroon was proclaimed.

The abolition of the federation confirmed to West Cameroonians that the Francophone led regime intended to confine them to playing inconsequential roles. This led to a growing feeling of marginalisation and alienation. The feeling of alienation was exacerbated by creeping 'frenchification' which took the form of insistence that Anglophones learn French while there was no corresponding insistence that Francophones learn English. This attitude was manifested in all other aspects of national life. There was also a corresponding deprivation of infrastructural development that would have led to self-sustaining economic growth in West Cameroon. This process was in parallel to the undermining of already existing economic structures which made West Cameroon to become increasingly dependent economically on East Cameroon. This meant that the negative impact of reunification fell heavily on West Cameroonians.

This chapter concludes by noting that it is rather too simplistic to present reunification as benefiting solely the Francophone elite, since a rump of the Anglophone bourgeoisie has participated actively and benefitted from the exploitation of West Cameroonians. Besides, the majority of the

Francophone masses, just like their Anglophone compatriots, suffered from the Ahidjo and subsequently Biya's authoritarian rule.

Chapter four analysed Biya's regime from 1982 - 1993. We are able to establish that the accession of Biya to power coincided with the intensification of the marginalisation of Anglophone Cameroonians, and the analogous development of resistance to this marginalisation. Here we brought out the nature of state power in Cameroon and how Biya instrumentalised it with the 'ethnicisation of power' to resuscitate ethnic tensions. This has come to compound the 'anglophone problem'.

We established that the process of 'cultural assimilation' epitomised in the near total absence of the English language on public radio and television has created a negative impression of the English language on the Anglophone youth.

Also an analysis of the distribution of political/administrative positions at senior levels of the public service and government was undertaken, and arrived at the conclusion that there has indeed been a systematic and institutionalised discrimination against Anglophone Cameroonians over the years.

We focussed attention on the advent of multiparty politics since 1990 and analysed its implications given the centrifugal forces at play in Cameroon. We observed that in spite of apparent opening up, the state has become increasingly more repressive as the Biya regime despite its unpopularity battles to maintain itself in power.

From our analysis of the October 11, 1992 elections, we drew the conclusion that discrimination against Anglophones is a Francophone elite phenomenon, as Francophones and Anglophones alike voted for one of the opposition candidates, John Fru Ndi, who happens to be an Anglophone.

We concluded that given the determination of Anglophone Cameroon to attain a federation, the Francophone led regime can only continue to ignore this agitation at its own peril, given the potential of radical groups in the Anglophone region destabilising the country.

Findings

This study establishes:

Firstly, that "national integration" and consequently "nation building" from the perspective of political integration as conceived by the Ahidjo -

Biya regime, has failed in Cameroon. This failure is not necessarily as a result of centrifugal pulls but mainly because of the attempt by the various Francophone led regimes to block auto-centred and balanced development in West Cameroon.

Secondly, that Anglophone Cameroonians had at reunification in spite of initial misgivings, aspired to develop with their Francophone compatriots, what Nfor (1980: 259) has described as 'qualitative integration' (see figure 5.1A). Qualitative integration meant the development of a nation with common values, based on equal participation and opportunities for the unifying regions.

Thirdly, that the Yaoundé authorities rather than allowing "national integration" to develop by ensuring social justice and equitable resource allocation, thought it could coercively achieve this through making the Anglophone elite and community completely dependent on Yaoundé for survival. The outcome has been a dependent elite, an exploited people, and an economically neglected region. This has engendered the widespread feeling of alienation and consequently, the rejection of "national integration".

Mal-integration (see Figure 5.1B) has meant the frustration of the aspirations of the Anglophone community, which has imposed on them the humiliating and undignifying status of second class citizens. As the aspirations of the Anglophone community has come to be at variance with that of the Francophone led regime, one can conclusively state that national integration as perceived by the Ahidjo-Biya regimes has failed in Cameroon. Thus, it is that Anglophone Cameroonians stated in the Buea Declaration (see Appendix III) that:

> As a people, our values, vision, and goals and those of our Francophone brothers in the Union are different, and clearly cannot harmonise within the framework of a unitary state...

Fourthly, that France has continued to play an active role in varying degrees in the administration and political evolution of Cameroon, as well as in financial and economic matters. While this is largely repugnant to the Anglophone elite, it would seem that the Francophone elite are at best indifferent to the phenomenon, if not completely acquiescent to it. Thus, when President Paul Biya describes himself as 'Francois Mitterrand's best pupil', he is not only making a statement of fact, but incarnates the

Francophone mind-set that sees nothing wrong in being Black, Cameroonian and at the same time being French.

Fifthly, that as a result of the exploitation and marginalisation of West Cameroon over the years, coupled with the spirited attempt of obliterating the linguo-cultural colonial legacy of the people of West Cameroon, "Anglophone nationalism" has developed. This has down played the negative role of ethnicity in the Anglophone consciousness. The growth of Anglophone nationalism is however distinctly different from Francophone chauvinism.

Figure 5.1A: DIAGRAM OF QUALITATIVE INTEGRATION

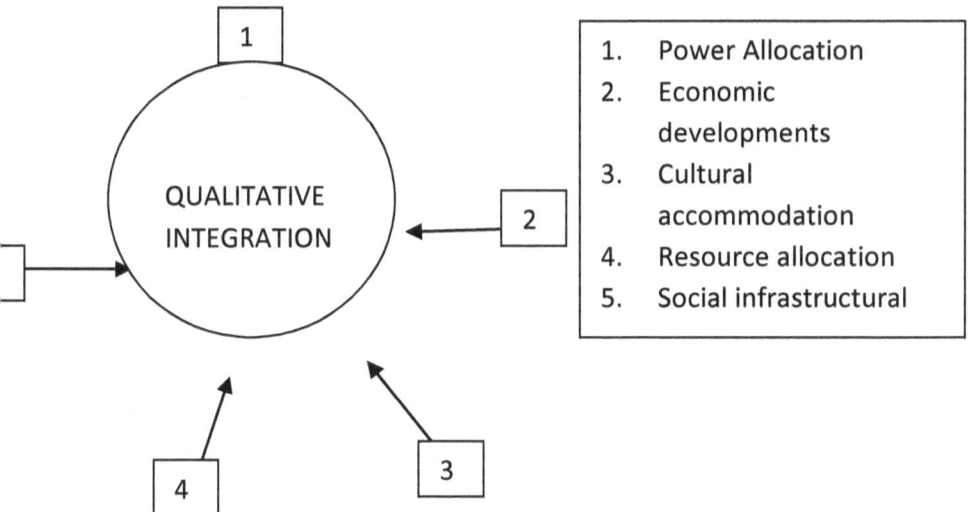

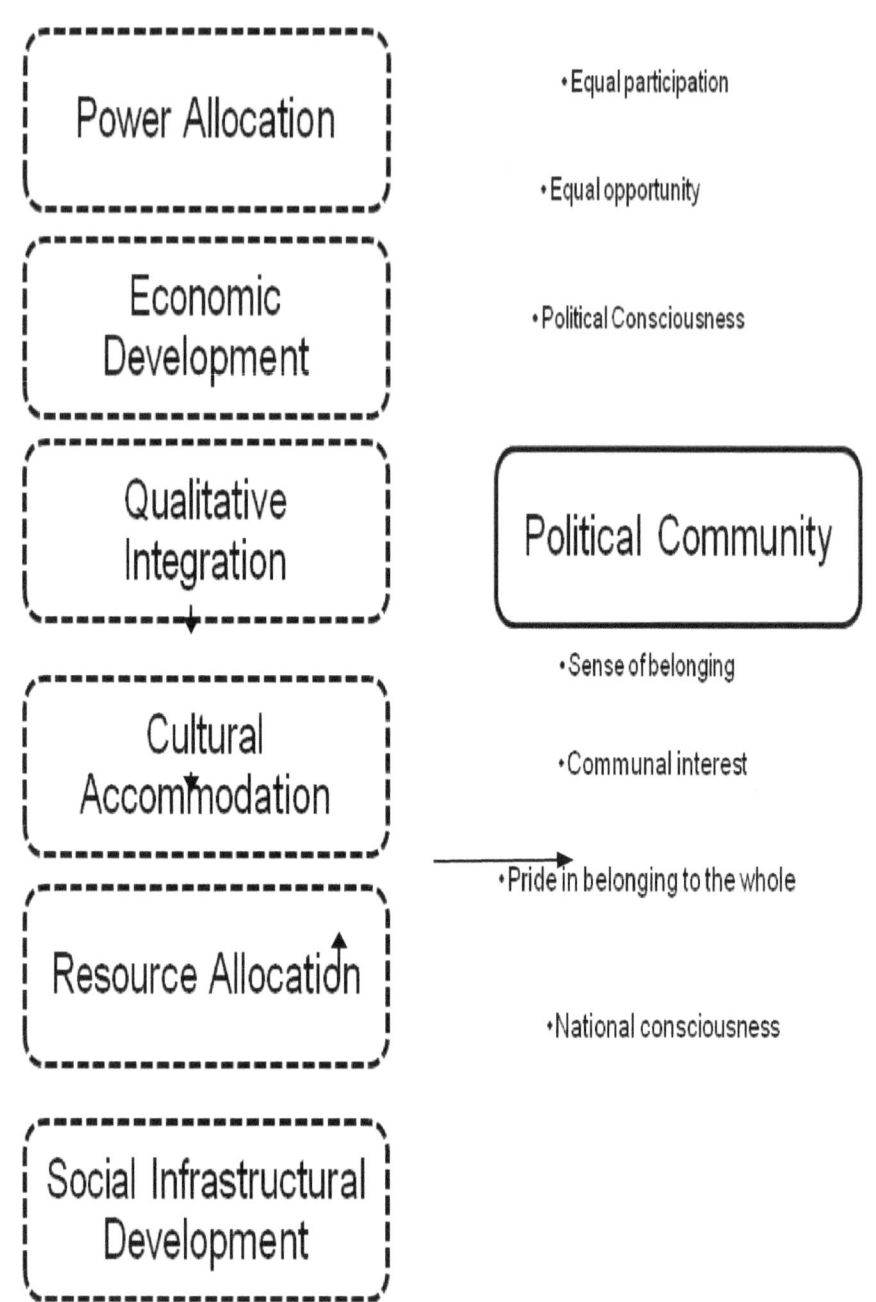

SOURCE: Nfor (1980) Cameroon Reunification: Costs and Problems of National Integration.

Figure 5.1B: DIAGRAM OF MAL-INTEGRATION

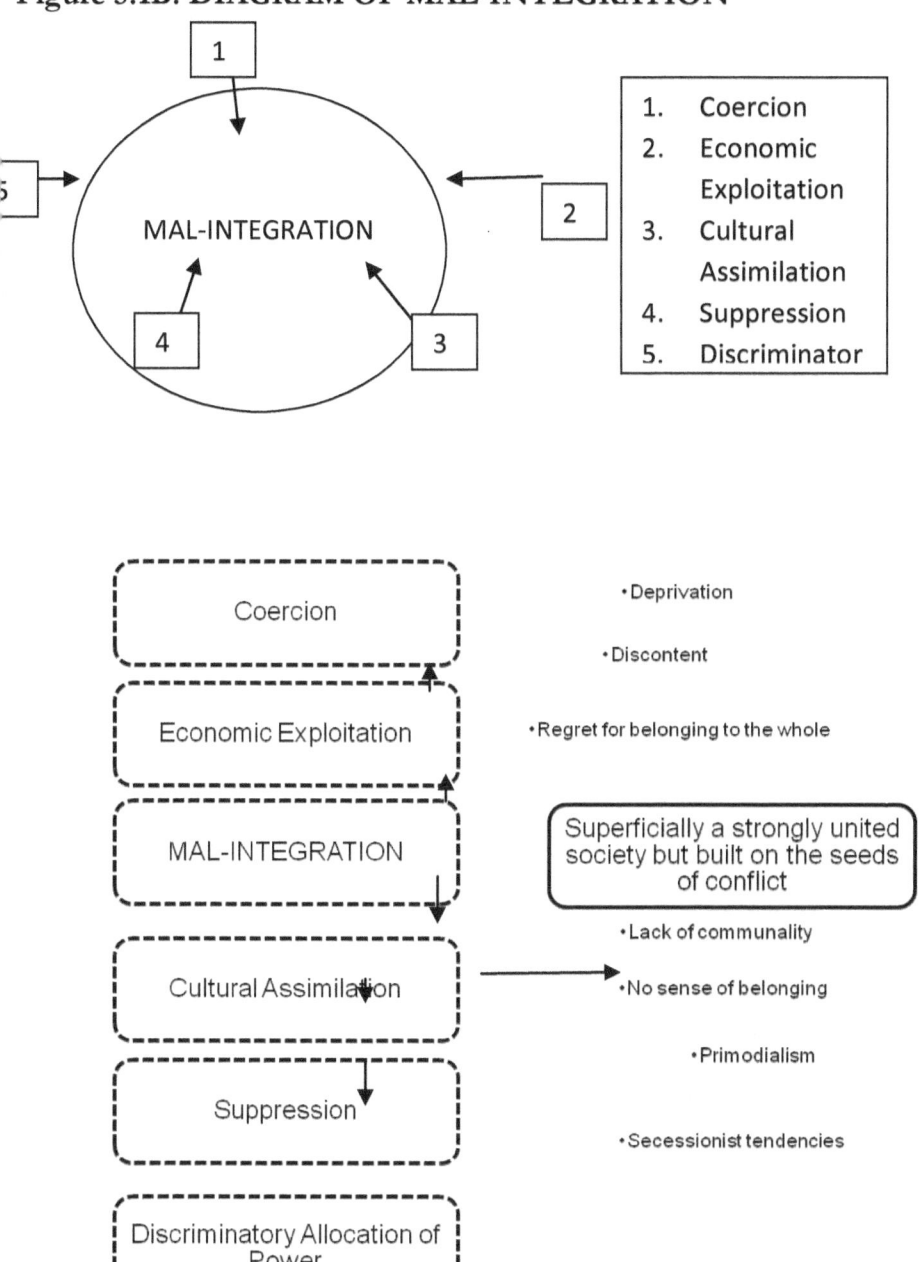

Source: Nfor (1980) Cameroon Reunification: Costs and Problems of National Integration.

Recommendation

In Chapter One (1.6.1 - 1.6.4), we examined the various means through which integration and 'unity' could be attained in a multicultural society. From our analysis of Cameroon, there is no doubt that it is a society made up of people with diverse cultural backgrounds. This is further complicated by the diametrically opposed legated colonial traditions. There is equally no doubt, from our analysis, that these colonial traditions have come to be the determining factors in the values of Cameroonians on both sides of the linguo-cultural divide: the long experience of local government practice, and self government led to the development of a liberal political culture in West Cameroon, whereas in Francophone Cameroon, the authoritarian nature of French colonialism and assimilation seemed to have been central to the formation of the Francophone mind-set.

As argued in Chapter One, federalism is not only a theoretically better option of organising the state in a multi-cultural society, since it best guarantees the rights of minorities, while at the same time preserving national unity, but with its system of constitutional checks and balances, is more practicable and inherently democratic.

Thus, it is only within a federal system that intricate details like revenue allocation formula, a rotational presidency, guarantee of equal opportunities and equal participation at all levels of government can be constitutionally entrenched. As such, adequate safeguards will be provided for minorities.

Conclusion

What makes the Cameroonian experience at 'national integration' very intriguing is that it has been an attempt at imposing a colonially legated and thus 'foreign' culture and values on people at the expense of another colonially legated culture and set of values. In the process no attempt has been made to develop an indigenous homogenous system – not that it is desirable for societies and states to aspire for homogeneity. This has led the two different groups to have diametrically opposed views on matters of education, administration, the legal system, etc.

Clearly, the failure of national integration has not been as a result of the lack of will on both sides of the linguistic divide, but because of the various attempts by one of the parties to the union to use its numerical superiority and its grip on the levers of power to impose its will on the Anglophone minority.

This imposition was facilitated by the nature of colonialism and the liberation struggle in the Cameroons. While France by the sheer power of military superiority successfully quashed armed nationalist struggle, and imposed on the Cameroonian people a regime acceptable to her, in the Southern Cameroons, the struggle for independence and unification was clouded by divisions within the ranks of the nationalists, and a lack of visionary leadership.

Since reunification meant that the losing side in the struggle for reunification could only guarantee for itself continued participation in the process of 'nation-building', as well as securing for itself part of the spoils of office by appealing for 'national unity', it thus became the champion in West Cameroon of the formation of a single national party.

The initial enthusiasm which West Cameroonians brought into the federation at its inception in 1961 was soon dissipated, as they soon perceived that their aspirations for the new nation differed fundamentally from that of their Francophone compatriots. This realisation soon turned into disillusionment, but rather than working towards attaining a federation that will protect and guarantee their interest as a people, the political class preferred to struggle for narrow interests and in the process, created room for Ahidjo to consolidate his grip on West Cameroon.

Inordinate ambition on the part of West Cameroon politicians facilitated the formation of a single national party. This meant that West Cameroon politicians had to articulate the interests of the region within the confines of the single national party. However, as the single party came to incarnate consensus, any contrary view to that of the party hierarchy was perceived as 'subversion'. The formation of the single party thus facilitated the abolition of the Federation in 1972, contrary to the 1961 Foumban Union Accord.

The emergence of the unitary state in 1972, while further marginalising the Anglophones, increased Ahidjo's authority and prestige. Anglophones continued to increasingly participate in national life, but in positions in which they could not contribute meaningfully to decision making. Ahidjo's authoritarian rule certainly played a role in cowering Anglophones who otherwise would have opposed him. The quest for individual self-fulfilment and grandeur clouded the judgement of the Anglophone political class, who often facilitated the repression of fellow Anglophones with dissenting views.

In spite of the democratic posturing of the Biya regime, meant essentially to satisfy the West, the regime became more repressive. With the growth of Anglophone nationalism, this implies that if the Francophone led regime is to avoid the looming and ever-increasing danger of separation, it will progressively succumb to Anglophone demands. There is as such the tendency that the Anglophones will become more assertive.

As pointed out earlier, it is important to note that there were fundamental differences from the onset to the nature and objectives of the Federation. West Cameroonians saw federalism as not only a means of bringing people of different colonial backgrounds together, but equally as an end in itself. As such, they insisted that the two states be maintained. East Cameroonians on their part understood federalism to be a stop-gap measure, which will help to facilitate the transition to a unitary state. The compromised outcome was a quasi-federal constitution. This, in the end, worked in favour of the Eastern State and led eventually to the gradual but complete absorption of the state of West Cameroon.

Whilst this study brings out the reasons for the failure of the federal experiment in Cameroon, what is of interest is how best to manage and satisfy minority grievances and aspirations, without this leading to disintegration? Given the centrifugal forces at play in Cameroon, recent examples of violent conflict as a result of skewed nation building abound: suffice to mention here, the former Soviet Union, Yugoslavia, Ethiopia (Eritrea), Somalia, the Sudan, etc. What is common in most of these countries is that they were forged and maintained with the use of force.

If West Cameroonians differ in the form of federation they aspire to, they are all agreed that they do require a federation which recognises and preserves the region's peculiarity. From our analysis, and given the present circumstances, it is obvious that the two main ideological forces, that is, the unitarists and the federalists, are on a collision course, given the obstinacy of the Francophone-led regime.

Whatever the case, there are two options opened to Cameroon: Anglophone Cameroon is determined to attain a federation which will allow it to have a degree of regional autonomy. Failure to achieve this may eventually lead to secession. The Francophone led regime on the advice of France, is not prepared to compromise on its unitarist stance, since this means losing some of its authority to the regions. As such, there is the serious possibility of an eventual violent conflict, since the authorities in

Yaoundé will try to resist any secessionist bid from groupings in West Cameroon.

The capacity for Cameroon to overcome the crisis of confidence and the failure of the unitary state depends on the ability of the Francophone-led regime to make concessions to the Anglophone minority, so as to preserve Cameroon's unity, and protect "national interest".

Appendices

Appendix I

Constitutional Position of the Southern Cameroons in the Event of It Electing to Become Part of the Republic of Cameroon

Communiqué

Considering that in the application of the Republic at the 14th session of the United Nations a plebiscite is to be organised in February 1961 to allow the people of the Southern Cameroons under British Trusteeship and the people of Northern Cameroons under British Trusteeship to declare whether they wish to join the Federation of Nigeria or to be united with the Cameroon Republic.

Considering that in the event of the result of this plebiscite being in favour of Reunification, the application of this reunification on a federal basis allowing for the particular conditions of each group, could not be automatic, but gradual,

Considering that the representatives of the Cameroon Republic and of the government party of the Southern Cameroons vigorously reaffirm the desire of their people to be reunited in one nation,

Considering that the political heads have already met twice to examine the broad outlines of the constitution of the two Federated states, they have, at the conclusion of their third meeting of the 10, 11, 12 and 13th October, 1960, decided to adopt the broad outlines of the constitution which they will adopt in the event of the plebiscite vote being favourable to them.

Joint Declaration

The representatives of the Cameroon republic and the Government party of the Southern Cameroons under British trusteeship met for the third time to continue their discussions on the projected constitution which would govern the reunified Cameroon.

At the conclusion of these talks, Hon J.N. Foncha , Prime Minister of the Southern Cameroons, His Excellency, M. Ahmadou Ahidjo, President of the

Cameroon Republic, and M. Charles Assale, Prime Minister and Head of the Cameroon government,

STATE:
1. That they wish to use every available means to bring to a successful conclusion the task of national reunification which they have set themselves;
2. That in no case will the United Cameroon be a part either of the French Community or the British Commonwealth;
3. That they wish to create a Federal State whose institutions could be broadly outlined as follows:

The Federal United Cameroon Republic will be a democratic state. It will have its motto, its anthem and its flag. The nationals of the Federated States will enjoy Cameroonian nationality. The Federated state in the first stage will have the power to deal with matters listed below as a minimum:

Public freedoms
Nationality
National defence
Foreign affairs
Higher education
Immigration and emigration
Federal budget
Posts and telecommunications

A list of powers which would fall within the competence of the federal government in the second stage will be set out in the constitution.

The federal authorities will be composed of:

A federal Executive headed by the President of the Republic, Chief of the Federal State, Federal legislature consisting of a federal legislative Assembly and a Federal Senate.

Certain federal laws will only be enacted in such a way that no measures contrary to the interest of one state will be imposed upon it by the majority (system of second reading with a qualified majority).

In the event of a conflict of laws between the Federal State and the Federated States, the federal law will prevail. In non-federal matters, the Authorities of each of the Federated States will be ruled by a Government and will have a Legislative Assembly.

A Federal Court of justice will have as its purpose to unify judicial systems and to act as the Highest Court of Appeal of the Federal State.

Federal Services will be established to carry out federal Administration. Legislation (or systems of legislation in force) will remain valid until the enactment of federal legislation.

4. The federation will be created by the Cameroon Republic and the Southern Cameroons under British Trusteeship. The two parties hope that the Northern Cameroons under British Trusteeship will also enter into this federation, either as a separate state, or as part of the Cameroons at present under British Trusteeship.

5. In the event of the Southern and Northern Cameroons voting in favour of reunification, those entrusted with the responsibility of the affairs of the Unified Cameroons would, through mutual agreement, specify the manner in which the populations of the Cameroons would be asked to express their opinion on the Federal Constitution.

Joint Communiqué

The representatives of the government party of the Southern Cameroons under British Trusteeship, led by J.N. Foncha, Prime Minister, on their return from London where they had talks with the United Kingdom Minister for the colonies on the future of their territory, had on the 1st and 2nd December a fourth meeting with the delegation of the Cameroon Republic, led by the President of the Republic, Ahmadou Ahidjo. The two parties were in full agreement:

1. That the United Nations General Assembly has stated with clarity the two questions which will be put at the time of the plebiscite on the 11th February, 1961, i.e.

(a) Do you wish to attain independence by unification with the independent federation of Nigeria?; or

(b) Do you wish to attain independence by unification with the independent Cameroon Republic?

2. That the two delegation whilst in agreement with the interpretation of the second question which was accepted in London, regret that the representatives of the Northern Cameroons were not present at this conference and ask:

(a) That immediately after the plebiscite and in the event of the people voting in favour of reunification with the Cameroon republic, a conference should be attended by the representatives of the Cameroon republic and the Southern and Northern Cameroons.

(b) That the conference, at which representatives of the Trusteeship authority and possibly those of the United Nations would be present, would have as its aim the fixing of time limits and conditions for the transfer of sovereign powers to an organisation representing the future federation.

Signed: FONCHA   Signed: AHIDJO

Appendix II

Open Letter to All English-Speaking Parents of Cameroon from the English-Speaking Students of the North-West and South-West Provinces

Summary: Realising that, with government indifference, the smouldering discontent in the English-speaking region of the country can only end up in war: knowing that we are those who thus will miss the peace and security we love; conscious of the pains and sorrows that are inseparable appendages to war: we call on our parents to press for a peaceful and permanent solution before it is too late. Done on the 20th August, 1985.

Dear Parent, Meeting in Kumba for students of the South West and in Bamenda for students of the North West on the 14th and 19th of August respectively, we, your children, resolved to launch to you this particularly important appeal to assume squarely your responsibilities before history. We deem it expedient that you appreciate fully the gravity of the country's situation. But first let us ask you some pertinent questions:

1. Tell us why for 23 years, the number of Francophone Cameroonians granted government scholarships yearly to study in France alone far exceed the total number of scholarships awarded English-speaking Cameroonians to study abroad. We have the statistics - see Cameroon Tribunes of 19th and 20th August, 1985. This year eight scholarships have been awarded the Anglophones to study in Britain, eight in Nigeria (one of whom is a Francophone), and one in Liberia and one in Sierra Leone, making a total of ten, whereas there are 1,000 (one thousand) scholarships granted Francophone students to study abroad in France, Belgium, etc. The Francophone will tell you that more of your children will be given scholarships after the GCE 'A' Level results are published. Last year, 50 were granted these scholarships and even if the figure were doubled (to be doubted) that would be nothing to the 1,000.

2. Tell us why the doors into most of the Higher Professional Schools in the country have been closed to us. This year again, none of us has been admitted into the National Polytechnic in Yaoundé.

3. Tell us why last year government decreed that students from commercial schools were free to register in the Yaoundé University, yet only the registration of the Francophone has been thereafter accepted.

4. Tell us why, with comparable, if not better qualifications than our Francophone counterparts, we must study in ENAM for five years whereas the former do only three years to obtain the same diploma.

5. Tell us why the inauguration of the construction work on only part of the Kumba - Mamfe road which is to start in December was so widely publicised whereas development projects in the Francophone areas of the country such as the construction of the Yaoundé - Sangmalima Highway, construction of the ultra-modern airport in Ebolowa, the opening of vast plantations in Ebolowa, etc, etc, remain closely guarded government secrets.

6. Tell us why bilingualism in Cameroon demands the mastery of the French language by Anglophones and not vice-versa.

7. Tell us how many kilometres of rail road exist in the English-speaking zone out of a total of 1,171km.

8. Tell us what has become of the Tiko, Mamfe and Nkambe airports, and the once busy Cross River Port.

9. Tell us why Radio Buea and Radio Bamenda are the laughing stock of the country though Radio Buea was created before Radio Douala, Bertoua and Garoua.

10. Tell us whether it is an accident that not a single industry exists in the North West Province which state of affairs obtains in no other province in the country.

11. Tell us what became of the Yoke power station of Powercam.

12. Tell us why all sign boards around SONARA Limbe, as well as all road signs in the country are solely in French.

13. Tell us why we participated in the recent Francophone games in Ivory Coast but never in the Commonwealth games.

14. Tell us why the majority of provincial chiefs in Buea and Bamenda are francophone where as we do not hold corresponding posts in the French-speaking provinces, or why out of over 25 secretary generals in the country only two are English-speaking.

15. Tell us why Bamenda and Kumba have two Francophone Primary Schools each whereas Yaoundé with a larger Anglophone population than the Francophone population in these two combined, has only one English

primary school, which, in addition, has been flooded by Francophone children.

16. Tell us why the North West and South-West provinces are respectively annexed to the West and Littoral provinces through the technique of basing so called regional offices of banks, corporations, computer services, and the army legions in the latter provinces.

17. Tell us what we really benefit from the sitting of few industries in the South West Province when all unskilled as well a majority of the skilled labour is recruited from the Francophone provinces while our brothers continue to roam the streets jobless.

So much unanswered and yet so much left unasked. These are not things that can forever be left unnoticed. Even the blind man when he stumbles against an obstacle knows that there is an obstacle here and shouts, or warns, or pleads that those with whom he lives see that such obstacles do not reoccur.

And we gladly accept to be the heirs to your toil and sweat. You should know, however, that the peace of Cameroon we are set to inherit is quite unguaranteed.

Still, let us recall some facts to your memory. Just as they constantly deride our persons and norms of behaviour, our Francophone friends have consistently denounced as base out system of education. The Ministry of National Education (MINEDUC) even tried to transform the Cameroon GCE from an internationally recognised certificate to a purely Cameroonian thing so that the bulk of English-speaking students who proceed to foreign universities should be stopped. We saw through the dirty tricks, and our opposition temporarily quashed the attempt. But it has not been abandoned. We are aware that its proponents are very alive and busy in the back seats of power seeking another outlet.

The latest unscrupulous attempt we recall with unquestionable bitterness. By issuing confusing announcements on public examinations, MINEDUC was responsible for thwarting the effort of many an Anglophone youth to better their futures and that of their families. These students did not sit in for Chemistry 'A' and 'O' level papers of the just ended GCE examinations. Though there is no doubt that irremediable damage has been done to some of the families concerned, nothing has been done or said to correct the situation. And, instead of calling for justice to fall on those involved in the scandal, the National Assembly takes it as an opportunity to press for harmonization of the educational systems (we might here ask what became of the GCE Commission?).

Now the simple question we ask is what to expect from someone who condemns a system and is given the opportunity and liberty to select from it? No doubt, total rejection.

Yet we like to make it clear that we cherish the principle underlying our educational system: emphasis is placed on understanding rather than on memorizing. The other principle which stresses the memory facilitates cheating at examinations, and turns out unqualified graduates unable to live up to the certificates they brandish, we hold as cheap, simplistic, and inadmissible.

Consider that the 1983 class boycott by students of the Yaoundé University, though it had the GCE problems resonating, was also sparked off by problems within the campus. Notably, there as the Chancellor's decision suspending the courses of Dr. Bisong in the 2nd year Economics degree class when the Francophone students complained about his teaching an important subject course in a FOREIGN LANGUAGE- that language being English. We decried this decision because all over the country's higher institutions of learning, English-speaking students are being frustrated in their academic career as they are forced to follow up studies in the French they have not mastered in programmes wholly divorced from the syllabuses they have studied. The President, in appealing to us to resume classes, said he would look into the problem. Two years have passed and we have been patient.

Spare some time more to look at our technical education. We who choose this section must end our studies in form four. In spite of its importance to the life of any nation, our technological education has been smothered. In the few technical schools provided by government, the students have to undergo studies in a language which is neither English, French, nor Pidgin, being a concoction of all three. This is because only Francophone teachers are sent to these schools. Afterwards, unfortunate as we are, we must compete, no longer at the City and Guilds examinations, but at a certain "CAP" with Francophone students who have studied in the security of their language and system. The examinations, if they are not in French, are very misleading English translations from the French (the French text being authentic). Not working on the authentic texts by which we shall be examined, we fail in our numbers. And our parents upbraid us!!

This is for the first cycle. Do we have second cycle technical schools at all? Two. At the end of these we present ourselves for the "Baccalaureate" in much the same conditions as for "CAP". The present final batch in the Bamenda Lycée Technique had 0 %. Over the years, between Kumba and Bamenda, success has been in twos and threes. Where do these proceed to? The Polytechnic College in Yaoundé? Entrance examinations to this college are wholly in French. So too are the studies there, and their books as well. Our technical education effectively ends therefore in an ungraduation class four. Mighty pity!

Those of us in grammar schools of general education must proceed into a civil service in which the English-speaking Cameroonian always remains a deputy. In the government set-up, despite the long lasting talk of the New Deal, the English-speaking Cameroonians are limited to a few skeletal Ministries reserved for them in the Old Deal! In these Ministries, the power has been devolved to the powerful Directors of Parastatals. Or else, they have to be Vices. Anglophones are craftily left out of the highest offices of the land, and given a stool presidency of a toothless voiceless rubber-stamp parliament with the excluding clause that he might not run for the Presidency of the Republic in the event of its vacancy.

Recently, we followed with undiminishing astonishment the Minister of State for Justice in his safari trip to Bamenda to castigate Anglophone magistrates for their ignorance, misinterpretation and contempt of the law. He was in truth passing shit on the legal system which gave these magistrates their undeserved titles – Ignorance. Misinterpretation, contempt, of the law! What a thing to say of all North-West and South-West magistrates! And in the open, too!

Tomorrow, when we are to become lawyers and magistrates in our turn, we think that we can work under the aegis of no better legal system than that in which the law is the last supreme authority in the land; a magistrate speaks his mind and is neither "of discreet" nor "reserved" towards any section of the community because his base is the law and is the truth.

Consequently, we advance our doubts on the workable nature of the harmonised law bill a Minister announces after first condemning the legal system of our cultural region. A harmonized law bill which we have to abide though it goes against our "convictions, customs and beliefs," a bill by which certain individuals cannot be arraigned before justice except after consultation of the chancellery. A bill to facilitate such filthy deeds as the

Honourable Minister's telegram No. 31/NJ/CAB/RP 77/75-1912 of 11th December, 1984 to the Public Prosecutor of the South West Province and to the Governor of the same province, both of which instructed these personalities to ensure that the fraudulent General Manager of SONARA who had stolen billions of francs from the sale of oil be not arrested. Certainly, a bill which denies the infallible equality of all before the law.

The file of grievance is interminable. While, for instance, there is a natural deep sea-port in Limbe, Government prefers to squander billions annually dredging the Douala port. These billions are pumped from the oil refinery in Limbe. They are billions necessary for the development of the nation. Then, when it comes to developing a second major sea-port, government talk is of according priority to Kribi. Limbe is in the English-speaking South West Province.

All these point to two things in particular: colonial status of our cultural region and assimilation of its members into full citizens of the other culture. No other persons than the French-bred and directed is more capable of combining these two. The conclusion is supported by the treatment we received at all levels and confirmed by the recent return to the name of the French Cameroon on Independence Day - Republique du Cameroun. It is also confirmed by the names given to our new party in French and English, respectively "Rassemblement" and Movement.

The Francophones, already settled, are gathering themselves round to enjoy the fruits of independence and some sort of democracy. The Anglophone, on the other hand, is still moving 'towards these goals as he still has to be fully integrated into the "Republique du Cameroun". No wonder, he has to wait until this is achieved before he can enjoy the fruits of development!! (The next thing we shall hear is that the French name only is authentic so our interpretation, misinterpretation rather, cannot be upheld. But this applies even to the constitution!!! Article 39).

Those who know what they say when they talk of integration know that it is a voluntary aspect of human cultures which happens when they are brought into peaceful contact and not forceful collision. It is achieved by endless exchange of ideas and cultural aspects, accompanied by intermarriages, through the ages, it perfects itself on the basis of natural selection not the biased selection by the men concerned. Nobody tries to force integration when facilities for endless peaceful contact and inter-communication have been attained. Except they are talking of something not so meritorious as integration.

It is for these reasons that we say that the peace of the Cameroon we are set to inherit is quite unguaranteed. For, if there is no permanent solution to the sectoral injustice and economic deprivation that we witness today, if there is no end to the assimilation destined towards us in the guise of integration; we, your children, assure you that sooner or later we shall have to smear the homes, streets, and gardens of this nation with blood. We won't accept to be eternally stigmatized as second class citizens, nor shall we want to be shorn of the cultural heritage which is ours, and which we recognize is of greater significance around the globe. So we shall fight for the justice we cannot otherwise have.

Yet, let it be clear to you that war holds no illusions for us. When we talk of fighting and bloodshed we do not mistakenly mean honour and ease. No! We fully understand the woes of war: inscrutable loss of life and communal bereavement, loss of husbands, fathers, children, relatives, and friends, whole communities made homeless, interruption of economic and social activities, unreserved destruction and devastation, general insecurity, and above all, uncertain results. We have no illusions about these but we shall boldly embrace them when no other course than war is left open to us.

That is why we make this solemn appeal to you to over-reach yourselves and ensure that things do not come to that stage. If you did suffer for your children, and do really love us, and would not knowingly cast and abandon us in a den without future, then you should spare no opportunity to seek in Cameroon a situation in which the fears, aspirations and rights of the minority will be constitutionally safe-guarded. By which we mean the drawing up of a new constitution. This, we assure you, is the only guarantor of a peaceful Cameroon. This, and this only. This, and nothing else.

Quit deceiving yourselves that all is or will be well. Any policy that refuses to recognize in Cameroon the two main cultures - a minority and a majority - is simply being delusive. Therefore, though you might not see with us, still do grant our request because of that precious blood of yours which flows in the veins of your children and grand children. Blood, which if all were to remain unchanged, would sooner or later paint red our pavements.

It is true that some of us, opponents of war, will refuse to participate in the fighting. But will that spare us, do you think, of the troubles that then would seize the country?

So put aside fears of imprisonment and death. Or would you have your children being shot at, and imprisoned in your stead while you live? In any case, your refusal to act will be construed as lack of sympathy or/and apathy towards the fate of your children. Then, much as we may sympathize with your 1961 fear of domination in the Federation of Nigeria, we shall be forced to the belief that our parents sold us: to slavery and butchery for their own ends. And, rather than revere your memories, your graves will be desecrated and bodily harm done those of you unlucky to be still alive then. These are things that condemn people before God; things not worth contemplating.

Therefore, come out of your reserve, speak your mind, and get things done, or was it our mothers who fathered us?

You each do have a voice, which, if used individually and in group, will not fail to yield dividends. In the party, at conferences, when in parliament, at the Central Committee and Political Bureau, during Ministerial Councils. In every other forum, you will devise, do it without fear; do it because your sons and daughters in agony over the future are pleading with you. You will be fighting to avoid disaster, and, no matter what is said, you will be working for a united, strong, peaceful, and prosperous Cameroon.

Let nothing baffle you that what we say about war will not come to pass. Abandon your let-us-sit-and-watch posture. You have certainly not been asleep wherever you are. Events, as you should have noticed, show that a storm is already gathering. We tremble at the thought of the lost and homeless; the moaning of the helpless and dying.

Certain things have to be done fast to arrest the deterioration of the situation. The aim should be to guarantee equality, justice and fair play towards each and all. Peace might abide with us today, but it is only these that can assure that the same remains with us for tomorrow and always.

Apart from drawing up a new constitution, justice always requires the establishment of a fully-fledged English-speaking University based on the educational principles we cherish. If we are frustrated in the Yaoundé University it is because of the French-dominated lecturers and the orientation of the studies which follow up the syllables of the Francophones from Secondary School but are quite strange to us. Everything there bears out the fact that it is a Francophone university. This was one of our grievances which, two years ago, the President assured us he would look into.

Especially, this University should be given a Polytechnic school to cater for our needs at that level, accompanied by a reinforcement of technical education in the North-West and South West Provinces at the basic level to feed this college. Then Cameroonians would be able to pursue their education unhampered until such a day as perfect bilingualism will be obtained to warrant the integration of these institutions.

Also, the Cameroonian constitution is clear on the fact that no citizen shall be arrested for his beliefs or opinions on whatever aspect of the country's life. The Universal Declaration on Human Rights, to which Cameroon is a signatory, also demands that nobody be arrested without charge nor detained without trial. We therefore plead with you to work for the release of Fon Gorgi Dinka from detention by the forces of oppression. It is surprising that no sooner is he made Fon of Fons that President Paul Biya decides to undermine the tradition and culture which has governed our people for centuries by having the Fon of Widikum locked up in the Yaoundé Brigade Mixed Mobile – BMM – place for common criminals.

If the Fon's release is not obtained with others, we are prepared to ask for it in our own fashion, and don't you raise your eyes at the casualties. We know ourselves well. Indeed, we have not been very tactful in opening all our mind. Everybody is now alerted and on guard but when the last straw drops, that will only mean more outrageous and internecine fighting. And, of course, more blood-baths.

We sincerely hope that such a time might never come particularly in the wake of the Papal visit to Cameroon; this country is not fitting ground for a fratricidal war. The Pope has upheld our Christian President, enjoined us to love and peace, and blessed our beloved fatherland. However, this glory shall be ours really, only if we take into consideration the rights and aspirations of every section of the population, and strive to satisfy a majority of the cross-section. Not by running too fast to the unripe harvest.

You should recall the Holy Father saying at the State House, to the President that is, "injustices committed by certain regimes concerning human rights or the legitimate demands of a section of the population which is refused participation or common responsibilities beget revolt of regrettable violence but which justice would have foreheld." Those words could not have come more to their home. They could not have been better timed.

May their wisdom, foresight, advice and the accompanying blessing be with us all and guard us in what we do so that the bad future is not permitted to occur.

Your kids

English-speaking students.

CC:
- All Party Chiefs
- All Mayors
- All D.Os·
- All Lawyers and Magistrates
- All Doctors and University Lecturers
- All Secretaries General and Provincial Chiefs of Services
- All Parliamentarians
- All Chiefs and Fons
- All Governors
- All Directors and Ministers
- Hon. S.T. Muna
- Dr. J.N. Foncha
- Dr. E.M.L. Endeley
- Mr. E.T. Egbe

Appendix III

The Buea Declaration of the All Anglophone Conference

In the name of the Almighty God from whom all life, protection, wisdom, power and glory emanate, we the people of Anglophone Cameroon represented by over four thousand delegates from all the thirteen Divisions of our territory, namely, Boyo, Bui, Donga-Mantung. Fako, Ngoketunjia, Kupe-Manenguba, Liebialem, Manyu, Meme, Menchum, Mezam, Momo, Ndian, and from all over the rest of Cameroon, and among whom, Elder Statesmen and Senior Citizens, Traditional Rulers, Religious and Spiritual Leaders, Leaders of political parties, Members of Parliament and of the Economic and Social Council, farmers, workers and elite of all professions meeting at the Mount Mary Maternity Centre in the historic town of Buea from 2nd to the 3rd of April, 1993 in an All Anglophone Conference for the purpose of adopting a common Anglophone stand for the announced national debate on constitutional reform and of examining several other matters related to the welfare of our territory and the entire Cameroon nation, DO MAKE THE DECALRATION, hereinafter contained for which we offer the following justification:

TODAY, no group of people who freely chose to join a political union want to accept to be treated as captive people. In 1961, the people of Anglophone Cameroon through a United Nations supervised plebiscite decided to enter into a political union with the people of La Republique du Cameroun and they did so, by the grace of God, freely and without the involvement of the population of La Republic du Cameroon. Their aspiration was to establish a unique bilingual federation on the continent of Africa, and evolve a bicultural society in which the cultural heritage of each of the two states would flourish. We believed that such a lofty goal was possible. Within this relatively short time however, our common experience in the union leaves us in no doubt that we are far from attaining these ends. We are a people with a problem.

Our problem, which the intolerant and hypocritical attitude of our Francophone partners would rather suppress, springs from a breach of trust from the part of the Francophone leadership and from a lack of openness in matters of public interest. Within these 32 years, our Union Accord has been violated, and we have been disenfranchised, marginalised, treated with suspicion, and our interests disregarded. Our participation in national life has been limited to non-essential functions and our natural resources have been ruthlessly exploited without any benefit accruing to our territory or its people. The development of our territory has been negligible and confined to areas that benefit the Francophones directly or indirectly. Through manoeuvres and manipulations we have been reduced from partners of equal status in the union to the status of a subjugated people.

As a people, our values, visions, and goals and those of our Francophone brothers in the union are different and clearly cannot be harmonised within the framework of a unitary state, such as was imposed on us in 1972. We are by nature pacifist, patient and tolerant. We have demonstrated these qualities since we came together to form this union. We fully subscribe to the statement of Voltaire, when he says, "I wholly disapprove of what you say, but will defend to death your right to say it." Our Francophone brothers believe in brutalisation and in torturing, and in raping our women and daughters, and in the use of the gun. We find such barbaric acts alien to us, indeed to the civilised standards of all democratic societies. Our idea of freedom of expression and of the press leads us to believe in the open discussion and understanding of public issues that affect our lives. Our Francophone brothers suppress freedom of expression and practise press censorship. The democratic principle of majority rule and minority rights leads us to believe in the rights and freedom of the minority. Francophone regimes pursue a policy of assimilation aimed at wiping our own identity. Thus, our vision of a bicultural society becomes an illusive, unattainable goal, and will remain so, until and unless we can find a better framework within which this aspiration can find expression.

In Buea today, we make an important decision, and for the benefit of those who hereafter may doubt the rectitude of our intentions, we place our records on the following facts:

1. The Pre-Plebiscite Accord

The United Nations document, entitled THE TWO ALTERNATIVES, which was widely circulated on the eve of the plebiscite to explain to the people the implications of their choice, and the JOINT DECLARATION by Prime Minister J.N. Foncha and President Ahidjo contained therein, made it clear to the people of Anglophone Cameroon that in the event of their opting for the second alternative, they would at independence, be forming a federation of two states with equal status.

It was clear that the majority in one state would not be allowed (As happened in 1972) to impose its will and interests on the other state.

2. The Constitution of the Federal Republic

The Federal Constitution of 1961 created the federation and preserved its unity. Article 47 of that constitution stated that the constitution could only be revised by a law passed by the federal parliament, and in that process 50% of the deputies representing any federated state could in fact veto the bill proposing revision of the constitution by voting against the bill. This article made it clear that no bill intended to impair the unity and integrity of the federation could be introduced.

3. Exploitation and Rape of the Economy

The illegal imposition of the Unitary Structure aimed not only at dismantling the state institutions of Anglophone Cameroon - that is, Legislature, Government, House of Chiefs - but at exploiting and raping the economy.

(a) The successive Francophone Presidents stepped up the exploitation of our natural resources, especially oil and timber.

(b) They destroyed an effective system of financing small scale industries which Anglophone Cameroon had established through the creation of the West Cameroon Development Agency and the Cameroon Bank. They abolished the bank.

(c) They looted the West Cameroon Marketing Board which Anglophone Cameroon had set up prior to independence and misappropriated its huge financial reserves of over 78 billion francs.

(d) They closed down POWERCAM, and our cheap source of hydro-electricity supply at Yoke, and compelled us to make use of theirs, which as a monopoly, is expensive and aimed at excessive profit making. They completely demolished all our hydro-electric installations instead of maintaining them as stand-by sources and confiscated the assets of the West Cameroon Electricity Corporation.

(e) They contrived to squeeze out Anglophone businessmen and have exclusive grasp and control of finance and business. As a result, familiar Anglophone business names like "Fomenky's Direct Suppliers," "Niba Automobiles," "Nangah Company," "Kilo Brothers," and "Che Company," are no more.

(f) They closed down our Agro-Industrial establishments of the Santa Coffee Estate, and later the Wum Area Development Authority and the Obang Farm Settlement.

(g) They closed down our sea and airports, and the present Bamenda Airport, abandoned with unfinished structures and insufficient equipment can in no way compensate for the closure of the Victoria Seaport, the Tiko Airport, the Besongabang Airport, the Bali Airport, the Weh Airstrip, the inland Port of Mamfe, and the beautiful Port of Ndian. The law abiding victims of all these acts were powerless because there was no legal framework within which victims could seek and obtain redress.

4. **Road Infrastructure**

The government of Anglophone Cameroon pursued a policy of maintaining all civil roads. For this purpose, difficult stretches like the Kupe Hill or Sabga, were tarred. The streets of our divisional headquarters were tarred. The Francophone led government failed to maintain all these. Worse than that, they destroyed what we had. Under the pretext of surfacing our roads, which were tarred before reunification, they destroyed them. For example, Kumba - Mbonge and Kumba -Tombel roads.

Today, the streets of Kumba are a pool of mud in the rainy season, while Nkambe and Kumbo have dust of one foot thick in the dry season. Twice, we have witnessed lavish ceremonies to inaugurate the Kumba - Mamfe road, when in fact till today, it has not been constructed. President Ahidjo had never cut a tape over an untarred road. He did that for the first time in Mamfe.

Before the elections, President Paul Biya publicly undertook to personally supervise the ring-road. We want to put it clearly on record that the two short stretches of roads in Anglophone Cameroon which are well done, that is Santa -Bamenda and Mungo – Victoria – Idenau, serve francophone interests.

5. Economic Rape

The question of the neglected roads in Anglophone Cameroon has had a wider implication as far as our economy and our development has been concerned. We had our trunk 'A' road stretching from Victoria through Kumba, Mamfe, Bamenda to Nkambe and Wum. Because of the deliberate attempts by our Francophone brothers to subjugate us, they abandoned the maintenance of these important roads, and instead, developed that of Douala - Bafoussam, so that our travel between Bamenda and Victoria or Buea is via their territory. The result is that our main towns in Anglophone Cameroon, which used to be booming commercial centres, for example, Mamfe, Kumba, Tiko, Nkambe, Wum, Widikum, Victoria, have been reduced to ghost towns, and our main trunk road is left as a farm track. In the meantime, no Francophone towns and cities have suffered any similar phenomenon. They are booming.

6. Road Check Points

The hundreds of check points on our roads today seem normal and acceptable to Francophones. They really make this country strange to Anglophones. Between Bamenda and Victoria, there are on average 35 check points. This unnecessary restriction on the free movement of people and goods serve no useful purpose because traffic cases rarely go to court. They originally well intended exercise has been reduced to a system of road tolls instituted by the Forces of Law and Order and the silence of the government on the matter is a tacit approval.

7. Divide and Rule

We achieved independence and went into the union as a single entity. They divided us into the Northwest and Southwest without consultations. They have continued with further attempts to fuse the Northwest into the Western Province, and Southwest into the Littoral Province, ostensibly to create bilingual provinces. These moves, in fact, are aimed at the cultural assimilation of Anglophones, and enforced uniformity which eventually should wipe out Anglophone identity and secure long term control of our natural resources for the benefit of France. It is unacceptable to

Anglophones. The greatest evil about this surreptitious plan is that it is being pursued by fanning Northwest and Southwest disunity through self-seeking individuals among us, and without consultations.

8. Marginalisation of Anglophones

From the inception of the Federation, Anglophone Cameroonians have only played second fiddle to the Francophones, starting with the first Prime Minister of West Cameroon, who assuming the role of Vice President of the Federal Republic, set the general pattern of the role of Anglophones since then. Anglophones have been appointed mainly into subordinate positions to assist Francophones, even where the latter were less qualified or less competent.

For 32 years now, some ministries such as those in charge of territorial administration, armed forces, education, finance and foreign affairs, commerce and industries, have never been occupied by Anglophones.

When a Francophone is Prime Minister, there is no Secretary General in the presidency and there is no Vice Prime Minister. The Prime Minister wields real power. When the post comes to an Anglophone, he is saddled with a Secretary General at the Presidency, and not one, but two Vice Prime Ministers on whom real power revolves. In the Foreign Service, Anglophones are rarely appointed Ambassador to London, Washington, Lagos, or Paris. These are reserved exclusively for Francophones.

In Home Affairs, as a general tendency, all top administrative posts: Governors, Senior Division Officers, Legion Commanders, etc in Buea and Bamenda are Francophones. Here are Anglophones today standing with cap in hand in their own home territory before Francophone administrators who will not allow them to use available structures to hold the All Anglophone Conference. How else can a subjugated people be treated?

9. Human Rights Abuses

Unlawful detentions, imprisonment, unwarranted searches, harassment by uncouth gendarmes, and torture by savage CENER agents operating la balançoire, are some of the intolerable realities of this country. In November 1992, late Che Ngwa Ghandi was tortured and regularly beaten by CENER agents and gendarmes until he died. Late Ghandi was only one of hundreds of Anglophone Cameroonians who have suffered either death or extreme cruel torture. As recent as Thursday, 25 March, 1993, gendarmes opened automatic machine gun fire on a group of peaceful demonstrators in Bamenda and killed three and wounded twenty. They claimed that the three were killed with dane guns.

On the 18th and 25th of March 1993, during a peaceful demonstration, 46 Anglophone Cameroonians were arrested, beaten, tortured, and detained in Victoria and two women were hospitalized.

10. Civil Liberties and the Due Process of Law

Before unification, we had our individual and civil liberties protected. One could not be arrested and left to languish in prison without a charge. It was unheard of for people's private premises to be searched without a warrant. The police did not carry guns all about. We knew nothing of the official night raids called "Kale-Kale". In fact, the opposition in Anglophone Cameroon who opposed unification warned about these forms of repression practised then in La Republique du Cameroun. Today, 32 years later, these things are unfortunately true.

In a real democracy, everyone is presumed to be equal before the law, and there is all certainty of enforcement of justice if the law is violated. On Monday, 23rd December, 1992, when the Bamenda High Court Ruling No. HCB-CRM 92 ordered that the 173 persons detained and tortured at the maximum security detention centre (BMM) be released, the minister arbitrarily ordered that they should not, in contempt of the high court ruling. These men and women were instead moved to Yaoundé in the most inhuman manner of transportation imaginable on the 27th December to be tried by a Francophone court. This teleguiding of justice by government is unknown to Anglophones.

11. International Isolation

By our special language of diplomacy, the peoples of Gabon, Central African Republic, and Chad are our brothers. Yes, each of these is a neighbour and 'a brother'. But when it comes to Nigeria and Nigerians, this our language of diplomacy is not consistent. Francophones blame Nigeria for practically everything in Cameroon. Consequently, our Mamfe/Ekok road -

one of the busiest in the country was neglected because it leads to Nigeria. It will be recalled that it was Anglophone Cameroon who left Nigeria to form a Cameroon Federation. If, therefore, there was a reason for any bias of whatever nature against Nigerians, it logically should come from Anglophone Cameroonians. Francophones forget that just like their 'brotherliness' with Gabonese and Chadians, etc is enhanced by their common francophone heritage, so Anglophone Cameroon and Nigeria too have a common cultural heritage. This attitude towards Nigeria is only one instance of a more general phenomenon, namely: the isolation of Anglophone Cameroon in international relations. Hence, the reluctance of the Francophone led government to fulfil the conditions for Cameroon's entry into the commonwealth.

12. Francophone Exploitation

Instances of Francophone exploitation are numerous. We state the following only:

i. After unification, all theatres in Victoria, Buea, Kumba and Bamenda were compelled to show only French films.

ii. When there is a football match in France, the whole nation is held to ransom by CRTV. CRTV does not do a similar thing when British teams play. Programmes originally in English are first translated into French before CRTV shows them to us.

iii. SONARA is predominantly staffed with Francophones.

iv. All oil money must be paid directly to Yaoundé.

v. SNH is predominantly Francophone.

vi. It was a Francophone who appeared in Victoria to buy the property of the National Produce Marketing Board when the organisation wound up.

vii. It was a Francophone who appeared in Buea proposing to buy all of Buea Clerks' quarters.

viii. It was a Francophone who appeared in Bamenda wanting to buy all of CAPME and its installations

ix. It was a Frenchman that was employed to liquidate PAMOL, Ndian. He has failed to do that job and he is instead exploiting PAMOL for personal ends.

We recall that before the attainment of independence in 1961, we practised parliamentary democracy, which was far more developed that what now obtains in Cameroon three decades later. We regarded democracy as a way of life, and an ideal to strive for. We were neither angels nor saints. Far from it. But from what we knew, we believed and still believe that whenever a government becomes fraudulent, intolerant and repressive, it is the democratic right of the people to change that government, and vote in another. We were spared such a task in Southern Cameroons by the relative uprightness of our government then, and our system of public accountability. Then, as will be recalled, our first government in Southern Cameroons, headed by Dr. E.M.L. Endeley of blessed memory organised a general election and was beaten by the opposition. Typical of our Anglophone conception of democracy, Dr. Endeley conceded defeat and there was a peaceful change of government.

Therefore, at this point in the history of our union, with La République du Cameroun, exactly 32 years, one month and 23 days since our people voted in a United Nations supervised plebiscite to form a federation with the people of La Republique du Cameroun, we find compelling reasons to declare as follows:

WHEREAS the people of Southern Cameroons, and they alone, voted freely in the 1961 plebiscite to achieve independence by joining La Republique du Cameroun, and whereas the basis of their union with La Republique du Cameroun was a decentralised federal structure,

AND WHEREAS, the provision of Article 47 of the Constitution of the Federal Republic of Cameroon preserved the unity of that Federation by prohibiting any amendments impairing the unity and integrity of the Federation,

AND WHEREAS, through the so-called "Peaceful Revolution" of 1972, a referendum was organised resulting in the imposition of a unitary state on Southern Cameroonians by the majority population of La Republique du Cameroun, contrary to the pre-plebiscite accord jointly signed by Prime Minister John Ngu Foncha and President Ahmadou Ahidjo, in the "TWO ALTERNATIVES," that no state shall be allowed to impose its will or interest on the other by its majority, and in violation of the constitution of the Federal Republic of Cameroon,

AND WHEREAS, we have patiently suffered these indignities and humiliations all these long years, while calling and waiting for redress, and whereas these our several and most humble petitions for redress have been repeatedly spurned, and callous deaf ears given to them,

AND WHEREAS the natural resources of our territory, our environment, and out cultural heritage are in imminent danger of being destroyed,
AND WHEREAS, in our relationship with the people of La Republique du Cameroun, the political leadership thereof has, time and again demonstrated its bad faith, breach of trust, unfulfilled promises and undertakings, and its relish for evil, corruption and manipulation,

BUT MINDFUL, of the fact that the good people, as distinct from the political leadership of La Republique du Cameroun, may still be desirous of maintaining some form of union with the people of Anglophone Cameroon,

AND WHEREAS, it is expedient that such a union, if it is to last, develop and prosper, must be built on a solid foundation and sustained in a clear atmosphere of openness, trust, mutual respect and a sense of belonging by all,

NOW THEREFORE, in order to secure these ends by laying a solid foundation for the union of the two Cameroons.
We solemnly make this declaration:

1. THAT THE IMPOSITION OF THE UNITARY STATE ON ANGLOPHONE CAMEROON IN 1972 WAS UNCONSTITUTIONAL AND ILLEGAL.

2. THAT ALL CAMEROONIANS OF ENGLISH-SPEAKING HERITAGE ARE HENCEFORTH COMITTED TO, AND WILL WORK TOWARDS THE RESTORATION OF A FEDERAL CONSTITUTION, WHICH TAKES COGNIZANCE OF THE

BILINGUAL NATURE OF CAMEROON AND WHICH WILL PROTECT THE CITIZENS AGAINST SUCH VIOLATIONS ENUMERATED HERE ABOVE. GOD BLESS ANGLOPHONE CAMEROON.

Done at Buea, this third day of April in the year of our Lord, One Thousand Nine Hundred and Ninety-three.

SIGNED: Participants at the All Anglophone Conference.

Bibliography

Articles in Books, Magazines, Newspaper and Journal Articles

AHIDJO, Ahmadou (1964) "The President speaks on Culture" (extract of message to the nation by H.E. Ahmadou Ahidjo, President of the Federal Republic of Cameroon, Buea, October 1, 1964) in ABBIA: Cameroon Cultural Review, No.7, October, CEPER, Yaoundé.

ANYANGWE, Carlson (1993) "A New Constitutional Order: Proposals for a New Constitution". Paper presented at the All Anglophone Conference, April 2, Buea.

ARDENER, Edwin W. (1958) "The Kamerun Idea I and II". West Africa 7th and 14th June.

-------------------------------- (1961) "Crisis of Confidence in the Cameroons," West Africa. 12th August, pp 878-879.

-------------------------------- (1967) "The Nature of the Reunification of Cameroon" pp 285-337 African Integration and Disintegration: Case Studies in Economic and Political Union by Arthur Hazelwood (ed), OUP, London.

BAMELA ENGO, Paul (1964) "Some Aspects of Legal Reform in Cameroon" pp 159-171 in ABBIA: Cameroon Cultural Review.

BAYART, Jean Francois (1973) "One-Party Government and Political Development in Cameroon" African Affairs 72, pp 125-144

-------------------------------- (1974) "Les catégories dirigeantes au Cameroun". Revue Française d'Études Politiques Africaines. pp 66-90

-------------------------------- (1978) "The Neutralisation of Anglophone Cameroon" pp 46-65, in Gaullist Africa: Cameroon under Ahmadou Ahidjo, edited by Richard Joseph, FDP, Enugu, Nigeria.

BENJAMIN, Jacques (1980) "The Impact of Federal Institutions on West Cameroon's Economic Activity." In An African Experiment in Nation-building, edited by Ndiva Kofele-Kale, pp 191-226, Westview Press, Boulder, Colorado.

BOU, Sammy Kum (1976) "How United is Cameroon?" Africa Report, November-December (New York). Pp 17-20.

CHUMBOW, Sammy Beban (1980) "Language and Language Policy in Cameroon," pp 281-311. In Kofele-Kale, op cit.

CLIGNET, Remi (1976) "The Impact of Educational Structures and Processes on National Integration in Cameroon," in The Search for National Integration in Africa, edited by D.R. Smock and K. Bentsi-Enchill, pp 139-158. The Free Press, New York.

CROWDER, Michael (1970) "Indirect Rule - French and British Style," in Markovitz (Ed.) African Politics and Society: Basic Issues and Problems of Government and Development. The Free Press, New York.

DERRICK, Jonathan (1985) "Cameroon, 25 Years of Independence" West Africa, pp 9 - 11, January 7.

DOYLE, Mark (1984). "Cameroon in Perspective: Biya's Nightmare Year". West Africa, pp 7- 8, January 7.

ENGERS, P.S. (1984) "Anglophone Cameroon: Drifting with a Rudderless Ship". West Africa, pp 1617-1618, August 13.

FONLON, Bernard (1963) "The Case for Early Bilingualism," ABBIA: Cameroon Cultural Review, pp 9 - 33, No. 5, March, CEPER, Yaoundé.

------------------------------ (1964) "Will We Make or Mar?" in ABBIA: Cameroon Cultural Review, pp 9-33, No.5, March, CEPER, Yaounde.

------------------------------ (1965a) "Under the Sign of the Rising Sun," Cameroon Times.

-------------------------------- (1965b) "Idea of Culture I," ABBIA, pp 5-29, No.11, November.

-------------------------------- (1967) "Idea of Culture II," ABBIA, pp 6-24, No.16, March.

-------------------------------- (1976) "The Language Problem in Cameroon: A Historical Perspective," in The Search for National Integration in Africa, edited by D.R. Smock and K. Bentsi-Enchill. The Free Press, New York.

JOHNSON, Willard (1970b) "The Union des Populations du Cameroun in Rebellion: The Integrative Backlash of Insurgency," in Protest and Power in Black Africa: 1886-1966. Edited by A. A. Mazrui and R. I. Rotberg, OUP, New York.

JOSEPH, Richard (1974) "Reuben Um Nyobe and the 'Kamerun' Rebellion," in African Affairs, October.

-------------------------------- (1976) "Economy and Society in Postcolonial Cameroon: A Critical Assessment," in The African Review. Vol.6, No.14.

Kofele-Kale, Ndiva (1987) "Class, Status, and Power in Post-reunification Cameroon: The Rise of an Anglophone Bourgeoisie, 1961-1980," in Irving Leonard Markovitz (Ed) Studies in Power and Class in Africa, pp 135-169. Oxford University Press, Oxford.

LE VINE, Victor (1961a) "The Other Cameroons," Africa Report VI. February.

-------------------------------- (1961b) "Calm Before the Storm in Cameroon," Africa Report, pp 3-4, May.

-------------------------------- (1963) "The Cameroon Federal Republic," in Five African States. Edited by Gwendolen Carter, pp 263-360. Cornell University Press, Ithaca, New York.

------------------------------ (1964a) "Cameroon Political Parties," in Political Parties and National Integration in Tropical Africa. Edited by J.S. Coleman and C.G. Rosberg, pp 270-284. University of California Press, Berkeley

------------------------------ (1976) "Political Integration and the United Republic of Cameroon," in The Search for National Integration in Africa, pp 270-284. Edited by D. Smock and K. Bentsi-Enchill. Free Press, New York.

------------------------------ (1986) "Leadership and Regime Changes in Perspective," in The Political Economy of Cameroon. Edited by M.G. Schatzberg and I. W. Zartman, pp 20-52. Praeger Publishers, New York, USA.

MBASSI-MANGA, Francis (1964) "Cameroon: A Marriage of Three Cultures," in ABBIA: Cameroon Cultural Review, pp 131-144. No.5, March.

MUKONG, Albert (1993) "Where Things Went Wrong," Being a paper presented to The All Anglophone Conference. April 3, Buea.

Munzu, Simon (1993) "Towards a Truly United Cameroon". Keynote Address Delivered at the All Anglophone Conference on constitutional reform, 2nd April, Buea.

NAWERI, Jasper Komla (1983) "The Beginnings of Freedom". West Africa. January 30, London.

------------------------------ (1984) "Restless Anglophones". West Africa, January 30, London.

NCHAMI, John (1992) "Of Constitutional Reforms and Federalism: The Anglophone Problem," in Times and Life Magazine. January, Douala.

NDONGKO, Wilfred (1980) "The Political Economy and Regional Economic Development in Cameroon". In An African Experiment in Nation Building: The Bilingual Cameroon Republic Since Reunification.

Edited by Ndiva Kofele-Kale, pp 227-250 Westview Press, Boulder, Colorado.

NFOR, N. Nfor (1984) "A Federation without Federalism: The Cameroon Experience in Nation Building: 1961-1972". Unpublished Seminar Paper, Department of Political Science, Ahmadu Bello University, Zaria, July 10.

NGOH, V.J. (1990) "A Walk Down Memory Lane: Cameroon's Reunification: A Who's Who," Cameroon Life, Vol.1, No.3, August, Mutengene.

NGOME, V. Epie (1993) "Cameroon: Anglophobia." Focus on Africa Magazine, Vol. 4, No. 3 July-September, London.

NOUCK, P.B. (1992) "A Legacy of Slaughtered Sheep and Broken Promises". Cameroon Life Vol.11, No.3, March, Mutengene.

NWOSU, H.N. (1976) "The Concepts of Nationalism and Right to Self Determination: Cameroon as a Case Study". African Quarterly, Vol.16, No.2, pp 1-26, New Delhi.

ROTCHILD, Donald (1966) "The Limits of Federalism: An Examination of Political Institutions Transfer in Africa." In Journal of Modern African Studies, Vol.4, No.3.

WELCH, Claude (1963) "Cameroon Since Reunification". West Africa, October-November.

Books

AFANA, Osende (1966) l'économie de l'ouest africaine: perspectives de développement. Francois Maspero, Paris.

AHIDJO, Ahmadou (1964) Contribution A La Construction Nationale. Présence Africaine, Paris.

AKIKA, Emmanuel et al (1990) Changer le Cameroun: Pourquoi Pas? Livre blanc par un groupe d'intellectuels: Edition C3, October, Yaounde.

------------------------------ (1992) Le Cameroun Eclaté? Une Anthologie Commentée des Revendications Ethniques, Editions C3, Yaoundé.

AKINYEMI, A.B. et al (1979) Readings on Federalism. Nigerian Institute of International Affairs (NIIA), Lagos, Nigeria.

AWA, Eme O (1976) Issues in federalism. Ethiope Publishing Corporation, Benin City, Nigeria.

AZARYA, Victor (1976) Dominance and Change in North Cameroon: The Fulbe Aristocracy. Sage Publications, New York.

------------------------------ (1978) Aristocrats Facing Change: The Fulbe in Guinea, Nigeria, and Cameroon. University of Chicago Press, Chicago USA.

BENJAMIN, Jacques (1972) Les Camerounais Occidentaux : la minorité dans un état bicommunautaire. Les presses de l'Université de Montréal, Montréal.

BETI, Mongo (1977) Main Basse Sur le Cameroun: autopsie d'une décolonisation. Francois Maspero, Paris.

BUELL, R.L. (1928) The Native Problem in Africa, Vol.11, Macmillan, New York.

CESAIRE, Aimé (1966) Discours sur le Colonialisme. Présence Africain, Paris.

CHAFFARD, Georges (1965) Les Carnets Secrets de la Décolonisation Tome 1. Editions Calmann-Lévy, Paris.

COLEMAN, James S. and Rosberg, C.G. (eds) (1964) Political Parties and National Integration in Tropical Africa. University of California Press, Berkeley.

CORBETT, Edward (1972) The French Presence in Black Africa. Black Orpheus Press, Washington DC.

DAVIS, S. Rufus (1978) The Federal Principle: A Journey Through Time in Quest of Meaning, University of California Press, Los Angeles, California.

DELAVIGNETTE, Robert (1950) Freedom and Authority in West Africa. London.

EYONGETAH, Tambi and Brain, Robert (1974) A History of Cameroon, Longman, London.

FONLON, Bernard (1966) The Task of Today. Cameroon Printing and Publishing Co. Ltd, Victoria.

GARDINIER, David (1963) Cameroon: United Nations Challenge to French Policy, OUP, London.

GIRADET, Raoul (1972) L'idée Coloniale en France 1871-1962, La Table Ronde, Paris.

GWEI, S.N. (1975) Education in Cameroon: Western Pre-Colonial and Colonial Antecedents and the Development of Higher Education. Unpublished PhD Dissertation, Department of Education, University of Michigan.

HAZLEWOOD, Arthur (Ed) (1967) African Integration and Disintegration. Oxford University Press, London.

HICKS, Ursula, K. (1978) Federalism: Failure and Success, A comparative study. The Macmillan Press, London.

JOHNSON, Willard R. (1970a) The Cameroon Federation: Political Integration in a Fragmentary Society. Princeton University Press, Princeton, New York.

JOSEPH, Richard (1977) Radical Nationalism in Cameroon: Social Origins of the UPC Rebellion, OUP, Oxford.

------------------------------ (1978) Gaullist Africa: Cameroon under Ahmadou Ahidjo. Fourth Dimension Publishers, Enugu, Nigeria.

------------------------------ (1987) Democracy and Prebendal Politics in Nigeria: The Rise and Fall of the Second Republic. Cambridge University Press, Cambridge.

KITCHEN, Helen (Ed) (1962) The Educated African, A Country-by-Country Survey of Educational Development. Frederick Praeger, New York.

KOFELE-KALE, Ndiva (Ed) (1980) An African Experiment in Nation Building: The Bilingual Cameroon Republic Since Reunification, Westview Press, Boulder, Colorado.

LE VINE, Victor (1964b) The Cameroons: From Mandate to Independence. University of California Press, Berkeley, California.

MACMAHON, Arthur W. (Ed) (1962) Federalism: Mature and Emergent. Russell and Russell, New York.

MARKOVITZ, Irving Leonard (Ed) (1970) African Politics and Society: Basic Issues and Problems of Government and Development. The Free Press, New York.

------------------------------ (1977) Power and Class in Africa: An Introduction to Change and Conflict in African Politics. Prentice-Hall Inc. Englewood Cliffs, New Jersey, 07632.

MAZRUI, A.A. and Rotberg, R.I. (eds) (1970) Protest and Power in Black Africa, OUP, New York.

MORTIMER, Edward (1969) France and the Africans 1944-1966: A Political History. Faber and Faber Limited, London.

MUKONG, Albert (1989) Prisoner Without a Crime. Editions NUBIA-NUBIA Press, Paris.

------------------------------ (Ed) (1990) The Case for the Southern Cameroons. CAMFECO, USA.

------------------------------ (1992) My stewardship in the Cameroon Struggle. Chuka Printing Co. Limited, Enugu, Nigeria.

NDIAYE, Jean-Pierre (1962) Enquête sur les étudiants noirs en France. Editions Réalités Africaines, Paris.

------------------------------ (1969) Elites Africaines et Culture Occidentale: assimilation ou résistance? Présence Africaine, Paris.

NDONGKO, A. Wilfred (1975) Planning for Economic Development in a Federal State: The Case of Cameroon, 1960-1971. Weltforum Verlag, Munchen.

------------------------------ (1974) Regional Economic Planning in Cameroon. Scandinavian Institute of African Studies, Uppsala.

NELSON, Harold D. et al (1974) Handbook for the United Republic of Cameroon. US Government Printing Office, Washington DC.

NFOR, N. Nfor (1980) Cameroon Reunification: Costs and Problems of National Integration. MSc thesis (unpublished), ABU, Zaria.

NGAYAP, Pierre Flambeau (1983) Cameroun: Qui gouverne? De Ahidjo à Biya, l'héritage et l'enjeu. L'Harmattan, Paris.

NGWAFOR, Ephraim N. (1989a) May Former Victoria Smile Again. Institute of Third World Art and Literature, London.

------------------------------ (1989b) AKO-AYA (An Anthology). Institute of Third World Art and Literature, London.

NGWANE, George (1990) The Mungo Bridge. Cosmos Educational Publishers, Limbe.

------------------------------ (1992) Fragments of Unity (to every son and daughter of the South West). Nooremac Press, Limbe.

------------------------------ (1993) Bate Besong (Or The Symbol of Anglophone Hope). Nooremac Press, Limbe.

NWANKWO, Arthur (1987) The Military Option to Democracy: Class, Power and Violence in Nigerian Politics. Fourth Dimension Publishing Co. Ltd, Enugu, Nigeria.

NYAMNJOH FRANCIS B. (1991) Mind Searching. Kucena Damian Nigeria Ltd, Anambra State, Nigeria.

OKADIGBO, Chuba (1987) Power and Leadership in Nigeria. Fourth Dimension Publishing Co. Ltd, Enugu, Nigeria.

OMBE-NDZANA, Vianney (1987) Agriculture, Pétrole et Politique au Cameroun: Sortir de la Crise? Editions L'Harmattan, Paris.

OYOVBAIRE, S. Egite (1985) Federalism in Nigeria. Macmillan, London.

PLEKHANOV, Georgi (1980) Selected Philosophical Works. Volume IV, Progress Publishers, Moscow.

SCHATZBERG, M.G. and Bartman, I.W. (Eds) (1986). The Political Economy of Cameroon, Praeger Publishers, New York, USA.

SCHNEIDER, Louis and Bonjean, Charles (eds) (1973) The Idea of Culture in the Social Sciences. Cambridge University Press, London.

SMOCK, D.R. and Bentsi-Enchill, K. (Eds) (1976) The Search for National Integration in Africa. The Free Press, New York.

SURET-CANALE, Jean (1971) French Colonialism in Tropical Africa. C. Hurst and Co., London.

SUSUNGI, N. Nfor (1992) The Crisis of Unity and Democracy in Cameroon: Can a country which has pronounced itself dead be saved by democracy? South Africa.

TITA, J, Che (Ed) (1993) A Time of Hope (Anglophones on the Anglophone Problem). Nooremac Press, Limbe.

WATTS, Ronald L. (1966) Dream of Unity, Pan Africanism and Political Unification in West Africa. Cornell University Press, Ithaca, New York.

WHEARE, K.C. (1963) Federal Government. 4th Edition, OUP, London.

WOOTTON, Graham and Ehrlich, Stanislaw (1980) Three Faces of Pluralism: Political, Ethnic and Religious. Gower Publishing Co. Ltd. Westmead, England.

YOUNG, Crawford (1976) The Politics of Cultural Pluralism. The University of Wisconsin Press, Wisconsin.

Documents and Official Publications

ANDERSEN, Kjell (1961) "Report on the Economic Aspects of Reunification". Presidency, Republic of Cameroon. February 18, Yaoundé.

APA (1991) "The Restoration of the State of West Cameroon: The Final Solution to the Anglophone Cameroon Question". Published for the Anglophone Patriotic Alliance by The West Cameroon Journal.

ATEKWANA, Akonji (1992) "Occupation of Posts of Responsibility and Tarred Road Infrastructure in Cameroon." CAM Research Team, 29th April, Yaoundé.

BERRIL (1960) "Rapport sur l'economie du Cameroun Occidental". Yaoundé.

BIYA, Paul (1991) Argument for real democracy: The Great Provincial Tour of President Paul Biya. August-October 1991.

CAM (1992) "A Memorandum Addressed to the Delegate General for National Security on the Aftermath of the Federation Day Celebration in Bamenda". Issued by the Cameroon Anglophone Movement. 30th March, Bamenda.

CAMEROUN 1982-1992: Des Faits et des Chiffres. Le Bilan de la Décennie Biya. September 1992.

ENDELEY, E.M.L. (1958) "A Statement of Policy". Published by the Federal Information Service, Lagos, 29th May.

------------------------------ (1961) "Plebiscite Message to all voters of the Cameroons."

FONCHA, J.N. (1985) "A Memorandum Addressed to His Excellency Paul Biya, President of the Republic of Cameroon on a University of Arts, Science and Technology in Bambili". 14th November.

------------------------------ (1990a) "A Brief Account of the Events which took place in the Bamenda Township on Saturday, 26th May, 1990 Culminating in the Shooting and Killing of Five Innocent Young Men and One Girl".

------------------------------ (1990b) "Letter of Resignation from the CPDM."

------------------------------ (1993) "An open Letter Addressed to the Government of the Republic of Cameroon on the Operation of Unification: Federal Republic of Cameroon. 1961-1971".

FONJOCK EKEANYA, B. (1993) "A Memorandum Presented Through the Chairman of SWELA to the All Anglophone Conference Holden at Buea on the 2nd Day of April 1993." 1st April, Mundemba.

"FOUMBAN Conference ends in Complete Agreement on Major Issues." Southern Cameroons Information Service, 24th July, 1961, Buea.

GORGI-DINKA, Fongum (1985) "The New Social Order"

------------------------------ (1990a) "Seating Ambazonia at the United Nations"

------------------------------ (1990b) "In the United Nations: Ambazonia versus La Republique du Cameroun."

Introducing the Southern Cameroons: A Symposium of the Southern Portion of the Mandated Territory of the Cameroons under United Kingdom Administration. Federal Information Services, Lagos, 1958.

(1985) "Memorandum Presented to the Head of State and Chairman of the Cameroon's People Democratic Movement by a Joint Committee of the Elite of the North West and South West Provinces Resident in the Littoral Province."

MUKONG, Albert (1985) "Open Letter to the First New Deal Congress." Bamenda.

MUNA, S.T. (1983) "Speeches by Mr. Solomon Tandeng Muna." President of the National Assembly. 1978-1983.

------------------------------ (1984) "Some Points of Social Justice." A Memorandum Presented to H.E. Paul Biya, President of the Republic of Cameroon by S.T. Muna, president of the national assembly.

(1985) "Open Letter to all English-speaking Parents of Cameroon from the English-speaking Students of the North West and South West Province," 20th August.

NTEMFAC, Ofege et al (1989) "Mono-cultural Cameroon Radio Television at the Service of Bi-cultural Cameroon." October 6, Yaoundé.

PHILIPPSON, Sydney (1959) "Report on the Financial, Economic and Administrative Consequences to Southern Cameroons of Separation from the Federation of Nigeria." Prime Minister's Office, Southern Cameroons.

SCHERR, Edmund (1973) "1992 Human Rights Report for Cameroon." January 19.

AAC (1993) "The Buea Declaration of the All Anglophone Conference." 3rd April, Buea.

(1961) The Constitution of the Federal Republic of Cameroon. 1st September, Yaoundé.

(1972) The Constitution of the United Republic of Cameroon. June, Yaoundé.

(1993) The Preliminary Draft Constitution of the Republic of Cameroon. May, Yaoundé.

(1961) "The Two Alternatives," Southern Cameroons Plebiscite.

TUNER, Frank L. et al (1965) The Economic Potential of West Cameroon. Stanford Research Institute, Palo Alto.

UNITED NATIONS (1961) A/RES/1608(XV) C.4 13 A/PV.994 /21 Apr. 1961/64-23-10 A/4737, The future of the Trust Territory of the Cameroons under United Kingdom administration, New York.

WONGIBE, Edwin Fon (1991) "The Social Democratic Front and the Thorny Road to Social Justice." 6th May, Bamenda.

Documents from Buea National Archives

FILE No. Qb/a 1966/1 Monthly Economic and Social Reports. West Cameroon, Ndian Division. "Extrait du Rapport Economique du Sous-Prefet de Bamusso."

FILE No.Qb/1 1964/10 Harmonization of Economic System of East and West Cameroon, 1964.

FILE No. Qb/a 1965/1 Second Five Year Plan. "Progress Report for 1966-1967 on the Second Five-year Development Plan," issued by the Ministry of Planning and Development, Yaoundé.

FILE No.Qb/a 1966/14 The Economic Situation of West Cameroon.

FILE No. Qi/1958/3 Export Control. "Permit to Import from French Territory by Way of Petty Trade."

FILE No. Qi/1959/3 Cameroon Air Transport 1959.

FILE No. Qi/1962/1 Cameroon Air Transport Limited 1962.

FILE No. Va.a 1962/1 Proceedings and Debates. Federal Legislature, 1962.

FILE No. Va/d 1960/2 Speeches by the Prime Minister.

FILE No. Va/d 1960/3 House of Assembly: Speeches. "Address to the Budget Session of the House of Assembly," 22nd March, 1961.

FILE No. Vc/b 1961/1 Record of the All Party Conference on the Constitutional future of the Southern Cameroons held at the Community Hall, Bamenda from 26th to 28th June, 1961.

FILE No. Vc/b 1961/3 Tripartite Conference Yaoundé, August 1961.

FILE No. Vc/n 1961/28 Constitutional Conference, 1961.

Documents from Hon. S.T. Muna's Library, Ngenmbo-Mbengwi

FILE No. 88/60 KNDP Meetings. "Memorandum presented to the President-General of the KNDP, H.E. J.N. Foncha, and through him, to the other KNDP members of the West Cameroon Executive Council by the Federal Parliamentary wing of the KNDP" by Hons. M.M. Fusi and S.T. Muna.

FILE No. 89/60 KNDP Speeches. "Speech presented by Hon. J.N. Foncha, Prime Minister of West Cameroon on the Occasion of Unification Day, 1st October, 1965."

FILE No. 89/68 KNDP Speeches. "Speech by the Hon. J.N. Foncha, Prime Minister on the Inauguration of the Youth Day in West Cameroon, on 11th February, 1964."

FILE No. 89/87 KNDP Speeches. "Presidential Address by H.E. J.N. Foncha to the 9th Annual Convention of the KNDP Held at Bamenda on the 15th August, 1963."

FILE No. 89/103 KNDP Speeches. "Hon. J.N. Foncha." 19th May, 1961.

FILE No. 91/43 KNDP Press Matters. "Speech by H.E. Dr. J.N. Foncha, Life President of the KNDP at the Party's 10th Annual Convention being held in Kumba from 23rd - 29th November, 1964."

FILE No. 91/376 KNDP Press Matters. "Press and Radio Statements" by J.N. Foncha, 14th September, 1965.

FILE No. 98/27 KNDP Correspondence. "To Hon. S.T. Muna. Summary Report on the KNDP: Bamenda NEC Meeting, 17th to 20th July, 1965" by Emmanuel Tabi Egbe.

FILE No. 98/37 KNDP Correspondence. "The Achievements of the KNDP" by J.S. Ndingsa, University of Nigeria, Nsukka.

FILE No. 98/57 KNDP Correspondence. "Letter to the President-General, Union Camerounaise, Yaoundé" by J.N. Foncha, 14th September, 1963.

FILE No. 98/72 KNDP Correspondence. "Report of the Central Working Committee on the Case of the Suspended Parliamentarians Submitted to the NEC on July 17th, 1965" by Dr. J.N. Foncha.

FILE No. 98/106 KNDP Correspondence. "The Split in the KNDP" by Nzo Ekhah Nghaky.

File No. 98/136 KNDP Correspondence. "Preliminary Submission and Consideration on the Case of the Suspended Parliamentarians' to the KNDP National Executive Committee by the Defenders."

File No. 98/160 KNDP Correspondence. "Muna in Fix" by NFOBIN, Charles, 1st November, 1965.

File No. 98/231 KNDP Correspondence. "Letters to Hon. S.T. Muna and E.T. Egbe" by William K.T. NKINEN, 14th June, 1965.

File No. 98/3485 KNDP Correspondence. "These Political Trends: Letter to the National President of the KNDP" by E.T. Egbe, 18th August, 1963.

Magazines, journals and Newspapers

ABBIA: Cameroon Cultural Review, Yaoundé.
Africa Report, New York.
Cameroon Champion, Victoria.
Cameroon Monitor, London.
Cameroon Life, Mutengene.
Cameroon Post, Limbe.
Cameroon Times, Victoria.
Cameroon Tribune, Yaoundé.
Challenge Hebdo, Douala.
Expression Nouvelle, Douala.
Focus on Africa Magazine, London.

Galaxie Media, Douala.
Jeune Afrique, Paris.
Jeune Afrique Economie, Paris.
La Détente, Douala.
La Gazette, Douala.
Le Combattant, Douala.
Le Confident, Douala.
Le Messager, Douala.
Le Quotidien, Douala.
L' Opinion, Douala.
SDF ECHO, Yaoundé.
The Herald, Douala.
The Messenger, Douala.
Times and Life, Douala.
Weekly Post, Yaoundé.
West Africa, London.

Names of individuals formally interviewed, and recorded viewpoints from the 2nd - 3rd April 1993 All Anglophone Conference

Carlson Anyangwe, Akonji Atekwana, Victor Ayuk, Michael Bame Bame, Ekotang Elad, S.M. Endeley, Martin Epie, Peter Ita Eta, Vincent Feko, Edwand Fon, John Ngu Foncha, Sam Nuvala Fonkem, Henry Fossung, S. Nfor Gwei, Hilary Kebila, Martha Lambi, Dan Lantum, Njoh Litumbe, Herman Maimo, Nnoko Mbele, Tatah Mentan, Justice Eyole-Monono, Diana Acha Morfaw, Albert W. Mukong, Akere T. Muna, Bernard Muna, S.T. Muna, Simon Munzu, Chief Namme, Augustine Ndangam, Stephen Ndi, V. Ombe Ndzana, E. Ngolle Ngolle, George Ngwane, V. Anomah Ngu, Jean Emmanuel Pondi, Jean Baptiste Sipa, Alexander Taku, Charles Taku, Christian Cardinal Tumi, C.P.N. Vewessee, Francis Wache, Azong Wara.

www.ingramcontent.com/pod-product-compliance
Lightning Source LLC
Chambersburg PA
CBHW050903300426
44111CB00010B/1361